THE DELUSIONS OF ECONOMICS

ABOUT THE AUTHOR

Gilbert Rist is professor emeritus at the Graduate Institute of International and Development Studies in Geneva. He first taught at the University of Tunis, became the Director of the Europe-Third World Centre in Geneva and, later on, Senior Researcher on a United Nations University Project. Afterwards he joined the Graduate Institute of Development Studies where he taught intercultural relations and social anthropology. His main interest is in an anthropological approach to our contemporary society. He is the author of *The History of Development: From Western Origins to Global Faith* (Zed Books, London, 3rd edn 2008).

THE DELUSIONS OF ECONOMICS

The Misguided Certainties of a Hazardous Science

GILBERT RIST

Translated by Patrick Camiller

ZED BOOKS

London & New York

The Delusions of Economics: The Misguided Certainties of a Hazardous Science
was first published in English in 2011 by
Zed Books Ltd, 7 Cynthia Street, London N1 9JF, UK
and Room 400, 175 Fifth Avenue, New York, NY 10010, USA

www.zedbooks.co.uk

Originally published in French in 2010 under the title *L'économie ordinaire entre songes et mensonges* by Presses de Sciences Po, 117 boulevard Saint Germain, 75006 Paris, France

Ouvrage publié avec le concours du Centre national du livre / Published with support from the National Book Centre
The translation of this book has been made possible through the generous support of SQLI Foundation http://fondation.sqli.com

Designed and typeset in Monotype Bembo Book
by illuminati, Grosmont
Index by John Barker
Cover designed by www.kikamiller.com
Printed and bound in Great Britain by
CPI Group (UK) Ltd, Croydon, CR0 4YY

Distributed in the USA exclusively by Palgrave Macmillan, a division of St Martin's Press, LLC, 175 Fifth Avenue, New York, NY 10010, USA

A catalogue record for this book is available from the British Library
Library of Congress Cataloging in Publication Data available

ISBN 978 1 84813 923 7 hb
ISBN 978 1 84813 922 0 pb

CONTENTS

INTRODUCTION

> The trouble with modern theories of behaviourism is not that they are wrong but that they could become true.
>
> *Hannah Arendt*[1]

Conventional thinking takes it as given that all human activities are now subject to an economic logic, yet this commonplace already raises a string of questions. Where did the 'subjection' originate? What is the basis for the respect given to economic 'laws'? Why has economics become a central category in the imaginary of social life? Why are its 'exigencies' so often regarded as final in all kinds of decision-making, especially in the realm of politics? By what token do the 'laws' of economics assert themselves with 'iron necessity', as Marx would put it? Should we be even doubting such a generally accepted view of the world, which corresponds to practices that are everywhere becoming more widespread?

These questions cannot all be answered straightaway in detail. But at least it should be made clear from the outset that the aim of this book is to overcome the sense of fatalism associated with economic logic, whose conclusions are presented as if they were inexorable. Since economics is only one possible view of the

1. Hannah Arendt, *The Human Condition*, Chicago: University of Chicago Press, 1958, p. 322.

world, not only is it legitimate to see things differently, but it has become necessary to throw off the constraints that economics imposes and to construct it in a different manner. In any case, those constraints are largely imaginary and often based upon unrealistic assumptions.[2] What is considered to be a 'science' is in fact a set of beliefs.[3] This is only partly reassuring, because we know that beliefs change more slowly than scientific truths. But it does not prevent us from trying our luck.

If we have reached this point, it is no doubt because over the centuries we have taken the hypotheses of economic 'science' to be not only plausible or probable but actually true; we have been won over by them, without questioning the assumptions on which they rest. It is exactly as if everyone had converted to a vulgar Marxist creed, in which the superstructure is straightforwardly determined by the economic base.[4] Economics is both everything and everywhere; nothing escapes its hegemonic grip on our way of seeing the world.[5]

---

2. The term 'assumption' is here used in the ordinary sense of a statement assumed to be true, though not necessarily verified, on which a chain of argument bases itself. It may therefore be thought of as synonymous with 'axiom': that is, 'a proposition, whether evident or not, which is not deduced from another proposition but is posited by a decision of the mind at the beginning of the deduction' (André Lalande, *Vocabulaire technique et critique de la philosophie*, Paris: Presses Universitaires de France, 1962). The term is close to 'premiss' or 'postulate'. Sometimes it denotes a simple prejudice.

3. Frédéric Lebaron, *La Croyance économique. Les économistes entre science et politique*, Paris: Seuil, 2000.

4. Engels explicitly rejects such vulgar Marxism in a letter of 21 September 1890 to Joseph Bloch: 'According to the materialist conception of history, the *ultimately* determining factor in history is the production and reproduction of real life. Neither Marx nor I have ever asserted more than this. Hence if somebody twists this into saying that the economic factor is the *only* determining one, he transforms that proposition into a meaningless, abstract, absurd phrase. The economic situation is the basis, but the various elements of the superstructure … also exercise their influence upon the course of the historical struggles and in many cases determine their *form* in particular.' Marx Engels, *Selected Correspondence*, Moscow: Progress Publishers, 1975, pp. 394–5.

5. The fact that most universities have a 'faculty of economic and social sciences' indicates the primacy (or even imperial authority) that 'economic science' arrogates for itself. There is also talk of a 'religious market' (or 'market in salvation goods') and a 'marketplace of ideas', and we know that the 'new' (neoclassical) economics has constructed a micro-economic theory of marriage, altruism and the political market (see Henri Lepage, *Tomorrow, Capitalism: The Economics of Economic Freedom*, London: Open

It is true that economic 'science' originally involved a high-minded ambition: the *doux commerce* exalted by Montesquieu was supposed to bring civil peace and general prosperity, after the religious wars that had recently steeped Europe in blood. But why is this optimistic vision so widely shared today, when living conditions are deteriorating for most people on the planet, social inequalities are worsening and the natural environment is suffering irreversible damage? Is it not apparent that the 'peace through commerce' project has given way to economic warfare, justified in the name of competition and matched by a war on nature? Mysteriously, economic theory continues to rule people's minds and actions, as if its prescriptions had the same kind of authority as astronomers' predictions about the phases of the moon or the appearance of planets in the sky.

The force of economic theory as a view of the world has to do not only with its focus on quantifiable material 'objects' (products for exchange and consumption), but also with its attempt to describe the world as it should be and, above all, with the way in which it has been gradually used to mould our behaviour to its principles. For example, the idea that everyone pursues their own interest is held to be self-evidently true in all circumstances; what started out as a mere working hypothesis ends up being affirmed as performatively true.

In fact, once we look at the results in practice, we can scarcely fail to question the mainstream economic doctrines that have been leading us all down a social and ecological blind alley. It is in their name that governments of both left and right see unbridled growth as a panacea for economic downturn and employment problems. But is not growth also the cause of the ecological dangers besetting us now and in the future?[6] Is it not socially and

---

Court, 1982). Nor should we fail to mention 'investment in human capital' and 'human resource management', or HRM for short.

6. 'One of the hardest lessons taught by climate change is that the economic model which drives growth, and the profligate consumption in rich nations that goes with it, is

politically unacceptable that inequality is on the rise in today's world, between those who are growing richer and those who, in ever larger number, are falling into poverty?[7]

The present work is a sequel to a critique of 'development' first published in English in 1997 and revised in 2002 and 2008, in which development is defined as the ongoing commodification of nature and social relations.[8] On reflection, this critique seemed to be not radical enough and to require extension to the very principles that make such commodification of the world possible. For the truth is that 'development' would never have seen the light of day, nor gathered around itself a consensus that has survived all the failures, if it had not been part and parcel of 'economic science'. The lessons of history and anthropology therefore had to be brought to bear upon the foundations of that science, without entering into the debates that take place inside it. This meant inserting economics in a new way into the whole field of the social sciences and ecology – a task all the more necessary since it was the attempt to assert its autonomy and primacy that led economic 'science' to commit some of its most grievous mistakes.

This being said, the object of the critique must be spelled out more precisely. It is clear that economic 'science' is not a homo-

---

ecologically unsustainable.' United Nations Development Program, *Human Development Report 2007–2008*, New York: Palgrave Macmillan, 2007, p. 15. Although the UNDP, for diplomatic reasons, singles out 'rich nations', it must be recognized that the 'economic model which drives growth' is now applied everywhere.

7. Some claim that inequalities are diminishing on a world scale, since 'living standards' are rising more or less everywhere, above all in the 'emerging economies'. But this choice of scale disguises the real problems (the most important ones) that exist within each country in both the South and the North (see Trent Schroyer, *Beyond Western Economics*, London: Routledge, 2009, pp. 1–2). A study published in 2005 (Carole Frydman and Raven Saks, 'Historical Trends in Executive Compensation, 1936–2003', 15 November 2005) shows that top company directors in the United States saw their salaries rise from forty times the average wage between 1940 and 1980 to three hundred times in the year 2000; while, according to Emmanuel Saenz, the richest 10 per cent of the population had half the total income in 2006. (Figures quoted from Hervé Kempf, *Pour sauver la planète, sortez du capitalisme*, Paris: Seuil, 2009, pp. 27–8.) Cf. Pierre-Noël Giraud, *L'inégalité du monde. Economie du monde contemporain*, Paris: Gallimard, 1996.

8. Gilbert Rist, *The History of Development: From Western Origins to Global Faith*, London: Zed Books, 2008.

genous body of doctrine: it includes a number of rival schools that have followed in succession or continue to oppose one another (classical, Marxist, neoclassical or marginalist, Keynesian, institutionalist, contractualist, monetarist, regulationist, neoliberal, socio-economic or evolutionary). This raises some uncertainty about the scientific status of the discipline, since the truths that it professes vary not only across history (which is perfectly normal) but also with one's ideological affiliation, which, despite claims that certain 'laws' or theorems are self-evident, is often a matter of the dominant political agenda.

Debates within the economics corporation therefore tend to be lively, and any kid gloves soon come off as the criticisms fly back and forth. It is therefore neither eccentric nor sacrilegious to pitch in with the aim not of supporting one school or another, but of questioning certain unexamined axioms that are common to them all. One of the characteristics of economic 'science' is its hierarchical compartmentalization, whereby the leading academics or researchers who publish in specialist journals are insulated from the 'organic economists' who appear on television or write in newspapers, or who hand out the rudiments in schools or undergraduate university courses. It is as if there are two styles or two forms of economic thinking: one takes pleasure in formal mathematical exercises, seeking to reconstruct in the laboratory – and hence to predict and control – the numerous interactions identifiable in economic processes; the other, sometimes referred to as 'mainstream', 'conventional' or 'normal' science,[9] is regularly sifted through by the media to justify company relocations, stock exchange fluctuations, the virtues of growth, public expenditure cuts, price rises and wage stagnation. The arguments of the latter are usually simple and stereotyped, and it is they which forge the

9. Thomas S. Kuhn, *The Structure of Scientific Revolutions*, 3rd edn, Chicago: University of Chicago Press, 1996, p. 37: 'One of the things a scientific community acquires with a paradigm is a criterion for choosing problems that, while the paradigm is taken for granted, can be assumed to have solutions.'

common sense and foster the 'economic culture' that everyone is supposed to possess for an understanding of the world around us.[10] Or, to put it in another way, their arguments are often no more than half-truths. Thus, for example, it is patently obvious that, if cars are to go on being produced in this or that European factory, the pay levels (of the workforce) will have to be cut to withstand competitive pressure from low-wage countries. But why not add that the opening of markets was imposed by governments in the name of 'pure and perfect competition', in whose theoretical benefits only economists continue to believe?

The present work, then, is devoted to a critique of this economic Vulgate. Consequently, its first objective will be to examine the validity of the fundamental theses from which everything else follows, and which form the minimum consensus among members of the profession belonging to the dominant current.[11] For what would be the point of highlighting, and perhaps trying to correct, defects in the upper storeys of a building, if the foundations are not sound? Of course, the criticisms presented here are not new. Some were formulated by economists themselves – most notably by members of unorthodox currents, who would argue that it is unjust, or even unjustified, to denounce all economists as such,

10. Those who consider themselves 'real' economists – and whose researches sometimes challenge the received wisdom – deplore the fact that these 'pseudo-experts' are favoured by the media. However, one wonders whether the compartmentalization of economic knowledge into specialist fields does not lead them to propose partial answers to general problems.

11. 'Refusal to debate whether its hypotheses are realistic is another article of faith of standard economics': Jacques Sapir, *Les Trous noirs de la science économique. Essai sur l'impossibilité de penser le temps et l'argent*, Paris: Albin Michel, 2000, p. 35. My approach is close to that of Stephen A. Marglin, who notes: 'I will be accused of setting up a straw man, an "economics" so drastically simplified and out of date that it caricatures the breadth and depth of the intellectual enterprise of contemporary economics. I have two responses. The first is that the enterprise of economics is better characterized by the content of elementary texts than by what goes on at the frontiers of economic theory. … Second, even at the frontiers, there is little questioning of the fundamental assumptions of economics' (*The Dismal Science: How Thinking Like an Economist Undermines Community*, Cambridge MA: Harvard University Press, 2008, pp. 4–5); and to that of Trent Schroyer (*Beyond Western Economics*), even if I do not share all his conclusions.

since they themselves have pointed to certain false assumptions and given up the beliefs typical of the discipline. The many references below to their work will show that their concerns have not been neglected; special mention should be made of the 'Mouvement pour une économie post-autiste' (or 'Mouvement des éconoclastes'), which was launched in France in the year 2000 and taken up in the English-speaking countries by the International Confederation of Associations for Pluralism in Economics (ICAPE).[12] On the 'orthodox' side, the polemic has been no less heated. Its representatives argue that in recent decades the 'economic approach' has devised all kinds of safeguards that make it possible to preserve the validity of the mainstream model. But it remains to be seen whether these changes are filtering through to the teaching of the 'elements' of economic science, or whether, as seems more likely, they reinforce a rather summary view of the benefits of market economics.[13]

It will probably come as a surprise that this book has not been written by a 'real' economist, and for many this will deprive it of all legitimacy. But the opposite case might easily be made, since a 'real' economist is rarely capable of tackling the principles of his own science. A proverb (doubtless Chinese) says, 'the fish is worst

---

12. Their work may be consulted at www.peacon.net. See also Edward Fullbrook, *Pluralist Economics*, London: Zed Books, 2008.

13. 'Reference to the market system as a benign alternative to capitalism is a bland, meaningless disguise of the deeper, corporate reality.... No economic power is invoked. There is nothing here from Marx or Engels. There is only the impersonal market, a not wholly innocent fraud.' John K. Galbraith, *The Economics of Innocent Fraud: Truth for Our Time*, Boston MA: Houghton Mifflin, 2004, p. 7. A little story may not be out of place here. When I was invited to speak about the assumptions of economics to a hundred pupils preparing for their baccalaureate exam at a French lycée, I decided to present some of the theses in this book and was rewarded with an attentive audience and a number of interesting questions. Still, I was rather afraid of how the teachers accompanying the pupils would react. What did they think of my critical arguments? Their reply was disconcerting: 'Of course we largely agree with your point of view,' they said, 'but we can't teach it. Our job is to get our pupils through the bac. And, as their papers will be corrected by external examiners, they would certainly fail if they deviated from the mainstream views in the syllabus.' This is how a lack of critical spirit and, ultimately, ignorance are transmitted.

placed to discover the existence of water'. And most economists are like a fish – totally helpless when it comes to fathoming the ideological and epistemological surroundings in which they move. Their interest centres on how the system functions – or on fragments of it that might provide material for an article – and they justify their hypotheses by constructing an ideal model on the basis of statistical elements. Just like classical mechanics or physics, which ignored air resistance or friction in establishing their laws, economists mostly operate in a social vacuum emptied of the specifics of human life. Such is the price of 'scienticity'. To achieve it, one has to leave out history, nature, social practices and relations, emotions – in a word, life itself. Nor is this all. Followers of mainstream economics are holed up in a fortress to which they alone have the keys, determined to ensure that no intruder, whether an economist or non-economist, discovers how to shake their certainties. As Steve Keen puts it, 'it is almost impossible to have an article accepted into one of the mainstream academic economics journals unless it has the full panoply of economic assumptions: rational behaviour (according to the economic definition of rational!), markets that are always in equilibrium, risk as an acceptable proxy for uncertainty and so on. When it comes to safeguarding the channels of academic advancement, little else matters apart from preserving the set of assumptions that defines economic orthodoxy.'[14] For a different world to become possible, however, the first step must be to imagine the possibility of a different economics, or even a pluralism of economics.

One problem in structuring this book is that the underlying assumptions of standard economic 'science' are so intertwined with one another, and so mutually supportive, that they should really be treated simultaneously. Since that is not possible, the task has been to disentangle and examine them in separate chapters,

14. Steve Keen, *Debunking Economics: The Naked Emperor of the Social Sciences*, London: Zed Books, 2007 (2004), p. 154.

before finally showing how they form a solid chain of debatable 'reasons'. This also explains why certain developments might have logically found a place in another chapter than the one in which they figure: the choice, though perhaps seemingly arbitrary, was necessary in order to avoid too much repetition. As to the copious notes, they make it possible to clarify particular points without overloading the text with quotations that might distract from the main argument. In any case, readers in a hurry can skip them and not feel that they have lost anything essential.

This book does not try to imagine the policies that a different conception of economics might inspire. Yet there is no shortage of ideas on how to tackle the key problems of social inequality and ecological threats. They cannot be solved separately, of course, since both result from the nature of the economic system dominant in today's world. Although it is often possible to give a patient some relief from the symptoms of his illness, everyone knows that it is preferable to act on the causes of it. Understandably, proposals are made for urgent social programmes to tackle poverty or for ecological taxes to correct the systemic aberrations and their resulting evils. Why not indeed? But, as those who support them both recognize and deplore, they will not change much that is fundamental. It is better to go to the root of the problems, even if it is masked by theoretical constructions designed to make us believe that it does not exist and that economic 'science' relates to the order of nature and necessity.[15] In any event, the central wager in this book is that it is possible to lay bare the roots of the situation we face today.

15. 'Nature is what remains when the effects of artifice and chance have been struck out from all things.... With this elimination of conceptual adjuncts, which it situates at the origin of its imagery and discourse, naturalist ideology possesses the most unspoken, and therefore the most secure, of its references: silent witnesses do not betray anything.' Clément Rosset, *L'Anti-nature. Éléments pour une philosophie tragique*, Paris: Presses universitaires de France, 1973, pp. 20–21.

I would like to express my deep gratitude to Marie-Dominique Perrot, François Bafoil, Jean-Noël DuPasquier, Philippe Durand and Frédéric Robert-Nicoud, who took the trouble to read a first draft and to supply exacting comments. Since they came from different disciplines and did not have the same opinions, I did not try to reconcile their sometimes contradictory remarks. But I learned a great deal from listening to them, and they allowed me to improve the argument considerably in the final version and to avoid a number of glaring mistakes. Those which remain are therefore entirely of my own doing.

This English edition has further benefited from the pertinent remarks of an unknown reader who had the task of advising the publisher on whether the book should be translated. I owe him or her my sincere thanks. Furthermore, recent reading of my own has prompted me to develop certain arguments and hence to improve the text in comparison with the French original. Lastly, I would like to express my gratitude to Patrick Camiller, who has the art of keeping my thinking to the point.

CHAPTER I

ECONOMICS BETWEEN HISTORY AND ANTHROPOLOGY

Let us first briefly consider what follows from treating economics as a social science that stands no higher than the other social sciences and has no special privileges in relation to them. This will imply an external critique: not because internal critiques are devoid of interest, but because they operate within a closed discipline gradually built up with the help of axioms or assumptions that supposedly define (and therefore separate) what is and is not an 'economic fact'.

The autonomy of economic 'science' from the other social sciences is fairly recent in origin; the different viewpoints that today characterize or identify the various disciplines were once quite closely intertwined. In the Age of Enlightenment, a thinker could be at the same time a doctor and physiocrat like Quesnay, a political theorist, anthropologist and musician like Rousseau, a moral philosopher and 'economist' like Adam Smith, or a polemicist and financier like Voltaire. It was not possible to say which 'competence' had the upper hand in each of these figures, unless and until one was content simply to ratify the verdict of history.

THE TRAP OF AUTONOMOUS DISCIPLINES

Historically, then, there was a kind of common ground in which various ways of looking at social facts had their roots. This is one reason why economics should be considered in relationship to other disciplines that share the same origin as itself. At the same time, it must be recognized that the eighteenth century marked a break with older ways of dealing with prices, commerce or production, and we may well wonder what this entailed for the 'well-being of society', to use an anachronistic expression.

Of course, ways of seeing the world change over the centuries, and there is general agreement that this should be attributed to the 'march of progress'.[1] Copernicus freed us from the illusion of geocentricity; Magellan finally demonstrated that the earth was round; Newton explained the laws of the universe on the basis of mathematics rather than theology.[2] So, why should we not salute Adam Smith and his disciples for putting an end to the contempt in which merchants were held, for discovering the best means of economic exchange and life in society, and for dispelling a variety of errors? The simple answer is that we are always at liberty to ask what we won and lost as a result of these 'historic advances'; and that, from the viewpoint of history and anthropology, there are many reasons to doubt some of the assumptions on which the early economists built their theories and which their successors neglected to verify (or lacked the courage to abandon).

Whereas, from Aristotle to the Physiocrats, the first outlines of economic 'science' presented themselves as no more than a theory to explain or interpret certain social phenomena, their sequels became more and more normative and prescriptive. They claimed to define an order that governs production and exchange and

1. This idea of progress, which was relatively new in the eighteenth century (Rousseau did not hold it!), resulted from the victory of the Moderns over the Ancients in the previous century. See Rist, *The History of Development*, pp. 35ff.

2. This despite the endearing fact that Newton was also a convinced alchemist!

ensures maximum satisfaction for all who engage in them, based on an anthropology (a vision of man, society and nature) with roots in the Enlightenment,[3] and a 'social physics' copied from the natural physics whose laws were beginning to be discovered at the time. For this programme to be realized, it was necessary that a number of hypotheses should be considered true. A provisional list of these would include: there is a 'human nature' that has been uniform and unvarying in all societies down the ages; individual behaviour can therefore be explained and predicted regardless of context; and one can devise models that enable the greatest number of people, if not all, to maximize their satisfaction and thereby contribute to their own happiness and the collective welfare.

These 'truths' were long held to be self-evident, even though studies of other societies – which began to appear in the early eighteenth century, but were either ignored or treated as marginal by economists[4] – called their universality into question. We should take a fresh look at those studies and compare them with the assertions of economic 'science' – not out of a passion for relativism, but to make economists focus on the range of different social practices, instead of describing an enchanted world in which it is exactly as if theory has taken the place of 'reality'.

3. 'Its peculiarity is ... its attempt to identify "is" and "ought", the actual and the obligatory, directly and without lengthy proofs; it simply equates reason and nature.' Gunnar Myrdal, *The Political Element in the Development of Economic Theory*, London: Transaction Books, 1990 (1930), p. 28.

4. In fact, an interest in 'savages' was already present in Montaigne, and the early eighteenth century saw the publication, most notably, of *Dialogues curieux entre l'auteur et un sauvage de bon sens qui a voyagé* and *Mémoires de l'Amérique septentrionale* by Louis Armand de Lom d'Arce, baron de Lahontan, republished by Gilbert Chinard for Johns Hopkins University Press, Baltimore, MD: 1931 (1703), and *Mœurs des sauvages américains comparées aux moeurs des premiers temps* (1724) by Joseph-François Lafitau.

CHANGING THE OPTIC

As Einstein showed, 'it is theory which decides what can be observed'. Thus, once economic 'science' established itself as the principal (or the only) conceptual grid for the apprehension of 'reality', it became difficult to avoid confusion between the level of theory and the level of the 'facts' deriving from it. But Einstein's statement has a corollary: 'reality' will appear differently according to the theory used to interpret it. For example, knowledge of the atomic system enables us to envisage matter otherwise than in previous conceptions. But, to define common salt as the grouping of two atoms of sodium and chlorine tells us nothing about its taste properties; or a tree will not be the same when looked at by a poet, a botanist and a forester evaluating it as a 'resource' (and converting it from a living being into a lifeless commodity). There are several ways of understanding the world, which differ with the spectacles we wear, and several ways of living in it, according to the purposes we have in mind. Why should the same not be true of 'economic goods'?

This work starts out from two assumptions: the first, rather banal, is that Western society is like all others (even if, like all others, it denies this and claims a pre-eminent position[5]); the second is that, in every society, there are 'theories' or 'ways of seeing' that combine a rational and an imaginary part, both accepted by all, which make the world intelligible and determine social practices. Simply put, we might say that in some societies people think (or believe) that all human beings are equal, while in others they think (or believe) that everyone belongs by birth to a particular caste. Furthermore, some think (or believe) that the

5. There seems to be no escape from this basic sociocentrism! As Lévi-Strauss showed, all societies think they are 'the best': the words *inuit*, *amazigen* (Berbers) and *muntu/bantu* all mean 'men' or 'humans', implying that anyone else is not human; Burkina Faso, the name of the African state, means 'homeland of real men' (implying...); China considered itself the 'Middle Kingdom' – that is, the centre of the earth; Cuzco is the 'navel of the world' (in competition with the Greek island of Delos), and so on.

earth is a mother goddess (the Andean *Pachamama*), while others think (or believe) that it is an exploitable 'resource'. The examples could easily be multiplied.[6] In each case, someone denigrates the 'beliefs' of others, because it is always unbelievers who think that others 'believe' (in wrong things). But the point here is not to decide one way or another, to say who is right and who is wrong. Whatever the 'beliefs' may be, they constitute – for those who subscribe to them – *practical truths* with which they have to comply: a Hindu will only marry within his caste, and an Amerindian *campesino* will not behave in the same way as an industrial farmer. If cows are 'holy', everyone will refrain from eating them and stop to let them cross the road.

Western society makes no exceptions to this rule. Nor does the economic theory that the West invented. By questioning its assumptions, it is possible to bring out the imaginary portion (of irrationality or belief) that is characteristic of it. To jump ahead a little, we may say that the non-spoken (or imaginary) element underlying economic theory belongs to the *paradigm of war* – war against nature, and war of humans against one another. Its assumption of original scarcity means that war must be waged on nature by exploiting all its resources, both renewable and, especially, non-renewable; and its assumption that in all circumstances everyone pursues only their own interest serves to legitimize competition and social inequalities. However, if it is true that we need a different paradigm (with another implicit imaginary) – one based on life in and with nature, on solidarity and disinterestedness – then some elements of an answer may be found in traditional or 'primitive' economic forms. Those who

6. Historically, there have been those who thought/believed that health depends on a balance of the four humours and those who thought/believed that there were such things as viruses; those who thought/believed that the earth was flat and dangerous to approach at its edges and those who thought/believed that it was round and could be circumnavigated. Today, some think that Africans 'believe' in the existence of witchcraft, while Africans confine themselves to noting that it does exist and is part of their everyday life.

live within those forms show that a different way of constructing the world is not only possible but exists in reality. To our Western eyes, of course, 'such people are crazy'. But what if we agreed to recognize the portion of craziness that we have turned into a practical truth that rules our lives?[7]

To draw on economic history and anthropology does not entail disturbing the dust that has gathered on obsolete practices, nor introducing exotic forms of behaviour into the picture, but it does force us *to see the world differently*. It dispels the illusion in which exchange is considered only in a narrow market perspective; no society would survive in the real world if it was limited to that. To be sure, 'real' economists are often distrustful, sometimes contemptuous, of anthropologists in the academic fraternity. The divergences between them are first of all methodological: anthropologists observe and record; economists calculate and think of what ought to be the case. Nor should we overlook the fact that most economists, won over by the ideology of progress, consider that history is 'moving forward' and that what was true or possible at an earlier stage is now consigned to oblivion, whereas others maintain that humanity (the quality of being human) develops only through respect for certain basic rules, including reciprocity and redistribution, gift and return gift.[8] This opposition threatens to persist for a long time still. So far as the enthusiasts of economic 'science' are concerned, what is at stake is the ideology of progress – an ideology which has been

7. Such a position will doubtless be branded as reactionary 'neo-primitivism' (see Jean-Loup Amselle, *Rétrovolutions. Essais sur les primitivismes contemporains*, Paris: Stock, 2010). I would still maintain that it is legitimate, however, since the aim is not at all to 'turn the clock back' – that makes no sense – but to change our epistemology (our theory of knowledge) and to become aware of the irrationality that is part of its make-up.

8. Adam Smith was right to say: 'Nobody ever saw a dog make a fair and deliberate exchange of one bone for another with another dog' (*The Wealth of Nations*, vol. 1, London: Methuen, 1961, p. 17). But it would be wrong to reduce his thought to a mere theory of self-interested exchange, as if he considered this the only means for an individual to gain 'the help of his brethren'. At the same time, we should always bear it in mind that Smith's knowledge of anthropology was cursory and prone to error.

losing momentum in recent years[9] – while for anthropologists the point is that the builders of economic models pay scant heed to the diversity of social practices. The aim of this book will be to cast some reflected light on the matter by 'observing ourselves in the face of others' – to use the fine expression of the sixteenth-century Genevan pastor Urbain Chauveton[10] – that is, by looking at our own society with the amazement of someone from a distant land used to other customs. This may help put an end to the sense of superiority, or even arrogance, that has been so characteristic of the West.

To avoid any misunderstanding, the approach adopted here should be spelled out even more clearly. With globalization triumphant, it might be asked, what point is there in referring to the customs of vanished or vanishing societies? Can we really learn anything from 'savages' who have now been marginalized or forced to integrate into the 'global village'? Does it make sense to address the problems of the twenty-first century with ideas that had currency in a bygone age or belong to traditions nullified and erased by modernity? Do we not risk drifting off in a 'reactionary' direction if we dwell too often on the ostensible harmony of earlier societies? Conventional thinking, nurtured as it is on social evolutionism, threatens to raise such objections whenever 'traditional' practices are held up as exemplary, seeing them not only as alien to reason but even as 'inhuman' in the scale of Western values. Yet the fact is that, far from having vanished, most of the practices and traditions in question are still very much alive – not only in the African countryside or the hedge-lined farmland of

9. See Pierre-André Taguieff, *L'Effacement de l'avenir*, Paris: Galilée, 2000.

10. Quoted in Gérald Berthoud, *Vers une anthropologie générale. Modernité et altérité*, Geneva: Droz, 1992, p. 11. A number of Chauveton's propositions are reminiscent of Montaigne. Compare, for instance, this snippet from Book 1, Chapter 30 of the *Essays*: 'I find that there is nothing barbarous and savage in this nation [Brazil], … excepting that everyone gives the title of barbarism to everything that is not in use in his own country. Indeed, we have no other level of truth and reason than the example and idea of the opinions and customs of the place wherein we live' (*Essays*, Chicago: University of Chicago, 1952, p. 93).

Normandy, but also in the cities of the industrial countries – and that they contain values of 'common decency' (as Orwell put it) which escape the mainstream liberal ideology of 'every man for himself'.[11] This is not at all to suggest that such societies are idyllic or conflict-free, but merely to point out that, despite the rivalries running through them, they also practise forms of exchange that challenge the assumptions of standard economic 'science'. Of course, as in all traditions, these practices undergo transformation over time, adapting to changes in the world in order to maintain their essential reason for existence. In this, they are like each and every one of us, who preserve our identity by constantly modifying ourselves. Frozen traditions would be dead traditions, good only to be displayed in a museum. But, fortunately, ways of acting and living that do not depend on the market are present all around us, even if the analytic grid that has been gradually imposed on everyone prevents us from seeing them.

We might even say, without too much fear of contradiction, that what remains marginal today is market economics, not traditional practices resting on reciprocity and redistribution! If market exchange is the only kind allowed into the equation, then it will be decisive for the simple reason that the conclusion is already contained in the premiss. But as soon as we widen the picture to include all forms of exchange – not only those involving monetary compensation (or corresponding to largely virtual financial flows) – we realize how important, at a global level, is everything that circulates 'outside the market' in forms and patterns, and in accordance with rules, that economic 'science' has chosen to ignore.[12]

---

11. See Jean-Claude Michéa, *L'Empire du moindre mal*, Paris: Climats, 2007, p. 54, and *Impasse Adam Smith*, Castelnau-le-Lez: Climats, 2002.

12. It would obviously be a futile exercise to quantify the scale of these transactions, giving in to the magic of numbers. Not only does economic calculation include flows that are often virtual in character (such as those in the financial economy), but the 'value' of the links forged outside the market is literally incalculable.

Of course, this opposition between neoclassical theory and 'traditional' practices is only one way of looking at things. Another, equally legitimate, approach would be to contrast mainstream economics with attempts to develop a form of social economics based on solidarity, in which cooperatives, mutual associations and exchange networks make it possible to escape the hegemony of the market. Similarly, it might be shown how long social struggles led to the 'free' availability of education, social protection and, in some countries, medical care. Although these public goods have a cost – and therefore a price, assumed by society as a whole – this is not set by the market, at least as long as the social state resists their privatization. Thus, as we said before, the market form is far from sweeping the board in social transactions. If economic anthropology decides to attack the fabrications of conventional (or neoclassical) economics, it does so for two reasons: first, to avoid limiting the debate to two economic forms ('capitalist' and 'socialist') which, even if they differ considerably in their practical consequences, largely rest on the same epistemological foundations; and, second, because (to quote Rousseau) 'When one wants to study men, one must consider those around one. But to study men, one must extend the range of one's vision. One must first observe the differences in order to discover the properties.'[13] This distancing or decentring, in both space and time, is thus a methodological requirement: we have to 'look into the distance' in order to understand what unites and divides the ways in which various societies think about the economy (modes of production, consumption and exchange) and the reasons they have thought up to establish rules for it.

13. Jean-Jacques Rousseau, 'Essay on the Origin of Languages', in *On the Origin of Language*, New York: Ungar, 1966, pp. 30–31.

FROM REDUCTIONISM TO COMPLEXITY

In what way will the new economic paradigm that should come into being differ from the one that is dominant today? At this stage of our enquiry, all we can say for sure is that it will be more diverse and more complex. People everywhere have been producing, consuming, saving, distributing and exchanging since time immemorial. That is not at issue. Just as the climate exists in the absence of meteorologists, 'the economy' has in a sense always existed, even if societies historically or geographically remote from our own have not regarded economic phenomena as distinct from social life, political power, religion, myths and social obligations.[14] Everything changed when economic 'science' chose to consider this vast set of relations only from the viewpoint of the division of labour, market exchange, individual rationality and the pursuit of utility, thereby flattening the diversity of human practices and reducing them all to calculable operations motivated by self-interest. What is unacceptable is the claim to impose a single, uniform 'economic logic', which ignores the many 'good reasons' for which human beings enter into relations with one another and give various meanings to the use they make of material goods.

This is why it is neither rational nor reasonable to put up with the reductionism that characterizes economic 'science'. Of course, we can accept that theoretical constructions supported by mathematical formulae are sometimes distant from the real world,

---

14. Hence the distinction between *substantive economics* (which, for Polanyi, means that people's livelihood everywhere depends on the environment and cooperation with others, and that economics is therefore 'embedded' in social relations) and *formal economics* (which corresponds to the rationality of *Homo oeconomicus* and market exchange). Some authors – e.g. Claude Lévi-Strauss, 'Productivité et condition humaine', *Études rurales* 159–60, July–December 2001, p. 130 – argue that the conflict between the two 'seems to be fading', on the grounds that traditional societies are devoid of neither rationality nor calculation, and even of certain forms of market, while market exchange does not explain everything in modern societies. In our view, however, the split certainly does exist, chiefly because of the intransigence of 'standard' theory in opposition to more unorthodox theories.

since any 'model' inevitably involves a degree of abstraction. But, beyond this methodological point, the main issue is the premisses and axioms on which the discipline rests. It is these implicit and explicit assumptions, not unlike acts of faith, which need to be questioned in the name of a rigorous approach that remains attentive to social practices.

CHAPTER 2

A FAILED SCIENTIFIC AMBITION

As in the case of other disciplines, the field of economic 'science' is beset with power struggles to gain access to prestigious jobs in academia, the civil service or international institutions, culminating in competition for the so-called Nobel Prize.[1] The top positions are held by people theoretically committed to mathematical modelling and a neoclassical vision of the world, who thus reproduce the ideal of economic 'science' as it is taught in the United States. That said, professional economists form a composite group in which corporate or banking employees rub shoulders with management specialists, teachers without access to the 'leading reviews', unorthodox economists, forecasters working for public institutions, and economics journalists. In the end, 'an "economist" is someone who manages to get himself recognized as such'.[2] The important point here is that, for the

1. I say 'so-called' because it is actually a prize created in 1969 by the Swedish central bank, 'in memory of Alfred Nobel'. No matter that Alfred Nobel's grandson protested at this misappropriation ('the Riksbank introduced its egg into another bird's nest'); the new prize has done much to break economic 'science' loose from political economy by lending it an aura of scientific authority. See Patrick Moynot, 'Nobel d'économie: coup de maître', *Le Monde*, 16 October 2008.

2. Frédéric Lebaron reached this seemingly disenchanted conclusion after a long field survey of economics in France: *La Croyance économique. Les économistes entre science et politique*, Paris: Seuil, 2000, p. 41.

'vanguard' of the profession – those at the top of the ladder – their work has a 'purely' scientific status characterized by mathematical formalization.[3]

The use of mathematical models is the subject of debate within the economics profession: not everyone has been won over to them.[4] Yet what better guarantee could one give of the pertinence of one's conclusions than to make them depend on a proof *more geometrico*, since the rigour of geometry is supposed to command universal acceptance? Unlike the other social sciences – which usually proceed by discursive or 'literary' argument – economics is able to express itself in formulas and equations. This is hardly surprising, when one thinks that it bases itself on the hypothesis of a rational, calculating *Homo oeconomicus*.

As we shall see, the scientific pretensions of neoclassical economics do not rest only on the formalism of the faction that dominates the field today. They go back much further in time – as far back as its original 'invention'.[5]

3. Ibid., p. 63.

4. 'Anyone who has studied the history of science a little knows that a fascination for formalism – and mathematics is by its nature a species of formalism – is an indisputable sign that science is slipping towards scientism. The spell of mathematics is a proof more of methodological weakness than of strength.' (Jacques Sapir, *Les Trous noirs de la science économique. Essai sur l'impossibilité de penser le temps et l'argent*, Paris: Albin Michel, 2000, p. 29.) The criticisms are much more violent in Bernard Maris, *Lettre ouverte aux gourous de l'économie qui nous prennent pour des imbéciles*, Paris: Albin Michel and Seuil, 1999/2003, which notes that the question most often treated in 'pure' economics is Arrow's impossibility theorem, a 'mathematical curiosity' for which 'mathematicians feel almost as much interest ... as for crossword puzzles' (p. 40).

5. See Serge Latouche, *L'Invention de l'économie*, Paris: Albin Michel, 2005. To some extent, the date of this 'invention' is obviously arbitrary. Some writers – Smith, Ricardo or Marx – go back to Aristotle; others to the mercantilists of the sixteenth and seventeenth centuries. Here we will settle on the eighteenth century, and particularly Adam Smith, even though his ideas have often been distorted to make out that he simply exalted the pursuit of individual self-interest as the means of achieving the general interest. The formulations in his *Theory of Moral Sentiments* (1759) are much more qualified, indeed different, in this respect.

THE TRIUMPH OF MECHANICS

In fact, we need to go back to the pivotal transition from philosophical reasoning to scientific reasoning, in the late seventeenth and early eighteenth centuries, when Descartes and Leibniz alike proposed a *mathesis universalis* (that is, a 'discourse without a subject') to make both the world and human relations (language) intelligible through mathematics.[6] For a long time these two systems – discursive and mathematical – supported and complemented each other, as we can see from Voltaire's attempt to put Newtonian physics 'within everyone's reach'[7] and from d'Alembert's and Diderot's publication of the *Encyclopédie ou dictionnaire raisonné des sciences, des arts et des métiers* (between 1751 and 1766).[8] This was also the period when academies on the model of the Royal Society were founded in Berlin (1700), St Petersburg (1725) and Stockholm (1739), when great enthusiasm was shown for the works of Leonhard Euler, when William Watson (1746) and Benjamin Franklin (1749) 'discovered' electrical phenomena (and Franklin invented the lightning conductor), when Carl von Linné undertook a systematic classification of nature (1735),[9] when La Mettrie published his *Machine Man* (1748), and when James Watt developed his steam engine, which became operational in 1786.

The Enlightenment therefore appears as an exceptional moment of Europe-wide scientific effervescence, in which early economists such as Turgot, Quesnay and Smith also participated.[10] None of

6. 'Nature is written in the language of mathematics', Galileo argued, against the Aristotelian tradition that distinguished between substance and form and identified earth, fire, air and water (or the hot, the cold, the dry and the wet) as the four elements.

7. Newton (1643–1727) published in 1687 his *Mathematical Principles of Natural Philosophy*, which dominated physics throughout the eighteenth century, and which Voltaire's *Élements de philosophie de Neuton* [sic] *mis à la portée de tout le monde* (1738) made accessible to cultured readers with an interest in physics.

8. We should note the primacy of science in the subtitle of the famous *Encyclopaedia*. The 'preliminary discourse' described physics or the study of nature as the key science that led to geometry, arithmetic and algebra.

9. In doing so, he spoke of the 'economy of nature', which made it possible to secure the best 'return' at minimum cost.

10. For a general overview, see the remarkable catalogue of the exhibition held in Paris

these founding fathers seems to have been personally involved in the debates and experiments that accompanied the birth of the new science. But, in keeping with the spirit of the age, they tried to understand their chosen field in terms of natural laws and value-neutral 'science', shaking off the constraints that had hitherto subjected production, consumption and exchange to the authority of the Prince or the Church.[11]

It is not without interest to note that Diderot admired the Physiocrats for 'giving birth to a new science specifically known as economic science'. 'All [their] works form a compact and clearly defined corpus, which reveals the natural law of men, the natural order of society, and the natural laws most advantageous for men gathered together in society.'[12] Dupont de Nemours, for his part, observed that 'since Quesnay, the ingenious inventor of the Economic Table, this science has become an exact science, all of whose points are susceptible of proofs as rigorous and indisputable as those of geometry and algebra.'[13]

This new science, which aimed to treat economic realities as part of a natural order (that is, of a society without actors), necessarily inserted itself into what Gusdorf calls the 'mental space' of the age, dominated by the mechanistic physics that offered itself,

in 2006: Yann Fauchois, Thierry Grillet and Tzvetan Todorov, eds, *Lumières! Un héritage pour demain*, Paris: Bibliothèque Nationale de France, 2006.

11. See, for instance, Adam Smith's account of 'natural price' (Book I, ch. 7) or 'the natural progress of opulence' (Book III, ch. 1) in *The Wealth of Nations* (vol. 1, London: Methuen, 1961). In Book IV, ch. 9 he writes that, if we disregard 'all systems of either preference or restraint …, the obvious and simple system of natural liberty establishes itself of its own accord'; this frees the sovereign from the impossible task of 'superintending the industry of private people' (vol. 2, p. 208). The founding works of political economy should thus be seen primarily as a critique of absolutism that closely links economic liberty to political liberty. At the same time, the theory of the harmony of interests makes morality unnecessary, by removing the disapproval that attaches to envy and the pursuit of individual interests. See Jean-Claude Michéa, *L'Empire du moindre mal. Essai sur la civilisation libérale*, Paris: Climats, 2007, p. 98.

12. Article on 'Agriculture', in *L'Encyclopédie*, quoted from Georges Gusdorf, *Les Sciences humaines et la conscience occidentale*, vol. 6: *L'Avènement des sciences humaines au Siècle des lumières*, Paris: Payot, 1973, p. 548.

13. Quoted in ibid., p. 549.

by virtue of its own successes, as a model for the human sciences too.[14] Social phenomena, conceived as effective homologues of natural phenomena, were to be explained in terms of 'laws' applicable to both, and in a vocabulary common to both, belonging as they did to one and the same 'natural order'.[15] Strictly speaking, then, although mechanics made its mark before economic 'science', the works of the early economists did not 'borrow' concepts from physics, but shared a single semantic world that guaranteed the scientific character of their propositions.[16] This is why economic 'science' founded its laws on concepts such as *equilibrium* (markets), *balance* (budgets, trade or payments), *mass* (money), *elasticity* (supply and demand), *forces* (market), *atomization* (market players), *circuit* (exchange of goods and services for money), *flows* (finance), *friction* (obstacles to competition), *leverage* (preference for credit rather than existing funds of capital), *boost* (economic revival), and so on.

This legacy bears the marks of an age completely geared to naturalization and rationalization of the world, including the social world, whose manifold phenomena became coherent through the discovery of 'laws' that made them intelligible, necessary and

14. For the Enlightenment, the Supreme Being was conceived as a 'great watchmaker' (Voltaire) or 'great architect' (the Freemasons) of the universe, in a final attempt to marry the natural order with theology. Nor was this mechanistic vocabulary absent from the political science of the age, which advocated 'checks and balances' to keep power in equilibrium and thus rested upon a 'political arithmetic' already present in Hobbes. This 'mental space', dazzled by Newtonian mechanics and attuned to the language of mathematics, existed in a universe of windmills, clocks, machines and newly ascendant steam engines (see Jacques Grinevald, 'Le sens bioéconomique du développement humain: l'affaire Nicholas Georgescu-Roegen', *Revue européenne des sciences sociales* 38 (51), 1980, pp. 62–3).

15. Pierre-Paul Le Mercier de la Rivière, *L'Ordre naturel et essentiel des sociétés politiques*, London: Jean Nourse, 1767.

16. 'The manner in which things exist and take place, constitutes what is called *the nature of things*; and a careful observation of the nature of things is the sole foundation of all truth. ... Political economy, ... in showing the manner in which events take place in relation to wealth,... forms a part of experimental science. ... Political economy, ... whenever the principles which constitute its basis are the rigorous deductions of undeniable general facts, rests upon an immoveable foundation.' Jean-Baptiste Say, *A Treatise on Political Economy*, 5th edn, Philadelphia: Claxton, Remsen & Haffelfinger, 1871, pp. xvii–xviii.

predictable.[17] However, this project to make economic 'science' a social physics, on the same footing as the natural (or physical-mechanistic) sciences, soon came to an end – for two reasons. First, the sciences of nature considerably altered their basic assumptions in the course of the nineteenth century – although economists did not try to take advantage of these new 'discoveries' in other disciplines. Second, and more fundamentally, the transposition of 'laws' from the natural world to the social domain had no legitimacy. For, even if one keeps adding ever more limiting assumptions, it will never be possible to explain the social system by the model of the solar system. In the social sciences, what Marglin calls 'algorithmic knowledge' has its limits.

THERMODYNAMICS AND THE IRREVERSIBILITY OF TIME

The classical mechanistic theory of Newton and Laplace had the characteristic of ignoring the temporal dimension, and therefore presupposed the reversibility of time. To put it simply, this meant that time had no importance, since one could always pass from situation A to situation B and subsequently *return* to an unchanged original situation. Meanwhile, of course, time passed 'normally' (hence irreversibly), but this did not affect the possibility of reproducing the phenomenon in the reverse direction. In celestial mechanics, bodies move regularly *ad indefinitum*; one can therefore predict their future position (or reconstruct their previous position) in a determinist manner, since the passing of time does not alter one's calculation. Evidently one cannot 'go back in time', but a given system that has been subjected to change can be restored

17. 'Nature, then, is what exists independently of human activity': quoted in Clément Rosset, *L'Anti-nature. Éléments pour une philosophie tragique*, Paris: PUF, 1986 (1973). To base economic 'science' on 'nature' makes it possible to disguise its historical and social origins. 'It is still in the name of ostensibly "scientific" knowledge that modern ideologies permit themselves to deploy their effects.' (Jean-Claude Michéa, *L'Empire du moindre mal*, Paris: Climats, 2007, p. 54.) Engels too claimed that socialism was scientific…

to its initial state if it is subjected to a reverse change.[18] Although it is not legitimate to generalize this theory – it has a foundation only at microscopic level, or in relation to celestial bodies (which move in the 'void', without friction) – critical appraisals of it took a long time to assert themselves. Without going further into the history, we may simply note that the first anomalies that called the mechanistic theory into question resulted from heat experiments: the fact that a warm body transmitted its heat to a cold body (until their temperatures equalized), never the reverse, indicated a real phenomenon of irreversibility.

The advent of thermodynamics thus rested on two fundamental principles. The first is that, in a closed system, the quantity of energy remains constant – or, in Lavoisier's aphoristic formulation, 'nothing is created, nothing is lost, everything is transformed'. The second is that, in a closed system, the 'useful' energy diminishes irreversibly and is transformed into 'disorder', or, in other words, into 'entropy', which cannot but increase over time.[19] Scientists did not admit it at once, but this was the end of classical mechanics and of its models based on reversibility.

But why are these considerations, even in the highly summary form given above, of concern to economic theory? For one simple reason. The 'scientific' claims of the early economists, based on physics as it was understood at the time, were thoroughly challenged by later paradigm shifts. For economic theory to retain the title of a 'science', it would have had to incorporate the results of the 'new physics' or thermodynamics (and also of the new sociology and psychology) in its way of posing problems, but

18. In economics this means that, if an event disturbs the equilibrium of supply and demand, the system is capable of spontaneously regaining the initial equilibrium.

19. The classical example is the piece of sugar that dissolves irreversibly into a glass of water; the reverse operation would evidently take not only time but a sizeable amount of new energy. These principles were first formulated by Sadi Carnot in 1824, and given general application by Rudolf Clausius in 1865. Clausius also introduced the concept of entropy, which corresponds to the degradation of 'useful' energy through its conversion into heat or mechanical work: a fuel that changes into heat and gas is irreversibly made unusable (and therefore loses its economic value).

instead it loftily turned its back on them. Having constituted itself as an autonomous 'science', economics thought it could go on constructing 'laws' on its original foundations, without facing up to questions about their validity.[20] In the course of the nineteenth century, economists did profoundly alter their approach to value: whereas the classics, from Smith to Marx, had based it on *labour*, the neoclassical economists (William Stanley Jevons, Carl Menger, Vilfredo Pareto, Auguste and Léon Walras) replaced this with *utility*.[21] What they did not give up, however, was their mechanistic ideal.[22]

Even in Léon Walras there is a kind of obstinate comparison of economic 'science' to mechanics and astronomy. For example: 'It is already perfectly clear that economics, like astronomy and mechanics, is both an empirical and a rational science. ... Then mathematical economics will rank with the mathematical sciences of astronomy and mechanics; and on that day justice will be done to our work.'[23] In another text, Walras at first seems eager to distinguish between physical facts (the objects of the physical-mathematical sciences of astronomy and mechanics) and psychic facts (the objects of the psychic-mathematical sciences – that is, of economics).[24] Does this mean that he has given up trying to keep economics within the fold of mechanics? Not at all. On the next

20. 'Advice derived from static reasoning, which ignores time, is often categorically opposed to advice derived from dynamic analysis, which takes time into account. Since the economy is fundamentally dynamic, static analysis is therefore normally dangerously wrong.' Keen, *Debunking Economics*, p. 81.

21. For an economist, the utility of a good is equivalent to its desirability: bread can be as 'useful' as poison.

22. The notable exception is Thorstein Veblen ('Why Is Economics Not an Evolutionary Science?', *Quarterly Journal of Economics* 12, 1898, pp. 373–97), who tried to interpret economics in the light of biology rather than physics, and who took into account the social and institutional changes that had made earlier assumptions obsolete.

23. Léon Walras, 'Preface to the Fourth Edition', in *Elements of Pure Economics*, London: George Allen & Unwin, 1954, pp. 47–8.

24. Léon Walras, 'Economics and Mechanics' (1909), in Philip Mirowski and Pamela Cook, 'Walras' "Economics and Mechanics": Translation, Commentary, Context', in Warren J. Samuels, ed., *Economics as Discourse: An Analysis of the Language of Economists*, Dordrecht: Kluwer, 1990, pp. 189–213.

page he states: 'It is easy to make mathematicians see that [the] procedure [of economics] is rigorously identical to that of the two most advanced and uncontested physico-mathematical sciences, rational mechanics and celestial mechanics.'[25] He illustrates this with several examples and suggests a set of equations to explain phenomena in both economics and 'celestial mechanics'. The article concludes: 'Mathematics would be the special language for discussing quantitative facts and it should go without saying that economics is a mathematical science on a par with mechanics and astronomy.'[26]

Nicholas Georgescu-Roegen points out:

> A curious event in the history of economic thought is that, years after the mechanistic dogma had lost its supremacy in physics and its grip on the philosophical world, the founders of the Neoclassical school set out to erect an economic science after the pattern of mechanics – in the words of Jevons, as 'the mechanics of utility and self-interest'.[27]

The fact is not only 'curious' but grave. In stubbornly seeking to build economic 'science' on the model of mechanics, when scientists themselves consider this to be obsolete, the neoclassical economists not only led their discipline into a dead end but undermined their own scientific pretensions. *Pace* Walras, economics is not only concerned with quantitative facts; it also addresses qualitative facts corresponding to the types of resources used (which do not produce entropy at the same rate). What is at issue is not the use of mathematics per se in economic argument, but reliance on models that are incapable of accounting for the irreversibility of the economic process, and therefore of its entropic nature (not to speak of social phenomena, which cannot be reduced to objects of natural science).[28]

---

25. Ibid., p. 208.

26. Ibid., p. 213.

27. Nicholas Georgescu-Roegen, 'The Entropy Law and the Economic Problem' (1970), in *Energy and Economic Myths: Institutional and Analytical Economic Essays*, New York: Pergamon Press, 1976, p. 53.

28. 'It is thermodynamics, through the Entropy Law, that recognizes the qualitative

One perverse effect of the mechanistic model may be seen in the circular diagram that economics manuals use to represent the economic process, in which the to-and-fro movement (by definition balanced) between production and consumption takes place within a closed, seemingly self-sufficient, system. In this schema, the economic circuit – or 'carousel'[29] – operates 'off the ground' and in an atemporal manner, taking no account of exchange with the environment, whether 'inputs' (natural resources, energy) or 'outputs' (degraded energy, waste), and forgetting that all production is matched by destruction and qualitative change in the environment.[30]

This leads to a surprising paradox. If the economic process really did unfold in a universe characterized by reversibility, scarcity would disappear since it would be possible to recover gas, smoke and ashes and to reconstitute the piece of coal one has just burned, and people might think that the needs of all could be satisfied at minimal cost.[31] Whereas in reality 'scarcity' underpins mainstream economic 'science', the mechanistic assumption of reversibility ought to lead it to ignore scarcity (which would leave economic 'science' without an object). So, in a way, economists must take the law of entropy into account (implicitly, without ever admitting it) in order to establish an original scarcity linked to their view of the unlimited character of needs, but then they overlook the effects of the degradation of energy–matter flows and continue to calculate in the enchanted world of classical

---

distinction which economists should have made from the outset between the inputs of valuable resources (low entropy) and the final outputs of valueless waste (high entropy).' Nicholas Georgescu-Roegen, 'Energy and Economic Myths' (1972), in *Energy and Economic Myths*, p. 9.

29. José Manuel Naredo, *La Economía en evolución. Historia y perspectivas de las categorías básicas del pensamiento económico*, Madrid: Siglo XXI de España, 2003, p. 68.

30. 'To equate the economic process with a mechanical analogue implies ... the myth that the economic process is a circular merry-go-round which cannot possibly affect the environment of matter and energy in any way.' Georgescu-Roegen, 'Energy and Economic Myths', p. 6.

31. Ibid., p. 9.

mechanics. It is exactly as if economic 'science' needed scarcity as its founding myth, only to rid itself of it through growth, whereas the contrary position holds that the actual economic process irreversibly degrades energy–matter and produces ever greater entropy that leads to scarcity, even absolute scarcity. The question then becomes whether scarcity lies behind us or in front of us.

THE IMPOTENCE OF ECONOMIC 'REASON'

To repeat: the mathematization of economics is not the issue: it is not the origin of some major aberration from normal economic 'science'.[32] Each science is free to choose its tools and modes of expression. The fundamental problem is not one of method but one of underlying assumptions. Let us simply note that the autonomy of economic 'science' (with its forms of calculation, its reduction of reality to questionable schemas, its ignorance of irreversible phenomena) rests upon principles that were generally accepted at the turn of the nineteenth century but that have since been consigned to the museum of naiveties of a bygone age; its only remaining believers are those economists who use mathematics to back up their scientific pretensions, without considering the validity of their initial (now anachronistic) hypotheses based upon mechanics.[33] The gravest consequence, over and above these

32. This is true even though the mathematization of economics continues to count as proof of its scientific character. We should also remind ourselves that Ricardo was not stinting with calculations and tables.

33. The classical economists are partly responsible for this false track. Apart from their ignorance of thermodynamics (which they can hardly be blamed for), they placed unshakeable trust in the cost-free 'bounty' of nature. Ricardo, for example, approved of Adam Smith's assertion that 'the rent of coal mines, and of stone quarries, ... is paid for the value of the coal or stone which can be removed from them, and has no connection with the original and indestructible powers of the land.' In plain language, this means that the cost of coal or stones corresponds solely to the cost of their extraction. 'Nothing is given for the use of air and water,' he continues, 'or for any other of the gifts of nature which exist in boundless quantity. ... In the same manner, the brewer, the distiller, the dyer, make incessant use of the air and water for the production of their commodities;

theoretical points, is that mainstream economic 'science' is not equipped to grapple with the ecological problems at the heart of present-day concerns. It is incapable of understanding the qualitative difference between what is produced by a machine running on renewable energy (wind, water, geothermal or solar energy) and by one running on non-renewable sources. Hence it cannot but encourage waste, rather than 'economize', since it takes no account of the fact that a large part of 'economic wealth' stems from ecological impoverishment. This is why it is insufficient to price in energy, waste or environmental degradation,[34] or to imagine that the market will necessarily restore equilibrium and solve the problems. Indeed, we have to recognize that time flows irreversibly, that the economic process takes place within an open system, and that many phenomena, far from tending towards equilibrium, are subject to a circular, cumulative causality that produces imbalances uncontrollable by 'market forces' alone. In the same way that *Homo oeconomicus* ignores society, the mechanistic model ignores nature and its specific temporality, which entails deep-seated uncertainty about future prices and defies all rational prediction.

In the end, if economics really were a science, it would not escape the paradigm shifts that are the fate of all the sciences. Contemporary physics, to take just one example, does not have

---

but as the supply is boundless, they bear no price.' At this point he quotes in a footnote from Book II, Chapter 9 of Say's *Treatise on Political Economy*: 'The waters of rivers, and of the sea, by the power which they have of giving movement to our machines, carrying our boats, nourishing our fish, have also a productive power; the wind which turns our mills, and even the heat of the sun, work for us; but happily no one has yet been able to say, "the wind and the sun are mine, and the service which they render must be paid for".' David Ricardo, *The Principles of Political Economy and Taxation* (1817), London: Dent, 1973, pp. 34–5.

34. Such prices are anyway patently fictitious. What is the 'value' of a landscape, a silence, a climate, or a threatened species of flowers, butterflies or birds, or a glacier? 'Faced with externalities, the issue for most economists is how to invent the missing markets or, failing actual markets, how to imitate the market mechanism. Hence the economist speaks of trade-offs between the environment and other goods, just as he or she speaks of exchanges between any two goods in the marketplace.' Marglin, *The Dismal Science*, p. 51.

much in common with the physics of the Enlightenment. The reason is simple: there came a point when the 'mainstream science' of that age could no longer explain certain phenomena; when the accumulation of 'anomalies' led scientists to reject an obsolete theory, sometimes with misgivings, and to replace it with a new one. It should be stressed that such 'scientific revolutions'[35] are not just a matter of a breakthrough in knowledge in a particular field; they involve a break between old and new knowledge, as the upheavals due to Copernicus, Newton and Einstein illustrate. 'Because it demands large-scale paradigm destruction and major shifts in the problems and techniques of normal science, the emergence of new theories is generally preceded by a period of pronounced professional insecurity.'[36]

Nothing of this kind is noticeable in economic 'science', however. This does evolve, of course, as it takes an interest in new areas and tries to take various phenomena on board. It recognizes that perfect free information (a precondition of Walrasian equilibrium) does not exist, and that we have to think in terms of asymmetrical information or imperfect competition. It asks questions about transaction costs, convergent expectations, trade agreements and institutions, and much else besides – all of which may involve novel approaches and a focus on particular issues. But nothing ever challenges the fundamental assumptions of the theory: we are always stuck with the supposedly utilitarian rationality of the individual subject and a universal axiomatics of interest. How can one fail to see, behind these notions of rationality (= calculation) and universality, traces of the mechanistic vision at the heart of Enlightenment science? Yet, more surprising still, economists do not change these premises even when they admit their reductionist character. Instead, they content themselves with minor adjustments, 'immunizing strategies' or ad hoc hypotheses

35. Kuhn, *The Structure of Scientific Revolutions*, 1970.
36. Ibid., pp. 67–8.

– for example, the introduction of 'limited rationality' (since *Homo oeconomicus* has never shown himself to be perfectly rational) to avoid giving up the principle of rationality as such.[37] Such touches are mainly designed to save the model on which 'normal science' is based, not to account for the way in which economic processes actually occur.

A report which, though now fairly old, was written under the aegis of one of France's most prestigious economists, Edmond Malinvaud, took a more nuanced position:

> Economic knowledge today finds itself in an ambiguous position. In part it originates in a genuine science, long autonomous but comparable in its ambitions and methodology to the sciences of nature and life. But the explanatory and prescriptive power of that science is rather limited. This is why our knowledge of economic phenomena also stems in part from a less rigorous discipline, which sometimes does not go much beyond mere historical description, but which is anxious to embrace every aspect of the economic impact on the life of human beings and societies.[38]

This is a strange admission: first, economics is a fully fledged science comparable to others; then it is unable to explain much, provides little guidance for decisions, and refers us, for an understanding of the world, to 'less rigorous' disciplines such as history, psychology, anthropology, political science or sociology. Others are much more outspoken:

> Virtually every aspect of conventional economic theory is intellectually unsound; virtually every economic recommendation is just as likely to do general harm as it is to lead to the general good. Far from holding the intellectual high ground, economics rests on foundations of quicksand. If economics were truly a science, then the dominant school of thought in economics would long ago have disappeared from view. Instead it

37. Philippe d'Iribarne, 'Comment l'économie assure-t-elle sa clôture?', *Revue du MAUSS* 15–16, 1992, pp. 58–78.

38. Quoted in Pascal Combemale, 'Ce qui se sait vraiment en économie', *Revue du MAUSS* 8, 1990, pp. 113–14. Edmond Malinvaud, Professor at the Collège de France, submitted this report in the late 1980s to the education ministry of the government of Lionel Jospin.

> has been preserved, not via greater knowledge, as its advocates might believe, but by ignorance.[39]

We cannot but wonder what economic 'science' is good for, apart from allowing economists to cultivate a little garden to which representatives of other disciplines are denied access.

If the term 'economic science' has become so widely used (but not 'psychological science', 'anthropological science' or 'geographical science'), is it not to lend authority to a single view of the world and to make us believe that none other is possible?

39. Keen, *Debunking Economics*, p. 4.

CHAPTER 3

HOMO OECONOMICUS: A DANGEROUS PHANTOM

Most economists, we must grant them that, admit that an autonomous rational *Homo oeconomicus* is a fiction. Yet his ghost keeps coming back to haunt the economic imagination. It is symptomatic that the standard version of mainstream (or neoclassical) economics supports itself upon a character who does not exist: entrance to the world of economists begins with trust in a model, not with questioning about social practices.

Homo oeconomicus appears as a rational (that is, calculating) individual, who disposes of scarce resources that can be allocated to various uses, but whose needs are unlimited, who makes self-interested choices, and who seeks to obtain the greatest satisfaction with the minimum effort. He is a consumer, but not a citizen.

The model has certainly evolved in the course of history – from the classical economists (Adam Smith) through the utilitarians (Jeremy Bentham), marginalists and neoclassicals (Léon Walras) to behavioural economics or theories of human capital (Gary Becker) that apply the economic model to the whole of human behaviour. But the basic hypotheses remain the same. *Homo oeconomicus* is always a rational, maximizing individual, without a history, an unconscious or a class identity, enjoying perfect information about prices and responding only to them. It is therefore easy to show that the real world is very different, that human beings live in society and act in accordance with a number of rationalities (not only self-interest), that they also observe various traditions or conventions, that they never know everything and have to make decisions in a situation of uncertainty, and so on. Hence the various special theories to meet these objections. But the ultimate purpose of the growing complexity is only to save the model.

Before we go any further, we need to say something about the famous Robinson Crusoe scenarios that Marx already ridiculed,[1] and which found their canonical form in Lionel Robbins's formulation: 'Economics is a science which studies human behaviour as a relationship between ends and scarce means which have alternative uses.' The first question is: what is specifically economic in the behaviour of the isolated *Homo oeconomicus* on Crusoe's island? It is true that he tries to 'economize' his strength and resources, and he wonders whether it would be better to use planks from the shipwreck to make a roof against the rain or to seal off his garden from wild beasts. Is his weighing up of effort against expected results (or risks against expected gains) not the kind of attitude that any sensible person would spontaneously adopt? How is it possible to reduce economics to simple husbandry, to the pure instrumentalism of cost–benefit calculations, without speaking at the same time of exchange? In all societies, 'intelligent' behaviour consists in organizing the available (limited) means to achieve certain ends. To define economics in this way is tantamount to claiming that economics is everywhere. But, before he met Friday – and hence before he practised exchange – did Crusoe engage

1. 'The individual and isolated hunter and fisherman, with whom Smith and Ricardo begin, belongs among the unimaginative conceits of the eighteenth-century Robinsonades, which in no way express merely a reaction against oversophistication and a return to a misunderstood natural life, as cultural historians imagine. ... In this society of free competition, the individual appears detached from the natural bonds etc. which in earlier historical periods make him the accessory of a definite and limited human conglomerate.' Karl Marx, *Grundrisse: Foundations of the Critique of Political Economy*, London: Penguin, 1993, p. 83.

in economics, or did he simply try his best to survive? If he did both – as most economists seem to think – the conclusion would have to be that economics is only the 'science' of survival,[2] and, above all, that economic 'science' places the isolated individual at the heart of its system, as if everyone lived only for himself, as if society did not exist.

In the eyes of mainstream economic 'science', the advantages of the model are its simplicity and its effectiveness: it employs a small number of hypotheses, yet makes it possible to explain a wide range of behaviour. To be true, however, this assertion needs to be qualified. Even if we assume that economic actors compare the possible choices and are consistent in their decisions (i.e. their preferences are stable and transitive), we must also recognize that their calculation has a cost and that, if this cost is greater than the expected gain (because the gathering of information itself consumes resources), it may be 'rational' to be irrational: that is, to forgo choice evaluation and to behave inconsistently. Moreover, it has been pointed out that, in the face of risks, the preferences of economic actors are most often inconsistent (paradox of Allais[3]). We could go on listing the objections – raised by economists themselves – which raise serious doubts about the validity of the model, or which considerably narrow its scope by excluding

2. James Buchanan remarked long ago that a Robbins-style definition of economics as 'the science of choices' reduced it to a mere calculation technique, whereas it should really start from exchange: 'Crusoe's problem is ... essentially a computational one, and all that he needs do to solve it is to programme the built-in computer that he has in his mind. The uniquely symbiotic [i.e. social] aspects of behaviour of human choice arise only when Friday steps on the island, and Crusoe is forced into association with another human being.' *Economics: Between Predictive Science and Moral Philosophy*, Austin: Texas A&M University Press, 1987, p. 27. By reducing economics to the calculation of opportunity costs, Lionel Robbins made the (political) discussion of goals beside the point.

3. This simply means that the transitivity of choices or preferences (if I prefer A to B and B to C, then I prefer A to C) is not always respected, especially in situations of uncertainty. In theory everyone is supposed to define their preferences without knowing or taking into account those of other people, and such preferences are assumed to be constant, even if the context changes.

the many situations in which it lacks explanatory, and *a fortiori* predictive, power.[4]

So, how can a model that is under attack from all sides, and that is constantly refuted by the facts, continue to provide the framework for mainstream economic 'science'? Although everyone agrees that it is excessively reductionist, many still cling to it because, once its assumptions are accepted, it offers a way to construct the basic theorems of microeconomics and to adapt them subsequently for macroeconomics. It therefore teaches us how the system should function if, and only if, we accept the premises on which the system is based. In a way, this kind of problem is also found in other disciplines. For example, the statement that 'a straight line is the shortest distance between two points' (or that parallel lines only meet at infinity) is true if and only if we are situated in Euclidean space. Geometers are well aware of this, and their science long ago developed complex hypotheses to account for more general cases, including curved or elliptical space. Similarly, even neoclassical economists might be expected to confine their model to situations that fit it, while devising others to account for the (much more numerous) circumstances that are exceptions to it.[5] Why not say outright that the theory

4. 'The economic approach implies that the actor is selfish (indifferent to solidarity), that his objectives are material (concern neither power nor prestige), that he always seeks to maximize his interest (is not content with suboptimal or merely "satisficing" gains), that he does not arbitrate by conforming to certain values (which would bar him from profit maximization), that he has precise information about prices, and that he disregards the impact his decision will have on other actors or the environment.' Philippe van Parijs, 'Le modèle économique dans les sciences sociales: imposture ou nécessité?', *Bulletin du MAUSS* 22, June 1987, pp. 70f.

5. 'I notice that there now reigns in the world a multitude of petty maxims that seduce the simple by a false appearance of philosophy. ... Such is this one: "Everywhere men have the same passions; everywhere amour-propre and self-interest lead them; therefore everywhere they are the same." When Geometers have made an assumption that from reasoning to reasoning leads them to an absurdity, they go back on their steps and thus demonstrate the assumption to be false. The same method, applied to the maxim in question, would easily show its absurdity.' Jean-Jacques Rousseau, 'Preface to *Narcissus, or The Lover of Himself*' (1782), in *The Collected Writings of Rousseau*, vol. 2, Hanover NH: University Press of New England, 1992, p. 194.

is true so long as one is speaking of market economics – where all actors pursue their self-interest (or maximize their utility), competition is perfect and transparency total – but that it does not apply to the majority of cases where actors are driven by different motives?[6] Instead, however, everything is done to save the model by making it more complex,[7] in order to explain decisions taken in a situation of uncertainty or to decipher the intersecting expectations that actors form on the basis of what they think others are thinking.[8] Economic 'science' is then forced to act 'as if' the model was true, while recognizing that it is not true in reality. It does not try to propose a different model, with greater explanatory or predictive potential, because its founding dogmas appear untouchable or their rejection would cost too much theoretically.

Standard theory, then, starts from the isolated individual, considering him as a special living being, an independent and autonomous subject, with no obligation to others. Well, one might

6. In fact, Carl Menger already insisted that the scope of his *Principles* should be restricted to the modern market economy (see Karl Polanyi, *The Livelihood of Man*, New York: Academic Press, 1977, pp. 22f.). This was also the position of Dudley Seers, in a famous article that has been too quickly forgotten ('The Limitations of the Special Case', *Bulletin of the Institute of Economics and Statistics* 25 (2), Oxford, May 1963, pp. 77–97). Seers was already arguing that Western ways of conceiving and teaching economics should not be extended to the countries of the South; that would, he said, be like calling *Treatise on Zoology* a work that dealt only with horses or fish, on the grounds that there were physiological similarities among all animals.

7. 'As ... Imre Lakatos explained, the central propositions of any theoretical framework are surrounded by a "protective belt" of "auxiliary assumptions" that prevent them from being refuted.' Rod Hills and Tony Myatt, *The Economics Anti-Textbook: A Critical Thinker's Guide to Micro-Economics*, London: Zed Books, 2010, p. 3.

8. Hence the famous metaphor of the beauty contest, which Keynes used as the basis for his theory of multiple equilibria (*The General Theory of Employment, Interest and Money*, London: Macmillan, 1961, p. 156). Speculators are compared to people who, having been shown photos of a number of pretty girls, have to say which would be designated as such by a majority of those present at the contest. 'It is not a case of choosing those which, to the best of one's judgement, are really the prettiest, nor even those which average opinion genuinely thinks the prettiest. We have reached the third degree where we devote our intelligences to anticipating what average opinion expects the average opinion to be. And there are some, I believe, who practise the fourth, fifth and higher degrees.' This points forward to the 'strategic rationality' of game theory, in which the environment changes as a function of the actors' decisions.

say, that is very simple and down to earth. Do we not daily meet 'individuals' about whom we know nothing, but whom we take to be visible examples of the human species? Yes, but do they conform to the definition that unknown economists give of them? Do they think of themselves as independent, autonomous and especially self-interested subjects?

THE UNLOCATABLE INDIVIDUAL

A brief anthropological excursus will give us cause to doubt it. Among the Peuls and Bambara, for example, a distinction is made between the 'container' or 'envelope' person (their relatively unimportant physical appearance, or *maa*) and the multiple 'personae of the person' (*maaya*), which vary unpredictably, even in a single day, and may change with the individual's age and involve changes in their name. In this perspective, man is not a monolithic (undivided) being but a totality in movement, not a closed entity but a being linked to others like him.[9] Melanesians, for their part, do not necessarily link their 'self' to their physical organism.[10] 'Individuals' are unknown: there are only *ka-mo* ('the wake'), and *do kamo* ('real humans') know themselves only through their relationship with others. 'Ego' is a kind of empty place that exists only as a function of other people, varying in accordance with the person in whose presence one finds oneself; hence the practice whereby a person is given different names by their father, uncle or sister, in addition to an ancestral name and a secret name. In such circumstances, how could anyone have an 'identity card'? Lastly, also in Melanesia, maternal uncle and nephew, father-in-law and son-in-law, grandfather and grandson,

9. Amadou Hampaté Bâ, 'La notion de personne en Afrique noire', *Colloques internationaux du CNRS* 544, 1973, pp. 181–92. Is this multiplicity of personae within a single person so far removed from our own culture, when we say, for example: 'it was too strong for me' or 'he was beside himself' or 'that wasn't like him at all'?

10. One can be accused of theft in a neighbouring village that took place while one was asleep.

are in a situation of reciprocity and call each other simply *duamata* (that is, 'our relative', without a proper name).[11] It would be easy to keep giving examples that challenge the universality of the notion of the individual. Let us take just two more. In Togo people draw *fa*[12] to determine whether a newborn child 'is' a grandfather or an uncle – which means that he will not be one 'individual' but two persons at once. Similarly, individualization has no meaning among the Cherokee: they say *tsi watah* ('I am a wolf') to underline that they are of the clan totem, since tradition has it that wolves created men.[13]

But how do these exotic references concern the paradigm of *Homo oeconomicus*? The simple answer is that economics assumes its model must be valid for all societies, but that this is largely an exaggerated claim – unless one considers that it can be imposed through the dominance of the market (which is now actually happening, not without resistance). Furthermore, the model of a 'standard' individual, free, autonomous and self-interested (who therefore always uses his freedom in the same way), became a possibility only in very special historical circumstances. Without going back to Aristotle, who defined man as ζῶον πολιτικὸν (a political or social animal, destined to live in society), we may recall that everyone in the *Ancien Régime* in France was defined by their estate or status: you were '*de* quelque part' (from somewhere),

11. Maurice Leenhardt, *Do Kamo. La personne et le mythe dans le monde melanésien*, Paris: Gallimard, 1985 (1947); *Do Kamo: Person and Myth in the Melanesian World*, Chicago: University of Chicago Press, 1979. It might be objected that all this material is old and that, as Leenhardt himself recognized, missionaries had helped to endow Melanesians with a body. Nevertheless, Jean-Marie Tjibaou agreed that the Kanak were far from having abandoned all their traditional conceptions: 'I am never I', he said, for example. 'I always exist with reference to someone.' And Achille Mbembé stated that the phenomenon of multiple personae still exists in Africa.

12. A method of geomancy that interprets signs from the position of a cowrie necklace thrown onto sand. For a more detailed account, see Edo Adjakly, *Pratique de la tradition religieuse et reproduction sociale chez les Guen/Mina du Sud-Est du Togo*, Geneva: Institut universitaire d'études du développement, coll. 'Itinéraires', 1985.

13. Jimmie Durham, 'Eloheh or the Council of the Universe', *Development* 3/4, 1981, Rome: SID, pp. 10–16.

prince or subject, member of a corporation (and therefore a body); or you were identified by your position in the family (Père Jean, Mère Marion, Antoine's widow or Pierre's son). Conditions were not uniform, and persons were not interchangeable; there was therefore no 'individual'!

It is indeed quite remarkable that the term 'individual' appeared in the social and political space only in the course of the eighteenth century,[14] when it served not to highlight particularity but to defend equality; universal suffrage thus 'abolished distinctions and privileges based on social order, category and class: everyone was only but totally "one".'[15] Only in the early nineteenth century did *l'individu* cease to designate equals and come to connote social egotism. And it was in the context of economic and political reflection that the new term *l'individualisme* made its debut between 1829 and 1835, in the works of Lamennais and then Balzac.[16]

Homo oeconomicus, the autonomous individual driven by self-interest, is generally accepted to be a mental concoction, but it is far from displaying the same properties everywhere (as the dominant economic current maintains). It could not come into being just anywhere or at just any time; its birth is purely contingent and coincides precisely with the invention of economic 'science'. This poses a formidable epistemological problem. How can one base a 'science' on the supposedly transhistorical and transcultural model of *Homo oeconomicus*, if the model first saw the

14. Of course the word already existed, but in different orders of discourse. For medieval scholasticism, *individuum* signified the indivisible or singular, that which cannot be divided without disappearing; it referred back to the Greek ἄτομος (literally 'indivisible'), which in its modern form, 'atom', was reserved for matter. The word 'individual' therefore did not apply to human beings, who were spoken of as 'persons' (from the Roman distinction between *persona* and *res*). Later, the word resurfaced in the life sciences, where it served to differentiate individuals from the genus and species. The French term *l'individu* appeared in the social-political order with Rousseau, Diderot and Condorcet, under the influence especially of Locke, whose works were translated soon after their publication in English. See Anne Viguier, 'Enfances de l'*Individu*, entre l'École, la Nature et la Police', *Mots* 9, October 1984, pp. 33–55.

15. Ibid., p. 51.

16. Ibid., p. 34.

light of day in the framework of that science and therefore depends upon a kind of cultural arbitrariness?[17] Beyond the conundrums about which came first, the chicken or the egg, it must at least be agreed that *Homo oeconomicus* is only a petty-minded provincial, who has hardly seen anything of the world and has a mere two centuries of history behind him. A solid dose of arrogance (and ignorance) is required to make him the ancestor of humanity, and to suggest that human beings have always naturally given themselves up to the joys of economics – especially since the 'rationality' of economic behaviour has often been imposed by violent authoritarian means, including the repression of workers' struggles in nineteenth-century Europe, the colonization of large parts of the world and, more recently, the imposition of IMF structural adjustment plans in the countries of the South.

HOW TO CONSTRUCT SOCIETY?

In social and political debate, the emergence of the individual raised (or re-raised) the old problem of how a society 'holds together' as a single entity. Antiquity already used the functional metaphor of the body and its limbs to justify the disparity of social conditions, allocating pre-eminence to the 'head', and the debate resumed with the social contract theories of Hobbes, Locke and

17. 'Economic Man is a bourgeois construction' (Marshall Sahlins, *Stone Age Economics*, Chicago: Aldine Atherton, 1972, p. 13). To be sure, Adam Smith became famous for his assertion that 'it is not from the benevolence of the butcher, the brewer, or the baker, that we expect our dinner, but from their regard to their own interest. We address ourselves, not to their humanity but to their self-love, and never talk to them of our own necessities but of their advantages' (*The Wealth of Nations*, Book I, ch. 2, p. 18). But that is far from conveying the whole of his thought. He also wrote: 'And hence it is, that to feel much for others and little for ourselves, that to restrain our selfish, and to indulge our benevolent affections, constitutes the perfection of human nature' (*The Theory of Moral Sentiments*, Oxford: Oxford University Press, 1979, Part I, Section 1, ch. 5.5, p. 25). Or again: 'That whole account of human nature, however, which deduces all sentiments and affections from self-love, which has made so much noise in the world, but which, so far as I know, has never yet been fully and distinctly explained, seems to me to have arisen from some confused misapprehension of the system of sympathy' (Part VII, Section 3, ch. 1.4, p. 317).

Rousseau. Of course, in keeping with the spirit of the times, these authors imagined human life in the state of nature (which did not have the sense of a prior historical stage) to be 'pre-political'. But this meant according a fundamental role to the individual parties to the contract, whose agreement (spontaneous or driven by necessity) established society, the nation or the social body. The minutiae, which have brought forth torrents of ink from political theorists, cannot be entered into here. However, two points closely relate to the way in which mainstream economists conceive of the world. First, methodologically, the very idea of grounding society on a contract, whatever its form, implied that the social dimension could be constructed through the aggregation of individual wills; this conflicted with the previously accepted notion that the unity of the social body rested upon a meta-social guarantor or on God himself (who legitimated the divine law monarch). It was a major innovation, which placed power in the hands of the contracting citizens (even giving them the right to behead the king!),[18] and which made it possible to explain the whole by the parts. Second – a point to which we shall return – the 'discovery' that the market maximized everyone's advantage, as the meeting place for the supply and demand of anonymous individuals eager to pursue their own interests, seemed to corroborate a theory that had originated in political philosophy (or political fiction). This put an end to the aristocratic ideal of honour and to the moral obligations of religion.

---

18. 'When I say "end of religion" I am referring to a quite specific phenomenon: the end of the principle of dependency structuring social space in all known societies prior to our own. ... The complete organization of the human-social sphere by religion is one thing: herein lies the historical truth of the religious phenomenon, and it is at this level alone that it makes sense to speak of the "end of religion"; but the role retained by religious beliefs in societies wholly organized outside religion is completely different.' Marcel Gauchet, *The Disenchantment of the World: A Political History of Religion*, Princeton NJ: Princeton University Press, 1997 (1985), pp. 163–4. Although Gauchet is right that the reference to God no longer structures our society, we would argue that economics has become a new form of religion. Religion is not disappearing: it is mutating, and reappearing where one does not expect it.

THE TAUTOLOGIES OF METHODOLOGICAL INDIVIDUALISM

So, the newborn *Homo oeconomicus* multiplied rapidly – or, to be more precise, his inventors hastened to 'clone' him theoretically as the representative of humanity, at once unique and innumerable. It was a dual *tour de force*, as well as a *coup de force*, which brought with it a new image of society as an agglomeration of mutually independent individuals, linked to one another only through fleeting acts of exchange that they see as serving to satisfy their interests.

This explanatory schema of human behaviour, which now goes by the name of methodological individualism, maintains that collective phenomena can be explained only on the basis of individual behaviour. It is a perspective that goes back to Jeremy Bentham, who wrote: 'The community is a fictitious body. ... The interests of the community then is [*sic*] the sum of the interests of the several members who compose it.'[19] More recently Margaret Thatcher vigorously proclaimed: 'There is no such thing as society.' Although mainstream economics has gradually refined its argument, accepting that individuals are not necessarily perfectly informed, that their rationality is sometimes limited, and that they may make decisions on the basis of prior experience, the fact remains that *Homo oeconomicus* is still concerned only with the maximization of his interests.

Raymond Boudon, who, though a sociologist rather than an economist, claims to be a follower of methodological individualism,[20] writes of it as follows:

19. Quoted from Keen, *Debunking Economics*, p. 28.

20. Compare the Public Choice school in the United States, founded by James Buchanan. Or this: 'We can explain even the most complex social phenomena by tracing them back to the individual and without invoking collective processes irreducible to the individual.' Henri Lepage, *Tomorrow Capitalism: The Economics of Economic Freedom*, La Salle IL: Open Court, 1978, p. 179.

> This principle means … that the sociologist must employ a method which considers the individuals, or individual actors, included in a system of interaction as the logical atoms of his analysis. … In each case, one can see an effort being made by the sociologist to analyse the reactions of the individual actors to the constraints defined by the system. It is necessary to add that these reactions are often established by an *introspective* type of method. … The sociologist reserves the right to resort to a universalist psychology. It implies, therefore, that the particular characteristics of the situation and of the context where the observed is placed will not affect his psychology to the point where his behaviour becomes unintelligible to the observer. If the behaviour of the observed appears to the observer to be difficult to comprehend, it is not due to the fact that their 'psychologies' are different but, for example, because certain elements of the system of interaction to which the observed belongs elude the observer.[21]

This definition, which includes a number of familiar points, displays the extreme poverty of the paradigm. First, it rests on the postulate of a 'human nature' common to all, which supposedly explains why, in like circumstances, people react in like manner, in accordance with their interests or a kind of 'rationality' that various authors define in various ways.[22] For the sociologist or economist, then, the task is like that of a policeman: 'to imagine what goes on in people's heads',[23] in order to reconstitute their motives 'with near-certainty' through introspection and

21. Raymond Boudon, *The Logic of Social Action: An Introduction to Sociological Analysis*, London: Routledge & Kegan Paul, 1981 [1979], pp. 36–7. See Raymond Boudon, 'L'individualisme méthodologique', in *Encyclopaedia universalis, Les Enjeux*, vol. 2, 1990, pp. 1134–8; and 'Individualisme ou holisme: un débat méthodologique fondamental', in Henri Mendras and Michel Verret, eds, *Les Champs de la sociologie française*, Paris: Armand Colin, 1988, pp. 31–45.

22. Apart from the 'pure' rationality of the neoclassical economists (rational choice or rational action theory), in which the calculating individual disposes of perfect information, there is also 'limited rationality' (Henri Simon) when the actor's information is imperfect and compels him to act in accordance with his existing knowledge, emotions and environment, or even a 'contextual rationality' (Alfred Hirschman) linked to the social (consumerist), institutional and political environment. Suddenly everything may become 'rational': everyone simply chooses their particular preference. This lands us in the realm of outright tautology. Although, in its early days, the theory of limited rationality recognized that the actor's self-interest was not always decisive, its conclusions still left no scope for other possible motives. See Jacques T. Godbout, *Ce qui circule entre nous. Donner, recevoir, rendre*, Paris: Seuil, 2007, pp. 241f.

23. Boudon, 'L'individualisme méthodologique', pp. 1136–7.

'universalist psychology'. Of course, it is necessary to take account of particular 'contextual constraints', never forgetting that, even if individual actors appear to act irrationally,[24] they have 'good reasons' for doing what they do in pursuit of their interests.[25] By this argument, one can always judge that the entrepreneur, mystic, altruist or thief is 'rational', in so far as he chooses the solution that seems best to him, but in the end the model does not explain much. Its underlying assumption is confirmed, in particular cases, only if it is accompanied with ad hoc hypotheses or contextual restrictions that make it slide into tautology.

Methodological individualism claims to explain numerous particular cases, but most often it does so *a posteriori*, by reconstituting them on the basis of assumptions that ratify the model. Thus, someone who chooses a life of pleasure is just as rational as someone who joins a monastic order; both 'are maximizing their satisfaction'.[26] The problem is that, if each actor is assumed to calculate or choose a rational course of behaviour, we need to know how and in which units he calculates, and how he compares the options that present themselves to him. That is never explained.[27] Finally, it is necessary to challenge the assumption

---

24. Boudon dwells more than once on the situation of Indian families with many children, which seems to go against their interests by limiting their standard of living. But, he argues, it is 'interesting' for them to have enough children to boost the family income by working, either on the land or in the city, so that it is not the 'weight of tradition' but a 'rational' attitude that accounts for the size of the family. What this rather trivial example overlooks, however, is that traditions are not necessarily irrational; it also presents as 'true' (because plausible) an assertion that has not been empirically verified.

25. 'The constraints determine the field of what is possible; they do not determine the field of what is real.' Boudon, 'L'individualisme méthodologique', p. 1138.

26. 'The maximization principle is a formalized expression of the belief of men of action and decision-makers (financiers, engineers, etc.) that calculation is the horizon of action in the world. Here too the strength of this belief, far from being reduced to the strength of the 'proof' resulting from a scientific controversy, finds its most solid foundation in the affinity that exists between the dispositions and social experience of certain actors and an economic vision of the world that gives them a kind of social "confirmation" or "validation".' Lebaron, *La Croyance économique*, pp. 134–5.

27. The exception is game theory – itself a kind of game, with models bearing evocative names such as 'The prisoner's dilemma', 'Scratch my back, I'll scratch yours', 'Deer-hunting', 'Centipede' or 'Chicken' – which makes it possible to imagine all kinds of situations,

of a 'human nature', which implies that all actors are endowed with the same psychology (the same as that of the sociologist or economist!) that makes them react in a uniform manner. In fact, nothing authorizes us to say that everyone has similar interests, motives or preferences independent of social determinants, moral obligations (duty) or historical location. If *Homo oeconomicus* was a universal character – as economists claim – how could social welfare insurance have developed, and how could we account for the existence of such a large number of charities? Maybe it will be said that generosity is itself 'self-interested', because it secures symbolic 'benefits'?

The first conclusion to be drawn from this discussion of *Homo oeconomicus* is that a huge gulf separates social reality from the model that claims to explain it.[28] Even allowing for the fact that it is a fiction, a simplified construction of human behaviour, we cannot but note that it accounts only for what happens in a 'perfect' market setting, which, as we know, is a rare case that scarcely exists outside the textbooks. The real problem, however, is the universalistic assumptions that underlie the model. That the model does not coincide with reality is fair enough; but not only does its formal construction have a highly tenuous bearing on the reality that it claims to 'simplify', it is largely contradicted by the observation of social practices. Since human beings are by turns wise and foolish, selfish and generous, autonomous and dependent, likeable and detestable, what entitles anyone to reduce them to a single aspect by decreeing that it alone is 'interesting'? To assert that *Homo oeconomicus* is calculating obviously enables the economist to calculate (which would not be possible if he thought of him primarily as generous), but does this simplification exempt one from taking other aspects of human life in society into account?

---

sometimes very remote from social reality, and to stage them in such a way that logical or mathematical reasoning easily manages to find the optimum solution.

28. See van Parijs, 'Le modèle économique dans les sciences sociales', pp. 67–85.

To consider the individual as free, autonomous and self-sufficient is an aberration: everyone exists only in the eyes of others and in their relationship to others, not to speak of the fact that social relations (and networks) are also power relations. On the other hand, there are facts in every society that face everyone as constraints that have to be incorporated by the individual.[29] It is therefore wrong to explain the social by adding up individual psyches: just as the atoms which form a molecule have different properties from those of the molecule itself, society has properties which the individual does not have. Mainstream theory claims the opposite, thinking it possible – by extrapolation – to aggregate the 'rational choices' (or effective demand) of all individuals making up society in order to reveal the 'social choice' (or general demand). But, as we have seen, this way of passing from individual to social demand is impossible, unless society is reduced to a single individual who has to 'choose' a certain quantity of a single good in accordance with his income. This dual condition – which is not only an abstraction but an aberration – does not discourage economists from proposing the fiction of a 'representative agent' that stands for the whole of society.[30] In the end, to depict society as a collection of individuals with nothing in common except utility maximization is to dispel any possibility of a social bond, unless one says that people have friends because it is in their interest or that marriage exists only because the spouses have an interest in staying together – which obviously explains nothing and sinks straight into tautology.[31] It is true that we should be

29. According to Durkheim, this is actually what is characteristic about social facts. You do not choose the rules of politeness or the list of prohibited foods.

30. This impossibility of reducing society to the sum of individuals who constitute it is brilliantly expounded in Keen, *Debunking Economics*, pp. 23–53 and pp. 260–61. See also Chapter 6 below.

31. Jean-Luc Migué, a great admirer of Gary Becker, summarizes his position on marriage as follows: 'Rather than incessantly and expensively renegotiating and supervising the innumerable contracts inherent in the exchanges of everyday domestic life, the two parties settle the general terms of the exchange in a long-term contract.' But he is still forced to conclude: 'The only element which distinguishes the classical firm analytically

wary of popular wisdom, but the saying that 'you stop counting when you're in love' is undoubtedly closer to the real practice of society than are the theories which claim that people calculate in all circumstances.

This obliges us to mention a final peculiarity. One would have thought that, in order to make their model of human behaviour more refined (or complex), economists might pay some attention to the work of psychologists, sociologists or anthropologists who have also set themselves the task of explaining it[32] – especially since nowadays it is no longer possible to submit a research project without inserting it, at least formally, into an interdisciplinary framework. The truth is, however, that in its quasi-autistic self-certainty economic 'science' claims to impose its model on all other disciplines (which it regards as pseudo-sciences of man). This imperialist ambition is present in the champions of methodological individualism as well as the adepts of the Public Choice or Human Capital school – Gary Becker, winner of the so-called Nobel Prize in 1992, is one of its leading lights – who propose an economic theory of marriage, health, altruism, popular customs, fashion, wage benefits for women who defer their first pregnancy

---

from the household is that inside the household, the relationship between the partners can be desired for its own sake' (the role of love). This qualification reveals the conundrum of a reasoning which, in seeking to explain everything, explains nothing. Lepage, *Tomorrow, Capitalism*, p. 171.

32. We should recognize, though, that some economists have concerned themselves with anthropology. Among these are: G.A. Akerlof, J. and J.L. Yellen, 'Can Small Deviations from Rationality Make Significant Differences to Economic Equilibria?', *American Economic Review*, 78, 1988, pp. 44–9; Kenneth Boulding, 'Notes on a Theory of Philanthropy', in Frank G. Dickinson, ed., *Philanthropy and Public Policy*, National Bureau of Economic Research, 1962, pp. 57–71; Peter Hammond, 'Charity: Altruism or Cooperative Egoism?', in Edmund S. Phelps, ed., *Altruism, Morality and Economic Theory*, New York: Russell Sage Foundation, 1975, pp. 115–31; Robert Sugden, 'Reciprocity: The Supply of Public Goods Through Voluntary Contributions', *Economic Journal* 94, 1984, pp. 772–87; and Colin F. Camerer, 'Gifts as Economic Signals and Social Symbols', *American Journal of Sociology*, 94, 1988, pp. 180–214. In addition to these articles (and to those, like Mark Granovetter, Viviana Zelizer and Amitai Etzioni, who define themselves as 'social economists') mention should of course also be made of Laurent Cordonnier, *Coopération et Réciprocité*, Paris: PUF, 1997.

for a few years:[33] in short, a theory of everything that underpins human relationships.[34] If this simplistic paradigm shows anything, it is that *Homo oeconomicus* is a *Homo miserabilis*.

33. Kasey Buckles has actually calculated that women who agreed to defer their first pregnancy could increase their income by 3 per cent over the year, and that other kinds of financial 'penalty' were in operation for women who had children ('Understanding the Returns to Delayed Childbearing for Working Women', *American Economic Review* 98 (2), May 2008, pp. 403–7). As if the wish to have children fitted together with economic calculation!

34. See the chapter 'The Gary Becker Revolution', in Lepage, *Tomorrow, Capitalism*, pp. 161–83; and, for a critical perspective, Gérald Berthoud, 'L'économie: un ordre généralisé? Les ambitions d'un prix Nobel', *Pour une autre économie, Revue du MAUSS* 3, 1994, pp. 42–60. We should note that Becker does not consider the individual to be totally egocentric: his well-being also depends on 'psychological benefits', and his desire for distinction may lead him to altruism. But if he gives, it is to receive.

CHAPTER 4

EXCHANGE

Marcel Mauss recommended that, before it is taken as a central category of economics, exchange should be considered a total social fact, at once legal, economic and religious, which sets society and all its institutions in motion.[1] Beyond the multiple practices of exchange – for people exchange not only goods or wealth but also courtesies, feasts, ceremonies, services, women, children, dances and festivals[2] – the question arises as to how society 'holds together', how order is organized in it, how the common good is pursued. On what does the social bond depend in the last instance? On a meta-social guarantor, on a god who unites all members of society around a set of obligatory beliefs and rituals?[3] On a common ancestor who welds together all who claim to follow in his footsteps? On a founding contract whose parties enter into obligations towards one another? On a multiplicity of individual interests that spontaneously ensure social harmony by forbidding anyone to gain the upper hand over others? Whichever

1. Marcel Mauss, *The Gift: Forms and Functions of Exchange in Archaic Societies*, London: Cohen & West, 1966, pp. 76f.

2. Ibid., p. 3.

3. This is, of course, Durkheim's position in *The Elementary Forms of Religious Life* (London: Routledge 1998 [1912]): 'the reality that religious thinking expresses is society'. The same is true of the *corpus christianum* in medieval Europe.

solution is chosen, it can be neither applied nor explained without reference to sharing and exchange.

This means that, according to how society represents the base on which it rests, exchange will take different forms for the achievement of different goals. Contrary to the views of Adam Smith – who thought he had established that people have a 'natural propensity to truck, barter and exchange', whereas 'nobody ever saw a dog make a fair and deliberate exchange of one bone for another with another dog'[4] – exchange is in no way 'natural' and its market form cannot condense all others. Not by a long chalk.

A quick incursion into the realm of philology will convince us of this, by identifying the origins of the words most commonly used for the operations that allow exchange to take place.[5]

THE RIGHT WORDS FOR IT

So, the primary meaning of the Latin *pacare* (from which our 'pay' is derived) is to 'calm' or 'appease' the partner we ask to hand over a counterpart; the Gothic verb *bugjan* (from which we get 'to buy') refers to the idea of 'freeing' by paying a ransom, or even of redemption (from *redimere*, ransoming) by a god. These verbs, then, primarily refer not to commodities but to persons – in this event, mere captives, who acquired the status of slaves by being bought (cf. the Latin *emere*, which, before it meant 'to buy', expressed the idea of 'taking or drawing to oneself'). As for selling, the Gothic *saljan* originally signified 'to offer as sacrifice to a divinity'.

In another emblematic register of exchange – the gift – the terms in use connote equally dangerous situations. The German homonym *Gift*, as is well known, actually means 'poison', which

4. *The Wealth of Nations*, vol. 1, Book One, ch. 2, p. 17.

5. All these remarks will draw on Émile Benveniste, *Indo-European Language and Society*, London: Faber, 1973 (1969).

suggests that there also exist poisoned gifts. This in turn refers back to the Greek *dosis* (δόσις), which defines the legal act of assigning a legacy, but also a medical prescription, a 'dose' of a remedy, which always threatens to turn into poison because such is the dual meaning of *pharmakon* (φάρμακον). As for the verb καταλλάσσω, it certainly meant 'to exchange', but also 'to reconcile', 'to make feelings change'. Finally, we should note that in the ancient Germanic languages the word *gelt* (which gave the German *Geld*, money) corresponded to a religious, economic or juridical sacrifice.[6] This is why the related Gothic *gild* primarily signified 'reciprocal tribute', a kind of entrance fee to join a *guilde* (that is, a fraternity that organized banquets or celebrations where one discussed 'the reconciliation of private enemies, the conclusion of family alliances, the choice of chieftains, peace and war'[7]). All these examples show that, far from concerning purely economic transactions, purchase, sale and gift-giving were primarily legal and religious themes, inscribed within visions of the world quite remote from the banality to which economic 'science' has reduced them. Far from being 'natural' (or 'free'), exchange is most often a risky business, because it commits the whole person within a complex institutional system that defines the rules of life in society.

So, we must be cautious in speaking of exchange: not only because of all its legal, religious and economic connotations, but also because it takes place in a variety of forms that include buying and selling, gift-giving and reciprocity, prestige expenditure, conviviality, hospitality and war (since the guest is often confused with the enemy[8]). For these reasons, exchange is to be both *feared* and *desired*.

6. Hence the German *Gottesdienst* (divine service or worship), derived from *gote-kelt* (payment or sacrifice made to God). Ibid., p. 58.

7. Tacitus, *Germania*, 22; ibid., p. 60. Benveniste also points out that *wergeld* ('man's price', because *wer* = 'man') is what is paid in atonement for the crime of murder.

8. *Hospes* is never far from *hostis* ('enemy', but primarily 'stranger') or *hostia* ('the victim who serves to allay the wrath of the gods'). Ibid., pp. 77ff.

PRESCRIPTION OR PROSCRIPTION

Anthropology largely confirms these conclusions by revealing multiple forms of exchange. First there is reciprocity, which may be *limited* or *symmetrical* when it only concerns two parties (persons or clans) or *general* when a larger number of parties are involved (A gives to B, who gives to C, who gives to N, who 'gives back' to A). This may sometimes express itself in ways that seem absurd (to us), as when – to use Bronislaw Malinowski's example – yams are exchanged for yams.[9] In fact, among the Trobriand Islanders, each man must provide for the needs of his sister's household – to eat produce from his own garden would be almost tantamount to incest – and he must perform this task with utmost care, since any oversight on his part would incur a loss of prestige.[10]

Redistribution corresponds to a *centralized* system in which everyone hands over their labour product (or what remains beyond subsistence) to a chief. He therefore has a considerable surplus at his disposal, but since he cannot use it all for his own ends he must redistribute it in the form of festivals and ceremonies, often marked by extravagant communal meals that keep alive the community that has contributed to them.[11] This does not necessarily mean that only the productive community itself benefits from

---

9. This will appear less absurd if we bear in mind that we exchange coffees for coffees when we go often to a café with the same friends. But this 'reversibility' of the gift does not mean that the return gift can be thought of as an equivalent.

10. Everyone therefore produces for another (in the *urigubu* system) and depends totally on someone else for their livelihood. Yet the situation is very different from the fable of the hunter who 'barters' a deer for two beavers (or two salmon), in which everyone counts on another to satisfy their needs in a framework of self-interested exchange (Ricardo, *The Principles of Political Economy and Taxation*, pp. 13, 16; and Smith, *The Wealth of Nations*, vol. 1, p. 53). This fable has a long history and may already be found in Turgot: 'Two savages come across each other on a desert island in the northern seas, one carrying more in his fishing boat than he can consume, the other carrying animal skins over and above what he can use to cover himself and make a tent' (quoted from Gérald Berthoud, 'Que nous dit l'économie?', in Serge Latouche, ed., *L'Économie dévoilée. Du budget familial aux contraintes planétaires*, Paris: Autrement, 1995, p. 63).

11. Although the chief only redistributes what others have given to him, this is a socially effective practice, rather like the present that a child buys for his father out of his pocket money.

the ritual largesse: members of one or more nearby tribes may be invited to take part, not only as a mark of honour but also to 'flatten' them (as Marcel Mauss put it), to dazzle them with a lavish display and therefore humiliate them, spurring them to do better still when the time comes for them to return the invitation.[12] Finally, we should mention the particular case of the Big Man, who, either by himself or with the help of his kinship group, originates the accumulation of goods and then solemnly distributes them to members of the group. Such is the price he must pay for keeping his title as chief; he literally works 'for the sake of glory'. Here it is exactly as if an idle society exploits its chief, making his prestige depend on his capacity to keep sharing out the fruit of his labours. As Pierre Clastres neatly puts it,[13] the chief is constantly indebted to the society that holds the power, and since the debt is inextinguishable he never accedes to power but has to content himself with the prestige resulting from his generosity.

Since exchange, in its early (non-market) form, always presupposes a social relationship, a way of being with others in the world, the goods are themselves 'embedded' in social relations.[14] Hence the intrinsic value of a good is defined neither by its relative scarcity nor by the utility that its acquirer can expect of it, but rather by the relationship between the trade partners. Members of some societies are not allowed to trade certain goods (food, for

---

12. The redistribution principle was in a way 'bureaucratized' in the great empires: ancient Egypt, China, the Inca empire. The surplus did, of course, make it possible to maintain the cohesion of the state, but thanks to new castes of priests, functionaries and warriors. See Karl Polanyi, *The Great Transformation*, Boston MA: Beacon Press, 1957 (1944), pp. 51–2. The social implications were obviously different: traditional chiefs could count on the respect inspired by their generosity, whereas despots required only that their subjects should bow in submission.

13. 'Préface' to Marshall Sahlins, *Âge de pierre, âge d'abondance. L'économie dans les sociétés primitives*, Paris: Gallimard, 1976 (1972), pp. 24–7.

14. 'Man's economy, as a rule, is submerged in his social relationships. He does not act so as to safeguard his individual interest in the possession of material goods; he acts so as to safeguard his social standing, his social claims, his social assets.' Polanyi, *The Great Transformation*, p. 46.

example) with their relatives but are perfectly at liberty to trade them with strangers;[15] whereas in other (Islamic) societies there is a complete ban on selling such precious goods as water or herbs, in order that no one should go without them.[16] Such practices, by the way, point ahead to the current debate on 'global public goods', which is closely bound up with the question of property systems.[17]

There are also prestige goods that can only be exchanged between equals. In Africa, for example, ceremonial goods (iron bars, grass skirts, cattle) circulate only among elders for the purposes of matrimonial compensation: they cannot be appropriated by the young or exchanged for other goods.[18] This is also true in the Kula system, except that, in this particular case, exchange does not 'compensate' for anything but serves only to acquire prestige. It is so well known, and so many shelves of books have been written about it, that we shall do no more here than recall its essential features. On the string of islands that form the Trobriand archipelago, the main activity of the chiefs is to exchange two kinds of prestige object (*vaygu'a*) at important ceremonies: long necklaces on which red shells move around clockwise (*soulava*), and armbands with white shells that move in the opposite direction (*mwali*); the parties to the exchange – who are linked by stable relations that may last a lifetime – can give armbands only to those from whom they have received necklaces, or vice versa, since no one ever receives both at once from the

15. Claude Meillassoux, *Terrains et Théories*, Paris: Anthropos, 1977, pp. 143–8. See Jean-Pierre Dupuy and Jean Robert, *La Trahison de l'opulence*, Paris PUF, 1976, p. 14; and Emmanuel Terray, *Marxism and Primitive Societies*, New York: Monthly Review Press, 1972 (1969).

16. Maxime Rodinson, *Islam and Capitalism*, New York: Pantheon Books, 1974 (1966), pp. 34ff.

17. This parallel was suggested to me by Jean-Noël DuPasquier. For a critical approach, see François Constantin, ed., *Les Biens publics mondiaux. Un mythe légitimateur pour l'action collective?*, Paris: L'Harmattan, 2002.

18. The anthropological tradition generally refers to these systems as 'fragmented markets', but the use of the word 'market' seems improper here.

same person. On the margins of these ceremonial exchanges and their accompanying magic rituals, a kind of real trading (or fierce bargaining) takes place over goods for personal use (*gimwali*).[19] But the core exchange of the Kula does not involve acquisition: possession of the necklaces and armbands is always provisional and serves only to cement social relations, permitting their holder to pride himself for a time on having access to an object all the more prestigious because of the long series of illustrious persons who have previously 'owned' it. Furthermore, the exchange is never simultaneous ('I give you a necklace if you give me an armband'), since everyone may have several partners at once (located at various stages of the process), and the game involves approaching the one who holds the most prestigious object.

These brief outlines will be sufficient to demonstrate the complexity of exchange systems, their accompanying precautions and rituals, their social implications, the symbolic value attaching to various goods, and the social control that is exercised over some of them. However, as Marcel Mauss showed in *The Gift*, it is possible to group the multiple practices under the general heading of *reciprocity* – or, in other words, the threefold obligation to give, receive and give back.

GIVING, RECEIVING AND GIVING BACK

First of all, we need to rid ourselves of the customary idea that the gift involves a free decision on the part of one side acting without ulterior motive. On the contrary, it should be regarded as a system that binds together at least three persons, who are constantly and simultaneously in the process of giving, receiving

19. See Branislaw Malinowski, *Argonauts of the Western Pacific*, London: Routledge, 1964 (1922). Together with Marie-Dominique Perrot, I have attempted a 'modern' approach to the Kula: 'Des Argonautes aux internautes', *Revue européenne des sciences sociales* 44 (134), 2006, pp. 203–14.

and giving back. This gift circulation has been represented since antiquity in the allegory of the Three Graces – three sisters, all daughters of Zeus, who stand intertwined or exchange three similar fruits with one another. Aristotle commented: 'That is why a temple of the Graces is set up in a place where it cannot fail to be seen and remind men to repay a kindness. To make such a return is the distinguishing mark of grace, for it is our duty not merely to repay a service done, but to do one ourselves on another occasion.'[20] Seneca gave an even more precise answer to the question of why the Graces were three in number:

> Some writers think that there is one who bestows a benefit, one who receives it, and a third who returns it; others say that they represent the three sorts of benefactors, those who bestow, those who repay, and those who both receive and repay them. ... It means that the course of a benefit is from hand to hand, back to the giver; that the beauty of the whole chain is lost if a single link fails, and that it is fairest when it proceeds in unbroken regular order.[21]

The gift cycle can certainly be broken down into three components, but it forms a single whole. In giving with pleasure, one often does no more than give back, and the one who receives hopes to give in turn.[22]

Second, we really are speaking here of a threefold *obligation*, which is characteristic of what Durkheim defined as a 'social fact':[23] to refuse a present is to open hostilities, by treating it as poisoned! But this obligation is paradoxical, since it combines generosity with constraint, the pleasure of giving freely with

20. Aristotle, *Ethics*, Harmondsworth: Penguin, 1955, Book Five, ch. 5, p. 151.

21. Seneca, *De Beneficiis*, Book I: 3, 2–4; Seneca on Benefits: N.S. Gill Ancient/Classical History Guide, http://ancienthistory.about.com/library/bl/bl_text_seneca_benefits.

22. The beggar who has just received a coin expresses this in his way by saying: 'May God reward you!' The person who pays for a round in a café is giving back what he has received. And he who says 'good day' expects his courtesy to be returned.

23. 'In spite of all these doctrines, social phenomena are things and ought to be treated as things ... Indeed, the most important characteristic of a "thing" is the impossibility of its modification by a simple effort of the will.' Émile Durkheim, *The Rules of Sociological Method*, New York: Free Press, 1962 (1895), pp. 27–8.

the self-interested expectation of something in return. Or, as Marcel Mauss put it, we need to study 'prestations which are in theory voluntary, disinterested and spontaneous, but are in fact obligatory and interested. The form usually taken is that of the gift generously offered; but the accompanying behaviour is formal pretence and social deception, while the transaction itself is based on obligation and economic self-interest.'[24]

Third, why do people give? Quite simply to create a social bond. What matters is not the actual gift but the relation of mutual dependence in which the partners stand to each other. This seems rather unusual, in a society where everyone's independence is highly valued and the ideal is to depend on nothing and no one. But the exchange of gifts, which accounts for only a small percentage of non-market exchanges, ratifies the social ties by alternating the positional hierarchy of those woven together by them. For the ritual in question rests upon a sequence of denials: the recipient hastens to say 'you shouldn't have!', underlining that the donor gave of his own free will; while the donor invariably continues 'it's nothing, really!', not only downplaying the importance of the gift but also implying 'it's nothing in comparison with the regard I have for you, and being nothing it puts you under no obligation, so if you give me something in turn you can do it just as freely.' The recipient may then express his thanks in various ways, perhaps by saying 'I'm much obliged' (the Portuguese *muito obrigado*): that is, I recognize my debt; the French *merci* also originates in this sense of obligation, of being at the other's 'mercy'. Then there may follow 'but you must let me pay you back sometime!', and the dialogue will end with 'I beg you, please don't mention it' (I beg you because I need you). As we know, it is always the 'little nothings' that keep a friendship going. Such stereotypical dialogues reveal not only the lack of social interest

24. Mauss, *The Gift*, p. 1.

in the actual gift (as opposed to the bond that it symbolizes[25]) but also a sequence of 'power reversals' (since each is caught in a range of obligations that must be denied in order to leave the other party free and to transform constraint into generosity). The one who gives always claims some power over the one who receives, in accordance with the saying that 'the hand that takes is always inferior to [*en dessous de*] the hand that gives'. But this dominant position is entirely provisional, since the gift will be returned and the alternation will restore power to the one who lost it. The passage of time makes the bond exist: the recipient constantly looks for an opportunity to pay the donor back – or rather to give in turn, not by 'returning' an equivalent gift, but by displaying even greater generosity and raising the 'level of the gift'.[26] Behind this game of mutual indebtedness, whether it is ritualized or spontaneous ('I owe him everything: when you love someone, you stop counting'), social relations take shape and persist through regular boosts over time.[27] Starting from a primal debt – we all receive life – society organizes itself in a 'fabric' made up of threads that tie everyone to others, through the exchange of goods, services, time, affection and civilities.

These remarks are evidently very far from exhausting the subject.[28] In any event, the focus of this chapter is not the

25. This explains why, in some societies, one never opens a gift in the presence of the person who gave it: it would be a source of embarrassment if judged too lavish, and appear a mark of disrespect if considered derisory.

26. Dominique Temple and Mireille Chabal, *La Réciprocité et la naissance des valeurs humaines*, Paris: L'Harmattan, 1995, p. 56. The expression is also found in Marshall Sahlins.

27. Gift and counter-gift should therefore by no means be reduced to a mere exchange of goods. 'All the testimony concerning gift exchange in traditional societies shows above all else that it involves reciprocal *recognition*, honour and displays of esteem.' Marcel Hénaff, 'De la philosophie à l'anthropologie. Comment interpréter le don?', *Esprit* 282, February 2002, p. 139 (emphasis in the original).

28. Apart from the works already mentioned, the reader's attention is drawn to three works by Jacques T. Godbout that deal with gift-giving in modern society: *Le Don, la dette et l'identité. Homo donator vs Homo oeconomicus*, Paris: La Découverte, 2000; *Ce qui circule entre nous. Donner, recevoir, rendre*, Paris: Seuil, 2007; and (together with Alain Caillé), *The World of the Gift*, Montreal: McGill–Queen's University Press, 2000.

innumerable forms of the gift and counter-gift, but rather exchange and the presuppositions underlying its market form. But, in order to disclose these presuppositions, a number of philological and anthropological preliminaries have been necessary to indicate the variety of rules and logics governing exchange practices, as well as the society-building purposes to which they can always be traced back in the end. For exchange is first of all a social relation, which comes before the invention of the market.

MARKET EXCHANGE OR INVERTED LOGIC

For pedagogical reasons, this section will take the form of a dichotomy between the logic of the gift and the logic of the market. This risks suggesting that they are two mutually exclusive realms between which people are summoned to choose – as if the gift were the reverse side of the commodity. But this is not the case, since the actual practices of every society belong to both registers,[29] different though these are in their importance and articulation (or hybridization). The 'great divide' that is supposed to separate modernity and tradition is largely fictitious,[30] and these categories have too often been misused, even in anthropology. The aim of what follows is not, therefore, to weigh a 'primitive' or 'authentic' world deserving of preservation or revival against a more or less depraved 'capitalism'; nor to identify the places where the 'purest' practices correspond to those logics. However, it does

---

29. 'We define the forms of contract and exchange in these societies, which, contrary to what has been suggested, are not lacking in economic markets; for the market is a human phenomenon which, in our view, is not alien to any known society, but whose exchange regime is different from our own.' Mauss, *The Gift*, p. 2, translation modified. Cf. Gilbert Rist, 'Préalables à une théorie générale de l'échange', *Nouveaux Cahiers de l'IUED* 7, Geneva: IUED/ Paris: PUF, 1998, pp. 17–40. See also the works of Godbout quoted in the previous note, as well as Laurent Bazin and Monique Selim, eds, *Motifs économiques en anthropologie*, Paris: L'Harmattan, 2001 and Jean-François Bayart, ed., *La Réinvention du capitalisme*, Paris: Karthala, 1994, who insist on the syncretic or 'makeshift' elements in the economy of contemporary Africa.

30. See Bruno Latour, *We Have Never Been Modern*, Cambridge MA: Harvard University Press, 1993 (1991).

seem legitimate to compare ideal types and to elicit what radically distinguishes them from one another. The fundamental texts of a theory, for example, can certainly tell us what it asserts and what it bases itself on, but it is more difficult to draw out what it does not assert or what it neglects, intentionally or unintentionally. Hence the heuristic power of comparison, in taking what exists in one case to show what is lacking in another case. We can 'identify' only by distinguishing, and an enumeration of the differences between one object or individual and another allows us to grasp what characterizes them and makes them unique. These precautions were necessary to avoid the reefs of 'primitivism' or old-style culturalism.

Ties and goods

As we have seen, the primary purpose of the gift is to create a lasting bond between exchange partners, who have to meet their respective obligations while denying that they exist. By giving freely, one deprives oneself of any right to something in return, so that the other is free to give in his turn. Paradoxically it is this 'obligatory freedom' that guarantees the counter-gift and prevents it from being confused with mere restitution: what one expects is never a *thing* but the confirmation of a bond that has been previously established. Hence the value of the exchanged object is first of all symbolic, even if it may sometimes be considerable and sometimes be reduced to 'nothing'.[31] Each party 'gives credit': that is, believes in the other and trusts him, sure of finding him again later.[32] Market exchange, by contrast, concentrates on the value of the good, expressed in its price, which in no way depends

31. The symbolic value is primary even when the exchanged object is 'utilitarian' (food, for example).

32. German is very clear about this: the *Gläubiger* (creditor) believes or has faith (*glaubt*) in the other. Cf. the root *kred – from which 'credence', 'credibility' and 'credit' are derived – which refers more to the sacred than to the economic: Benveniste, *Indo-European Language and Society*, pp. 143–8.

on the relationship between the parties to the exchange (who think of themselves as perfect strangers). Once the contract has been completed, then, each party should preserve his freedom or anonymity, considering himself 'quits' and taking his leave of the other; individual freedom is gained through refusal to enter into a personal relationship. This is the 'degree zero' of relationships: the introduction of money to pay for goods or services breaks the social bond.

Power between generosity and interest

In the logic of the gift, power is obtained through giving: generosity allows one to 'make a name for oneself', and credit is acquired especially from a host of social networks within which gifts and counter-gifts circulate. The various parties involved in gift-giving live through a succession of alternating inequalities, defined by whether they give or receive. In the logic of the market, power belongs to those who accumulate without taking anything but their own interests into account. Even if there is talk of 'give and take' (implying equality with regard to property), all that counts is what is received – that is, gained. Social credit or recognition depends on the accumulation of possessions and wealth, as the saying 'people only lend to the rich' makes clear.

Raising the stakes and equivalence

The logic of gift-giving does not support equivalence: to give the same thing back would be an affront. One must know, if not how to 'give without counting', then at least how to give back a little more than one has received (but not too much – to avoid 'flattening' the other!). What we see, then, is a kind of raising of the stakes, or of the 'level' of the gift, which prevents one from gaining at the other's expense. There is nothing of the kind in the market system, where money serves as the general equivalent. Debt to other people quickly becomes intolerable: no one wants to be 'outdone' by another, and therefore in his debt, and all try to 'settle their account'. The equality and liberty of individuals implies a balance in their transactions with one another.[33]

Time and space

Here again the two logics are in opposition. Since gift and counter-gift take place only between partners who know each other personally, they can produce effects only within precise spatial limits (even if there is a considerable geographical distance between the partners, as in the classical case of the Kula, but also in transnational social networks linked to contemporary migration[34]). On the other hand, their long time scale guarantees the permanence of the social ties: a gift immediately reciprocated would kill the relationship; each gift is thus a kind of wager on the future justified by the trust (credit) that one partner places in the other, who is obliged to reciprocate it. By contrast, market exchange is in principle instantaneous (if we leave aside forward transactions); payment must not be delayed, or must even be in cash, thereby 'settling' the transaction. The parties to the transaction do not need to enter into a personal relationship with each other, and so there are no spatial limits; the goods alone matter, regardless of their provenance. In this way, exchange can be de-territorialized or globalized.

Denial and boasting

The giver plays down the value of his gift: 'it's nothing', he says, since a nothing is enough to create a bond. Meanwhile the

---

33. Credit operations or 'trading debt' (to a bank, for example) are also a form of 'settling one's account', since the repayment terms and interest rate are clearly specified in advance. This has nothing to do with the hope of a counter-gift based on the partner's generosity.

34. See the important study: Alessandro Monsutti, *War and Migration: Social Networks and Economic Strategies of the Hazaras of Afghanistan*, London: Routledge, 2005, which shows that the ancient *hawâla* system enables migrants to transfer often large sums of money to their families in Afghanistan in the absence of postal or banking services: the whole system rests on trust and the players' personal knowledge of one another.

recipient claims that the other 'shouldn't have'. Both sides play at denial. Their relationship is forged in what is implicit, in what is unsaid – or even, as Marcel Mauss put it, in 'social deception'. No one must either glory in their generosity or present their gift as something that was owed. The point is to 'bow' to the threefold obligation, and also in a way to one's partner. In the market system, by contrast, it is not forbidden to boast of 'striking a good deal' – which means that one gave less than one received, that one came out on top, that one knew how to assert one's interests against those of the other party. Here the main thing is the acquisition of a good, not the relationship forged during a transaction, in which the object of exchange is often merely a pretext.

Pleasure and fear

Politeness teaches children to say 'please' when they ask for something. This means implicitly 'please me by granting what I wish', but it also – perhaps mainly – means 'do it only if it pleases you too'. The gift must be a shared pleasure, an exchange in which one is freely involved. One should take part only if it 'pleases' – otherwise one might as well pack it in. Market logic, characterized by the lure of gain, does not know the pleasure of giving; it is obsessed instead with the fear of losing if equivalence is not respected. Market transactions go ahead not because they give pleasure but because they secure an advantage.

At the end of this inevitably schematic account, we therefore see two different worlds appear: on the one hand, Mauss's threefold obligation of 'give, receive, give back'; on the other, the opposite imperatives – 'take, refuse, keep' – of a realm completely ruled by the commodity.[35] Fortunately, the real world does not function in accordance with the binary logic of 'either/or'. No one can

35. Alain Caillé, *Dé-penser l'économique. Contre le fatalisme*, Paris: La Découverte/MAUSS, 2005, p. 17.

entirely shake off their social obligations of reciprocity: many of our activities do not fall under the sphere of the market; no company could operate if its employees refused to 'give it their all'; large corporations form agreements with one another because personal relations are often preferable to strict economic rationality; economists periodically remind us that trust is necessary for good business, since 'naked self-interest' is not enough; every executive knows that gifts ranging from 'business lunches' to backhanders are sometimes necessary; advertising people try to persuade consumers that a particular brand throws in something extra 'for free', that it has not completely abandoned disinterested behaviour, and so on. So, we live in a hybrid system, even if the logic of the market is preponderant and tends to blot out the others.[36] Gifts are often adulterated and placed in the service of the market. Yet the market is never 'free': it is an institution that obeys certain rules governing competition or the quest for profit maximization.

This said, the two logics refer us to two models of society, whose exchange practices have completely different meanings since they rest upon different values and institutions.[37] Thus, the market form of economy does not at all go without saying; it does not derive from a 'natural penchant', as Adam Smith claimed. In a way, it too is 'embedded' in the society that gave birth to it. Its triumph required that society be defined as a sum of free and equal individuals, linked to one another by the fiction of

36. In addition to the 'gift economy' and the market economy, mention should be made of the 'autonomous' (home-grown, partly 'informal') economy that escapes the reach of the market. See Alfredo L. de Romaña, 'Une alternative sociale en émergence: l'économie autonome', *Interculture* 22(3), 1989, cahier 104.

37. 'There came a time when everything that men had considered as inalienable became an object of exchange, of traffic, and could be alienated. This is the time when the very things which till then had been communicated, but never exchanged; given, but never sold; acquired, but never bought ... when everything, in short, passed into commerce. It is the time of general corruption, of universal venality, or, to speak in terms of political economy, the time when everything, moral or physical, having become a marketable value, is brought to the market to be assessed at its truest value.' Karl Marx, *The Poverty of Philosophy*, London: Lawrence & Wishart, 1966, p. 29.

an original 'political contract' (as in Hobbes, Locke and Rousseau) that finds concrete expression in the multiplicity of private purchase and sales contracts that members of the society agree among themselves.[38] It was then necessary to explain how these self-interested individuals find an advantage in the contract (since a gain on one side was long thought to correspond to a loss on the other) and also have an interest in living alongside one another.[39] Classical economics gave a twofold answer: the famous 'invisible hand'[40] reconciles private interests, since 'by pursuing his own interest' the individual 'frequently promotes that of the society more effectually than when he really intends to promote it';[41] but, above all, while preserving individual autonomy, the division of labour generalizes the dependence of all upon all, which for Adam Smith is the consequence of our natural propensity to exchange.[42] This evidently results in a kind of natural social consensus, since everything is then supposedly in equilibrium.[43] Exchange is therefore primary: it explains why people 'live together' and cements

38. None of this calls into question the distribution of 'initial endowments', which, though unequal, are regarded as given.

39. In a consequentialist ethical perspective, actions are judged by their consequences rather than the intentions behind them. Beginning with Mandeville and Adam Smith, the public sphere was considered in terms of the effects produced by individual actions, and the private sphere in terms of the actors' intentions. See Marglin, *The Dismal Science*, p. 111.

40. The importance of the term in Adam Smith has doubtless been exaggerated. In fact he uses it only three times: in his *History of Astronomy* (1755); in *The Theory of Moral Sentiments*, Part Four, ch. 1 (1759, 1790), to show that people are equal in face of 'life's necessities'; and in *The Wealth of Nations*, with reference to the unintended consequences of the maximization of personal profit. It is difficult to see here a 'doctrine' that structures his work, even though the formulation has been taken up and repeated thousands of times.

41. *The Wealth of Nations*, vol. 1, Book Four, ch. 2, pp. 477–8. Cf. Ricardo's formulation: 'This pursuit of individual advantage is admirably connected with the universal good of the whole': *Principles of Political Economy and Taxation*, ch. 7, p. 81.

42. 'It is the maxim of every prudent master of a family never to attempt to make at home what it will cost him more to make than to buy. The tailor does not attempt to make his own shoes, but buys them of the shoemaker. The shoemaker does not attempt to make his own clothes, but employs a tailor. The farmer attempts to make neither the one nor the other, but employs those different artificers.' *The Wealth of Nations*, vol. 1, Book Four, ch. 2, p. 478.

43. 'There is endogenous production of externality: one might speak of self-

society, but it also implies that they produce in order to buy and sell; it ultimately rests upon the interest we have, not in others, but in the things that others produce and are prone to sell us, and hence upon the advantage we might derive from them – 'society itself grows to be what is properly a commercial society.'[44] This marked a shift to a new vision of society, not only because this 'opened out' beyond the (politically established) state frontiers to the de-territorialized, homogenous space of the market,[45] but above all because self-interest or the desire for gain, hitherto morally condemned as concupiscent, lay at its foundation.[46] This

---

transcendence of the Market.' Jean-Claude Liaudet, *Le Complexe d'Ubu ou la névrose libérale*, Paris: Fayard, 2004, p. 181.

44. *The Wealth of Nations*, vol. 1, Book One, ch. 4, p. 26. Although this perspective came to dominate economic 'science', it cannot be regarded as a summary of Adam Smith's position. Indeed, he thought of market relations as a kind of *pis-aller*: 'All the members of human society stand in need of each other's assistance. ... Where the necessary assistance is reciprocally afforded from love, from gratitude, from friendship, and esteem, the society flourishes and is happy. ... But though the necessary assistance should not be afforded from such generous and disinterested motives, though among the different members of the society there should be no mutual love and affection, the society, though less happy and agreeable, will not necessarily be dissolved. Society may subsist among different men, as among different merchants, from a sense of its utility, without any mutual love or affection; and though no man in it should owe any obligation, or be bound in gratitude to any other, it may still be upheld by a mercenary exchange of good offices according to an agreed valuation.' *The Theory of Moral Sentiments*, Book Two, ch. 2, pp. 85–6. Nevertheless, Smith's conception of each man as a 'kind of merchant' appears all the more novel if we compare it with medieval canon law (Gratien's twelfth-century Canon 11), which stated: *homo mercator, vix aut nunquam potest Deo placere* ('only with difficulty, if at all, can the merchant be pleasing to God'). Quoted in Max Weber, *General Economic History*, New Brunswick NJ: Transaction, 1981, p. 357.

45. There is thus a shift from the market as a place ('the marketplace') to the market as a network, as Marie-Auffray Seguette aptly puts it in *Les Biens de ce monde. L'économie vue comme espace de recomposition de la religion dans la modernité*, Paris: EHESS, 2008, p. 178.

46. Thus *avaritia* (cupidity), or the immoderate love of possessions condemned by theology, gave way to the principle of abundance. 'I flatter myself to have demonstrated that neither the friendly qualities and kind affections that are natural to man, nor the real virtues he is capable of acquiring by reason and self-denial, are the foundation of society; but that what we call evil in this world, moral as well as natural, is the grand principle that makes us sociable creatures, the solid basis, the life and support of all trades and employments without exception.' Bernard Mandeville, *The Fable of the Bees* (1723), ed. E.J. Hindert, Indianapolis: Hackett, 1997, p. 148. Individual immorality is 'offset' by the fact that it contributes to the common good, which is conceived only from the point of view of economic prosperity (no longer from that of relations among men). Some have pointed to the affinity of this position with the dogma of original sin, which, while

brought with it a new social project: 'Consumption is the sole end and purpose of all production; and the interest of the producer ought to be attended to only so far as it may be necessary for promoting that of the consumer.'[47] As Marx saw, however, this primacy of the commodity transforms social relations, since 'to the producers ... the social relations between their private labours appear as what they are, i.e. they do not appear as direct social relations between persons in their work, but rather as material [*dinglich*] relations between persons and social relations between things.'[48] In other words, human relations vanish behind these 'social things', taking the 'fantastic form of a relation between physical things'.[49]

All this does not happen of necessity, but stems from the world-view of the eighteenth century. This historical contingency of the model – which has evolved and grown more complex in various contemporary schools – raises the formidable question of whether it is fit to grasp the multiple forms of exchange outlined above, which intermingle in varying degrees within all societies. That markets exist and people exchange goods to satisfy their interests is a valid statement, but only if we immediately add that that is not all they do. And, to do other things, they must have recourse to forms of exchange that radically diverge from the market form. The notion of market hegemony is therefore a type of reductionism – but today this reductionism claims to establish its hegemony over all the social sciences. Mainstream economics has pulled sociology and even psychology in its wake, as if the market model of exchange could explain the whole of human behaviour. But it is a theory built upon a kind of vow of ignorance, which turns a blind eye to the other kinds of

---

considering man 'incapable alone of any good', anticipates his salvation through divine grace (now become 'the invisible hand').

47. *The Wealth of Nations*, vol. 2, Book Four, ch. 8, p. 179.

48. Karl Marx, *Capital*, Volume 1, Harmondsworth: Penguin/NLR, 1976, p. 166.

49. Ibid., p. 165.

exchange that exist in every society, not only 'savage' society, and concentrates only on the market form. By a deft reversal, it would now have us believe that the particular case has universal validity – rather as if our knowledge of only one grammar meant that it was the only one possible.

We should resist the temptation to dichotomize, however, since there are many different forms of exchange. In *The Gift*, Marcel Mauss noted the possible remnants (or metamorphoses) of 'archaic exchange' in modern societies, including the 'legislation on social insurance' (an already accomplished measure of 'state socialism') or 'the movement for compulsory unemployment insurance'. And he concluded: 'The themes of the gift, of freedom and obligation in the gift, of generosity and self-interest in giving, reappear in our own society like the resurrection of a dominant motif long forgotten.'[50] We are speaking of hybrid forms, of course, but they merit attention because they revive ancient principles of solidarity and reciprocity while also being the product of social history, and because they betoken an attempt to escape the ravages of individualism without appealing to a radical gift economy (which it is impossible to generalize in societies beyond a certain numerical threshold). They are therefore paths that should continue to be explored. Negative testimony to the promise they hold is the virulent opposition of US lobbies to a system of (nearly) universal medical cover, or the major tendencies to privatization of the educational system that are evident nearly everywhere. The solidarity society, the beginnings of which Mauss thought he could detect in the early twentieth century, is today threatened by mainstream economics, in the name of a doctrine that still claims to achieve the greatest happiness of the greatest number.

The point of these considerations is not to write off altogether the market form of self-interested exchange, in favour of a 'perfect' form of gift and counter-gift. It is simply to acknowledge that

50. Mauss, *The Gift*, pp. 65–6.

different forms of exchange, resting upon fundamentally different principles, exist alongside one another. While it is legitimate to want to acquire certain goods without entering into ties with other people, it is also legitimate – and necessary – to enter into the logic of gift-giving, 'which prevents humans from becoming things'.[51]

DO THE AXIOMS OF SELF-INTEREST SERVE THE INTERESTS OF EXCHANGE PARTNERS?

We have so far let pass the founding idea of 'standard' economic theory, according to which exchange is mutually advantageous if both parties pursue their own interest. As Milton Friedman put it:

> The prices that emerge from voluntary transactions between buyers and sellers – for short, in a free market – [can] coordinate the activity of millions of people, each seeking his own interest in such a way as to make everyone better off.... [E]conomic order can emerge as the unintended consequence of the actions of many people, each seeking his own interest.... The price system works so well, so efficiently, that we are not aware of it most of the time.[52]

However, this conclusion is not only debatable but false! Stranger still, economists themselves have demonstrated its falsity, by combining methodological individualism with the game theory that occupies such an important place in contemporary economic research.[53]

What 'standard' theory ignores (or leaves out of account) is the problem of cooperation between exchange partners, or the mutual

51. Godbout, *Ce qui circule entre nous. Donner, recevoir, rendre*, p. 371.

52. Milton and Rose Friedman, *Free to Choose: A Personal Statement*, New York: Harcourt Brace Jovanovich, 1980, pp. 13–14.

53. Game theory is mainly used to explain the labour market, unemployment, organizations, contracts, institutions, and situations where competition is absent (or, more generally, exchange situations that bring into relation with each other two individuals, or groups of individuals, whose actions are liable to influence the behaviour of others). 'Strategic' rationality implies that the environment (or the decisions of other players) is influenced by individual choice, whereas in 'parametric' rationality the environment is taken as constant or given.

trust that must be established between them for the exchange to be worthwhile to each. The simplest case is that of mail order or advance purchases, where the buyer pays 'up front' and has to trust that the seller will honour the contract, despite his evident interest in keeping the sum received without completing the order.[54] Let us simply note that, if the buyer is distrustful, he or she will not place an order and the seller will gain nothing – which is the least favourable solution for both parties.

To crystallize the perverse effects of economic rationality taken to its extreme, economists generally refer to the so-called 'prisoner's dilemma'. Two men suspected of armed robbery (which they did in fact commit) are arrested, even though there is hardly any evidence against them. It is then explained to them that:

—if neither confesses to the crime or incriminates the other, they can only be charged with the lesser offence of illegal possession of a firearm, which carries a tariff of two years' imprisonment;
—if both of them confess, they will be liable to the maximum penalty of ten years, but this will be reduced to five years in recognition of their cooperation;
—if only one of them confesses, he will be released, while his accomplice (whom he has incriminated) will be sentenced to ten years.

This may be expressed in the following table:

		B: *confesses*	B: *doesn't confess*
A	*confesses*	5/5	0/10
A	*doesn't confess*	10/0	2/2

54. The following pages are largely inspired by Cordonnier's *Coopération et Réciprocité.*

Clearly, the optimum strategy would be for each not to confess, so that they both get only two years' imprisonment. But, even if they agree beforehand, how can each be sure that the other will keep his promise not to confess? Given the uncertainty, each will have an interest in confessing, since there is a danger that, if he keeps his mouth shut and the other confesses, he will go to prison for ten years. If each is 'rational' and strictly pursues his own interest, the indicated solution (the dominant strategy) is therefore not mutually advantageous, since by both confessing they incur a greater penalty than if they both remain silent. This means that, 'in pursuing their personal interest a little too closely, the players risk missing opportunities for mutual gain'.[55] In other words, when exchange theory adopts a purely individualist perspective, it does not show a way towards cooperation or reciprocity. The consequences are harmful to both parties: individual interest contradicts mutual interest; if each persists in wanting more for himself, both will end up with less. 'If the lesson of the prisoner's dilemma is reliable, it places in doubt the very possibility of market exchange. For it suggests that the exchange will everywhere break down because of each player's greed – a conclusion that remains valid so long as we stick to the usual hypotheses of economic theory.'[56] Moreover, according to the prisoner's dilemma, the dominant strategy is damaging to both parties, while in 'normal' market practice the stronger side wins at the expense of the weaker.

Laurent Cordonnier's use of the 'archaic' theory of exchange (gift and counter-gift) shows that the dire outcome predicted by game theory is not inevitable, so long as both players are aware they can avoid it if they stop trying to impose their selfish interest.[57] Since 'being the only one to cooperate' (in this instance, by

55. Ibid., p. 50. 'You risk losing all by seeking to gain more' is the moral of Fontaine's fable of the Heron (VII/4).

56. Ibid., p. 186.

57. Cordonnier partly bases himself on the fact that, according to Marcel Mauss,

keeping quiet) carries the maximum risk (ten years in prison if the other confesses), and since it therefore cannot be accepted as a rational solution, how can one imagine cooperating in such a way as to push the other to cooperate in turn? The answer is to think that 'the players have the power to alter the behaviour of others, and therefore to be partly "under their influence"; this is as clear as daylight in the other social sciences, which recognize that individuals are directly joined to one another by a *social bond*.'[58] Exchange does not take place in a social vacuum, then, and the logic of gift and counter-gift actually gives effect to the cooperative solution (the one most favourable to both players within the constraints of the prisoner's dilemma).[59] There are two reasons why this is so: first, the fact that partners in the gift/counter-gift system do not choose each other but are socially assigned (groups that exchange women or services, relatives who exchange food, etc.) rules out any competition with other players; and second, no bargaining is allowed between the parties to the exchange. Furthermore, there is a time lapse between gift and counter-gift: the obligation to give back is certainly part of the rules of the society, but it implies trust in the other party (who might always fail to discharge his debt). It is not the market that leads to the optimum solution. Rather, an institutional structure makes it clear that 'what is in keeping with people's interests is not necessarily obtained by letting their interests express themselves'.[60]

---

the threefold obligation of giving, receiving and giving back is not exempt from self-interested motives – although, as Mauss also points out, 'there is an interest, but it is only analogous to the one which we say is our guiding principle.' *The Gift*, p. 73. See also note 29 above.

58. Cordonnier, *Coopération et Réciprocité*, pp. 196–7.

59. 'The exchange-gift, as we have depicted it, is the process through which the cooperative outcome of the prisoner's dilemma asserts itself' (ibid., p. 175). 'The gift/counter-gift may be analysed as the movement of exchange that shifts individuals from the non-cooperative to the cooperative outcome of the prisoner's dilemma' (p. 180).

60. Ibid., p. 176.

Although Laurent Cordonnier takes some liberties with certain themes of classical anthropology,[61] his account is interesting because it brings out the aporias of 'standard' economic theory, which asserts without further ado that exchange is mutually advantageous when each player pursues his own interest. The truth, as we have seen, is very different. Unless 'free' exchange is framed by a set of rules, whether imposed or internalized, it cannot but lead to disaster for the contracting parties.

Economists are by no means unaware of these baneful consequences of an exclusive pursuit of self-interest, in the particular circumstances defined by the model of the prisoner's dilemma.[62] One might have thought that this would temper their devotion to the virtues of the market, but 'standard' economic theory continues to prosper and still teaches that the market enables an optimum allocation of resources. In other words, economists have various models at their disposal, which allow them to prove one thing or the opposite as circumstances dictate.

Lastly, we should ask ourselves whether the generalization of the market – which economists present as a 'natural' advance devoutly to be wished – is compatible with a 'human' society. Karl Polanyi doubted it: 'Our thesis is that the idea of a self-adjusting market implied a stark utopia. Such an institution could not exist for any length of time without annihilating the human and natural substance of society; it would have physically destroyed man and transformed his surroundings into a wilderness.'[63] Note that these lines, written in 1944, employ the past tense, as if the utopia of the self-adjusting market had disappeared in the turmoil of the 1930s. We must therefore recognize that Polanyi was mistaken:

61. In particular, following Marshall Sahlins, he insists on the continuum between general, balanced and negative reciprocity, and hence between unconditional gift-giving and frenzied haggling (ibid., pp. 166–7). He also freely admits that his perspective is somewhat reductionist (p. 149), which we should not hold against him.

62. Indeed, 'the prisoner's dilemma is undoubtedly the strategic interaction most widely discussed, commented upon and utilized by economists' (ibid., p. 61).

63. Polanyi, *The Great Transformation*, p. 3.

the 'great transformation' that he thought would result from the failure of the market has not taken place; market economics is still alive and kicking. On the other hand, he was right to say that the self-adjusting market destroys man and transforms his surroundings into a wilderness. Why, then, do we pretend not to realize it? Should this collective blindness not be attributed to our economic imaginary, to the false assumptions and hidden prejudices that lie beneath the appearance of reason and common sense?

CHAPTER 5

THE FAIRY TALE OF SCARCITY

Is scarcity part of 'nature' or of the primal scene that institutes economic 'science'? A simple fact of life or just a way of looking at things? A reality unnoticed by previous generations or a timely invention to make economic discourse more credible? Certainly the idea of an original scarcity opens most of the economics textbooks.[1] But is human existence really determined by the struggle against scarcity and the quest for abundance? Should we not rather think that the twin assumption of scarcity and limitless needs[2] was needed to get *Homo oeconomicus* down to productive labour (at long last!),[3] thereby triggering the process of economic growth?

---

1. 'Human activity presents an economic aspect when there is a struggle against scarcity. ... Scarcity of means, choice of ends, measurement of costs: these are the three ideas that allow us to understand the essence of economic activity. ... Economics is the science of the administration of scarce resources.' Raymond Barre, *Économie politique*, vol. 1 (10th edn, Paris: PUF, 1975, pp. 13, 15, 20). This implies that, if the struggle against scarcity was crowned with success, economic 'science' would no longer have any meaning. That, no doubt, is why needs must be considered limitless.

2. The concept of 'need' is itself highly implausible, being a first approximation to the naturalization of human wants. Basing itself on the supposed incompressibility of physiological needs – an idea widely rejected by anthropologists – economic 'science' has built up a 'theory of needs' (disguised as so-called 'preferences') that legitimizes economic growth. I hope to have shown elsewhere that it is wrong to think of needs as self-evident: see Rist, *The History of Development*, pp. 167ff. and bibliography.

3. It is worth noting that, before it became the 'substance of value' (in the classics and Marx), labour was widely looked upon with contempt. Antiquity consigned it to slaves, and in keeping with its etymological roots in *tripalium* medieval France regarded *le travail*

THE TWO FACES OF SCARCITY

Before looking more closely at the concept of scarcity,[4] we should make an initial distinction between two very different forms. On the one hand there is *finitude-scarcity*, which is a *given*: gold or oil is scarce because it is a non-renewable resource that exists in finite quantities, like the paintings of Rembrandt or Matisse. This is the kind of scarcity that occupied the early classical economists – only they used it as a criterion for the *exclusion* of scarce goods from economic theory, on the grounds that these were literally 'priceless'! Ricardo, for example, wrote: 'In speaking … of commodities, of their exchangeable value, and of the laws which regulate their relative prices, *we mean always such commodities only as can be increased in quantity by the exertion of human industry*.'[5] Classical economics, then, did not concern itself mainly with 'scarce', non-reproducible goods; the exception was land, whose price regularly increased because of its original 'scarcity'.[6] However, the reason for excluding scarce or non-reproducible goods was that their value depended not upon the labour socially necessary to produce them (since they were either 'given' by nature or the fruit of a vanished genius[7]) but solely on what Ricardo called the 'caprice of demand'.

---

as a form of torture. Judging by the case of Vauban, French cities in the eighteenth century had between 130 and 150 days off a year (including Sundays) – a considerable number, even if the working day was longer than it is today. (Bruno Caceres, *Loisirs et travail du Moyen Âge à nos jours*, Paris: Seuil, 1973, pp. 30–32, quoted in Alain Caillé, 'Deux mythes modernes, la rareté et la rationalité économiques', *Bulletin du MAUSS*, 12, December 1984, p. 28.) For a long time idleness was considered an aristocratic (and then bourgeois) privilege; only in the mid-eighteenth century did economists begin to criticize the 'unproductive' or 'sterile' classes.

4. Scarcity is, let us remember, the core of *Homo oeconomicus*, who has scarce resources but limitless needs and therefore constantly has to make choices.

5. *The Principles of Political Economy and Taxation*, p. 6; emphases added.

6. This explains why ground rent, paid by the farmer to the landowner, increases as population growth makes it necessary to develop less and less fertile land and offers an advantage to the owners of more fertile land (since the rent is fixed at the cost level of those who produce under the worst conditions).

7. This gave rise to statements that seem quite staggering today. Jean-Baptiste Say, for example, wrote: 'Natural riches are inexhaustible, for otherwise we would not obtain

On the other hand, there is *shortage-scarcity* socially created by the market; any good may suddenly *become* scarce because demand outstrips supply. In fact, the works of the neoclassical school made this new concept of scarcity *the universal principle explaining value.*[8] Why? The reason is that they disregarded the specificity of naturally scarce goods (finitude) and chose to base the value of all goods on their utility alone. For the neoclassical school, then, there is no difference between a Picasso painting, a piece of land by the sea, a motor car, a barrel of oil and a sack of potatoes. They are all 'useful' goods that satisfy people's wants, and not existing in unlimited quantities they are therefore 'scarce'. In a way, the neoclassical economists *reversed* the logic of the classical school, by extending the theory of rent to all commodities and making 'need' the sole criterion of value. All that counted for them was the price established by the 'law' of supply and demand – or, to be more precise, by the all-decisive 'caprice of demand' – which jumbled everything together in the market.[9]

This is why the 'new' (i.e. neoliberal) economists, who think of themselves as faithful disciples of the neoclassical (or marginalist, or subjective theory of value) school, can claim:

> It is enough to start from the banal, but often neglected, observation that we live in a world where *everything is scarce* by definition: not only natural resources, raw materials, energy or money … but also *time* (the scarcest of all our resources because it can never be extended), *information* (which mobilizes time, research efforts and energy), imagination, action

them for nothing. Incapable of being either multiplied or exhausted, they are not the concern of economic science.' Quoted in Latouche, 'L'économie paradoxale', in *L'Économie dévoilée,* p. 23.

8. See Paul Fabra, *Capitalism versus Anti-Capitalism: The Triumph of Ricardian over Marxist Political Economy*, New Brunswick NJ: Transaction, 1993, pp. 3, 315ff. As Fabra also notes, far from being continuators of the classical school, the 'neoclassical economists' are actually its contradictors (p. 3).

9. 'In the phenomenon of exchange … demand ought to be considered the principal fact and supply the accessory fact.' Walras, *Elements of Pure Economics*, p. 89; translation modified.

or decision. ... Since everything is scarce (the principle of economics), there is necessarily *choice*, and *nothing is free*.[10]

This apparent piece of common sense, which uses a 'banal observation' to dish out supposedly self-evident truths, reveals a strange confusion. For it brackets together such disparate things as natural resources, time, information and imagination, as if the supposed scarcity that makes them the subject of economics were of the same order for all. That is indeed the logical consequence of the neoclassical position.

To put it in another away, what is at issue here is the origin of commodity (product) flows, which may be either resource stocks or capital funds.[11] The speed at which flows can be produced from a stock is not time-dependent: the same stock of petrol can be used in one day to run a hundred cars or in a hundred days to run a single car. The end result is the same: the stock is exhausted. Funds, on the other hand (a field, a workforce, a hotel room), produce flows (wheat, labour, takings) only at a particular rhythm: one harvest a year, a working day that can never exceed twenty-four hours, only one room booking per night. Moreover, unlike stocks, funds have to be maintained and used carefully to preserve their productivity.[12] The fundamental difference, then, has to do with the fact that flows deriving from (non-renewable) stocks, unlike those produced by funds, are not reproducible. Such flows also have a different temporality, since the speed at which stocks

10. Lepage, *Demain le libéralisme*, pp. 27–8; emphases in the original. Scarcity of time is here presented as a natural fact that does not need to be justified, probably in the belief that everyone thinks their life (or their day) is too short. However, Africans or Latin Americans would not understand the idea that time is a 'scarce commodity'. Benjamin Franklin's quip that 'time is money' is not universally valid.

11. All non-renewable resources are by definition stocks (but stocks of commodities can also be created with renewable resources, through the production process). Here I am referring only to stocks of non-renewable resources.

12. This means that flows (products, revenue, services) produced on the basis of funds may also dry up in the event of over-exploitation (soil erosion, over-fishing, material wear and tear, burnout of the workforce, etc.). Classical economists ignored this, believing like Ricardo in the 'original and indestructible powers of the soil' (*The Principles of Political Economy and Taxation*, p. 33).

are used up is left to their owner's judgement, whereas the rhythm of fund-generated flows is determined by their specific nature.[13] The problem arises when the value of flows deriving from stocks and the value of flows deriving from funds are homogenized within the same price system. It is ignorance of this difference which explains why the price of oil is set solely on the basis of supply and demand, no account being taken of its gradual but inevitable depletion; the formal rationality of 'standard' economics concerns itself only with the potential revenue from a flow, so long as there are consumers willing to pay the price regardless of where the flow originates (in funds or stocks). In fact, the price rises through which the market signals a shortage are in no way proportionate to the finitude of the resource;[14] all they do is record that the producer's expected revenue is out of line with what consumers are willing to pay to obtain the good in question. This, by the way, contradicts the constant refrain that the market permits optimum resource allocation, by establishing the most satisfactory price possible for buyers and sellers. For the simple fact is that the market ignores an important variable relating to the origin of the flows.

THE MEANS OF ABUNDANCE

So, with the hegemony of the neoclassical school, scarcity became the basis of economic 'science', and the struggle to overcome it was supposed to stimulate never-ending growth. But how did people live before this 'discovery' came to overturn social practices? The answer is given by those anthropologists who argue

13. Thus, if I inherit a 'stock' of a million dollars, I can spend it as I see fit (in one day, one year or fifty years). But if I inherit a field, I cannot sell today the harvests it will produce next year or over the next ten years, even if certain kinds of forward contract may allow me to 'secure' a future sale in advance. The rhythm of disbursement is therefore totally different with regard to stocks and funds.

14. The actual 'proportionality', of course, is known as price in the language of economics.

that traditional societies are societies of abundance.[15] This may seem somewhat of an exaggeration, but that itself reveals how the meaning of the word has evolved. As it is conceived today, abundance connotes a profusion or surfeit of resources, whereas for traditional societies it corresponds to a state of satisfaction with frugality that condemns personal enrichment in order to safeguard the social bond.

That said, we should not be too naive. In addition to the two previously mentioned forms of scarcity (finite stocks and market-induced shortage), there are situations resulting from external factors such as an earthquake, prolonged drought, a cyclone or tsunami, which can happen any time and throw a society off balance. This kind of 'conjunctural scarcity' may even affect traditional societies that normally have no experience of the phenomenon.[16]

Surprising though it may seem, given the image of people living at the edge of survival, traditional societies are so far from constantly battling against scarcity that they are unaware of its supposed existence. Of course they could produce more, but their social system forbids it.[17] The fact is that it would be easy to work longer in these societies, to form reserves and increase

---

15. The key reference here is Marshall Sahlins's *Stone Age Economics*, the French translation of which is actually subtitled 'The First Age of Abundance'.

16. We shall confine ourselves here to natural risks. Unfortunately, civil or international wars are the most frequent causes of the destitution that afflicts many societies. In tribal society, Karl Polanyi writes, 'the individual's economic interest is rarely paramount, for the community keeps all its members from starving unless it is itself borne down by catastrophe, in which case interests are again threatened collectively, not individually' (*The Great Transformation*, p. 46). Or again: 'the amount of hunger increases relatively and absolutely with the evolution of culture' (Sahlins, *Stone Age Economics*, p. 36). Sahlins's observation that primitive society admits shortage for all but not accumulation for all has its counterpart in today's world, where workers in a self-managed enterprise might agree to reduce their working time (and their pay) in order to overcome a period of crisis.

17. To describe what he calls the 'domestic mode of production', Sahlins speaks of an 'anti-surplus' mentality, deliberate 'underproduction', or even 'anti-production'. These terms are questionable, for they assume a threshold beyond which there would be a 'surplus' or an optimum or maximum production level, which is here very difficult to determine. However, the social practices on which Sahlins bases his account are no less deserving of attention.

the collective wealth. But that is precisely what they refuse to do. Why would a Bushman tire himself out, if it is enough that 65 per cent of the population works a third of the time to satisfy the needs of all? Nor does that rule out festivals, unproductive expenditure or squandering of goods patiently accumulated by the 'big men' (with the help of their spouses and kin), who thereby gain prestige without acquiring any power.[18] Lizot showed that the daily work requirement for subsistence among the Yanomami varied between two and a half hours (in the dry season) to four and a half hours (in the rainy season), and that the young and the old did not take part in labour but received 'assistance' under kinship obligations.[19] His conclusion is clear: 'To speak at all costs of scarcity in primitive societies sometimes leads to the most absurd situations.'[20]

The hypothesis of original scarcity is therefore by no means borne out by the practices that actually characterize 'traditional' or 'primitive' societies. To be sure, people in them live soberly or frugally, without wishing for more or seeking to accumulate when that is a possibility. They do this for two reasons. First, their aim in life does not lie in consumption: work is not highly valued and they prefer to chat among themselves, to listen to the chief – or the elders – to tell stories or relate the founding myths, or to organize feasts. Second, since personal enrichment always carries a risk of envy and violence, those who have obtained a better harvest thanks to hard work or favourable circumstances, or who have brought home an especially large game animal, are forced to redistribute their goods in order to ensure social

18. Of course, the goods accumulated by 'big men' are perishable, especially in the case of food. Redistribution is therefore a necessity. Things would probably not be the same in a society where money could be hoarded to one's heart's content.

19. Jacques Lizot, 'Économie primitive et subsistance. Essais sur le travail et l'alimentation chez les Yanomami', *Libre*, 4, Paris: Petite Bibliothèque Payot, 1978, p. 85. This confirms Sahlins's point that 'structurally, the economy does not exist' in traditional societies (*Stone Age Economics*, p. 76).

20. Lizot, 'Économie primitive et subsistance', p. 106. Among the Yanomami, what is scarce is neither material goods nor food but women!

harmony. Besides, hunting and work in the fields are most often collective activities whose fruits are shared among all. That solves the problem at source, so to speak.

The scarcity assumption is necessary for the economic ideology, since only scarce goods are economic – unlike so-called 'free goods', which can be enjoyed without the need to sacrifice anything to obtain them.[21] But this is not without consequences for the way in which life in society is conceived.

HOW TO CONQUER VIOLENCE IN SOCIETY?

To place scarcity at the origin of things means considering it, implicitly or explicitly, as the prime cause of social violence. If, by hypothesis (or rather, by social construction), goods are defined as scarce, one must expect struggles in which everyone tries to control or appropriate them; *homo homini lupus*, the war of all against all, can then begin. To escape from this anarchic and dangerous 'state of nature', the only solution – if one follows Hobbes – is for everyone to agree on transferring their rights to the Leviathan, who will promulgate laws to which everyone is subject. This is not so far from Rousseau's social contract, where 'each one, uniting with all, nevertheless obeys only himself and remains as free as

21. In economic theory, such 'sacrifice' – that is, the forgoing of one thing to obtain something considered more desirable – is called 'opportunity cost'. Two remarks should be made here for the sake of completeness. Traditionally, air and water have been considered 'free goods' (see Barre, *Économie politique*, p. 17), but we know that this is already less and less the case for water (and will be tomorrow for air). Water is becoming more and more scarce, owing to extra demand (shortage-scarcity) as well as pollution (finitude-scarcity due to human activity); its price is therefore rising, to offset the costs of purification and because of increased demand. Marginalist economics explains prices in terms of utility: a thirsty traveller in the middle of the desert, for example, would pay different prices for a first and a tenth litre of water, since he would derive greater satisfaction from the first than from the tenth (hence the 'marginal utility' of a litre of water would decline). But this theory does not do away with the assumption of scarcity; it merely shows that the value of a good is not necessarily tied to its production cost (to the 'labour incorporated in it', as classical economists would have said).

before; … as each gives himself to all, he gives himself to no one.'[22] Although the two solutions are different, they both risk conferring excessive power on the sovereign – for, even if the sovereign is none other than the people, it can compel respect for the general will only by 'forcing dissidents to be free' (a formulation whose ambiguity never ceases to provoke comments).

From the same starting point as that of contract theories, where everyone fights over the right to dispose of a scarce resource to satisfy limitless needs, economists conjured up a new solution in which scarcity is replaced with abundance. It was enough to think of it[23] – especially as they had already established that, if everyone pursues their own interest, it will permit the spread of prosperity and the harmonization of private interests. Hence, there are no longer any grounds for the kind of renunciation that Hobbes and Rousseau urged for the constitution of a civil society at peace with itself. On the contrary. Nothing needs to be given up: the task for everyone is to engage in competition, since 'the study of his own advantage naturally, or rather necessarily, leads him to prefer that employment which is most advantageous to the society.'[24] To put an end to the violence that comes from envy of the goods that others have managed to acquire, it is necessary to make prosperity general (this was Marx's position too). And that means stepping up production and labour ('working more to earn more'), increasing the number of mutually beneficial exchanges, encouraging competition for the general good, and promoting economic growth to reach an idyllic state where no one lacks for anything. So many false promises, never kept but constantly renewed.

This new vision evidently conflicted with the opposition to personal enrichment or accumulation prevalent in traditional

22. Jean-Jacques Rousseau, *On the Social Contract*, New York: St Martin's Press, 1978, p. 53.

23. 'Economics can posit unlimited wants as a universal axiom only because it takes the assumptions of modernity as its own while imputing them to human nature.' Marglin, *The Dismal Science*, p. 201.

24. Smith, *The Wealth of Nations*, vol. 1, p. 475.

societies.[25] What used to be forbidden was now prescribed. Fear of attracting the 'evil eye' because of excessive riches mutated into a quest for social prestige.[26] Collectively chosen frugality became a sign of 'poverty'. Social violence, once contained through the duty to redistribute wealth, now had to be mastered by the hope of collective prosperity. This had the effect of making growth 'the only *real* foundation for the modern social bond'.[27] In 'rich' societies a hard-won political equality made light of economic inequalities, while in 'traditional' societies people readily put up with political hierarchy so long as it was tempered by material equality. That democracy is preferable to all forms of authoritarian rule is beyond question. Yet, for all the promises at election time, it is not enough by itself to guarantee economic justice. Indeed, we can see today the anti-democratic effects of extending the economic paradigm to all spheres of the state, especially health and education. Is a society still genuinely democratic when it tolerates the explosion of inequalities and social segregation? Do such 'aberrations' not sap that confidence in institutions which is the bedrock of society? As for hierarchical societies (even ones preserved from the virus of personal enrichment), they are not necessarily more economically egalitarian than our own, but they encompass social constraints that promote redistribution: 'The premium set on generosity is so great when measured in terms of social prestige as to make any other behaviour than that of utter self-forgetfulness simply not pay.'[28]

As we shall now see, the new economic 'science' that claims a neoclassical inspiration does not only turn the older world-views upside down. It slides into a dual paradox.

---

25. This opposition was shared by European societies before the logic of the market swept the board.

26. It is possible to interpret the evil eye as a kind of scrutiny of the other's wealth.

27. See Jean-Claude Michéa, *L'Empire du moindre mal*, Paris: Climats, 2007, p. 101.

28. Polanyi, *The Great Transformation*, p. 46.

THE DUAL PARADOX

The wish to consume incites an obligation to produce and trade. And, for this to continue, a sense of scarcity or lack must be constantly re-created – a kind of permanent frustration, so that each individual feels convinced that the road to happiness passes through the satisfaction of new needs (eating exotic food, spending the Christmas holidays in the Maldives, buying a new car model or a second home), which both stimulate growth and confirm social status. New products must therefore keep appearing on the market, and they must soon come to be seen as indispensable. How could people live before the spread of the motor car, the mobile phone or electronic mail?[29] The system imposes constraints that induce us to conform, and are difficult to shake off. Once upon a time, it was enough to have a home of your own for people to take note of you. Now you have to have an electronic address. Our 'needs' no longer depend on our free choice: they are shaped by a system that forces them upon us. As Baudrillard said long ago, 'there are only needs because the system needs them'.[30] Scarcity is not only part of the founding myth of economics; it must be constantly maintained through the illusion of its possible disappearance on the horizon of history.

The second paradox has graver consequences, which go well beyond the subjective sense of a permanent lack. For, in order to extend its sway, the market must make scarcity general, not only for non-renewable resources but also for 'reproducible' ones such as water or fishing produce.[31] Once no more than the founding

29. This is not to deny certain benefits of 'progress', although too many cars actually limit mobility and technological obsolescence forces us to keep buying new electronic devices. The key point is the constraint on us to conform to the customs of 'modernity'.

30. Jean Baudrillard, *For a Critique of the Political Economy of the Sign*, St Louis: Telos Press, 1981 (1972), p. 82.

31. The theme of the 'tragedy of the commons' (see Garret Hardin, 'The Tragedy of the Commons', *Science* 162, 1968, pp. 1243–8) means that over-exploitation is inevitable when several players compete for a limited but freely accessible resource such as collective fields or the ocean depths, since each tries to maximize his advantage at the others' expense and

postulate of neoclassical economics, scarcity has turned into the end goal towards which the 'exigencies' of the economy are leading us; a working hypothesis is in the course of becoming reality. Excess demand (shortage) and resource depletion (finitude) are thus combining to make everything scarce, so that it will no longer be possible to disentangle the two variants we identified at the beginning of this chapter. Economic 'science' thereby justifies its theory by conflating that which is part of nature and that which depends on society.[32] But this theoretical 'success', if that is what it is, is derisory in comparison with the founding fathers' declared goal of leading society along 'the road to plenty'. The facts are perfectly clear. Far from fulfilling its promises, neo-classical economic 'science' achieves their opposite and results in absolute scarcity. Most astonishing of all is that this turnaround, which many reports have shown to be happening, never leads economists to question their thinking; they just go on hoping that 'market mechanisms' (plus technological innovation) will be enough to solve the crises ahead.[33]

---

thereby provokes resource depletion. In theory, the solution is either to restrict access to the resource (quotas) or to privatize it (on the grounds that its owner will not act against his interests). However, history shows that 'collective land' is not necessarily over-exploited but is usually well managed. In fact, most of the commons is not something freely available for anyone to appropriate, but is mainly established by an institution that sets the rules for its use and prevents intrusion by 'profiteers'. This is why, in the case of fishing (where it is impossible, or too burdensome, to exercise collective control), quotas are always exceeded and the privatization of fishing areas that some would like to see is difficult. So, although economic theory offers a solution in principle to the dilemma, market practices do not conform to the goals of rationality and effectiveness set by that theory, and actually result in the tragedy they were meant to ward off.

32. Bruno Ventelou (*Au-delà de la rareté. La croissance économique comme construction sociale*, Paris: Albin Michel, 2001) also stresses that classical (or standard) theory engenders scarcity and in a way makes it come about (pp. 14, 41, 106 and *passim*). But his Keynesian perspective of cooperation, meant to allow scarcity to be overcome through positive externalities, appears over-optimistic when we think that the capitalist system is forced to extend the realm of the commodity and to continue along the path of accumulation.

33. For example, Robert Solow (Nobel prizewinner in 1987) writes: 'If it is very easy to substitute other factors for natural resources, then there is in principle no "problem". The world can, in effect, get along without natural resources, so exhaustion is just an event, not a catastrophe' ('The Economics of Resources or the Resources of Economics', *American Economic Review* 64 (2), May 1974, p. 11). Similarly, Lawrence Summers did

Thus, in grounding their 'science' on the assumption of scarcity, neoclassical economists have not only introduced a totally new vision of society but also shaped society in accordance with it. No doubt the scarcity postulate was necessary within the terms of their own discourse, to underpin theories that would otherwise have been groundless and incomprehensible; there can be no other explanation for their stubborn defence of the founding myth. The question, however, is not whether economic theories are consistent or inconsistent (one does not discuss the validity of an equation), but what social consequences they entail once they become self-fulfilling. As they are presently formulated, all variants of the theory focus exclusively on the functioning of the market (since the axioms on which they are based preclude an interest in anything else). It is always easier to keep doing what you have always done – and know how to do – instead of considering that you might do things differently. Since the market is the only form of exchange susceptible to formal models, it occupies the whole terrain, not only in theory but also in social practices.[34] The 'needs' of the consumer flow into the 'needs' of the market: both the one and the other must grow incessantly. And, as all production is accompanied with destruction, the dead end of general scarcity lies at the end of the road.

---

not hesitate to declare in 1991, when he was chief economist at the World Bank (before becoming treasury secretary in the Clinton administration, and later chairman of the National Economic Council in the Barack Obama team): 'There are no … limits to the carrying capacity of the earth that are likely to bind us at any time in the foreseeable future. … The idea that we should put limits on growth because of some natural limits is a profound error.' Quoted in Richard Douthwaite, *The Growth Illusion: How Economic Growth Has Enriched the Few, Impoverished the Many and Endangered the Planet*, Totnes: Green Books, 1999 (1992), p. 201.

34. Economists such as Gary Becker do not think twice about reducing all social relations to market relations.

CHAPTER 6

UTILITY AND FUTILITY

As we know, the concept of utility occupies an important place in economic 'science', as a kind of pendant to the concept of 'need', whose degree of satisfaction it is supposed to measure. However, before we come to what economists consider to be useful, it may help to clarify matters if we take a brief look at the work of Jeremy Bentham, the acknowledged father of utilitarianism,[1] who was first and foremost a moral theorist concerned with institutional reform.

> The end and aim of a legislator should be the happiness of the people. In matters of legislation, general utility should be his guiding principle. The science of legislation consists, therefore, in determining what makes for the good of the particular community whose interests are at stake, while its art consists in contriving some means of realization.[2]

1. There was also a form of utilitarianism in antiquity. According to Aristotle, 'it is because of happiness that we each act in all our life's encounters', and Saint Augustine reported in *City of God* (Book XIX) that all the philosophical sects of philosophers held that the 'securing of happiness' was the starting point of philosophy. Cf. Luc Marie Nodier, 'Définition de l'utilitarisme', *Revue du MAUSS*, 6, 1995, p. 18. Hobbes, for his part, noted that each man desires what is good to him and shuns what is evil ('On Man', in Hobbes, *Man and Citizen*, ed. Bernard Gert, Indianapolis: Hackett, 1991, p. 47). And, finally, Bentham himself owes a large debt to Helvétius.

2. Jeremy Bentham, *Principles of Legislation* (translated from the French abridgement of Étienne Dumont, 1802), London: Oxford University Press, 1914, p. 1. Cf. Bentham, *Introduction to the Principles of Morals and Legislation*, ch. 17, §1: XX.

So, it is the 'happiness of the people' that primarily concerns Bentham, even if he decides to start from the individual to realize it:

> Nature has placed mankind under the governance of two sovereign masters, pleasure and pain. To them we owe all our ideas: to them we refer all our decisions, every resolve that we make in life. … This maxim, unchangeable and irresistible as it is, should become the chief study of the moralist and the legislator. To these two motives the principle of utility subjects everything. … The principle of utility, accordingly, consists in taking as our starting-point, in every process of ordered reasoning, the calculus or comparative estimate of pains and pleasures, and in not allowing any other idea to intervene.[3]

In this version at least, Bentham's argument is clear enough – 'none of your subtlety, none of your metaphysics'[4] – but the fact remains that the quest for 'the greatest happiness of the greatest number' raises a number of questions, of which we can mention here only the most significant.

QUESTIONS FOR JEREMY BENTHAM

(a) Until the beginning of the eighteenth century, the task of political (or moral) philosophy had been to reflect upon the conditions of life in society, on the relations among people or forms of government.[5] From then on, the legislator was expected to be guided by 'the public good' or 'public happiness', or by the aim of general prosperity. Already embryonic in Mandeville, for example,[6] this tendency reached a peak with Bentham: social

3. Bentham, *Principles of Legislation*, pp. 3–4; cf. *Introduction to the Principles of Morals and Legislation*, ch. I, i–ii. In a note added to Chapter I of the *Introduction* in July 1822, Bentham said that the utility principle was synonymous with the 'greatest happiness' or 'greatest felicity' principle. As Alain Caillé has pointed out, we are still in the world of Newton: there is an attraction to pleasure and a repulsion from pain; individuals behave like atoms subject to the law of universal gravitation.

4. *Principles of Legislation*, p. 4.

5. This is especially true of Rousseau's article 'Économie ou Oeconomie (Morale et Politique)' that he wrote for the *Encyclopedia*.

6. See Louis Dumont, *From Mandeville to Marx: The Genesis and Triumph of Economic*

morality no longer concerned itself with organizing relations (egalitarian or hierarchical) among the members of society in order to ensure civil peace or social harmony, but made the collective happiness depend on their relationship with things (which brought them pleasure or pain). This was a major reversal, since it broke the immediacy of the social bond by introducing an 'economic' mediation: the legislator's job was no longer to define a political system or forms of power, but to attend to the satisfaction of the greatest number.

(b) How do individuals calculate? Apart from the fact that there is no 'unit of account' that can be applied to pleasure or pain, it must be recognized that there is most often no common way of measuring pleasures for the same individual. How would one compare the pleasures of a good meal and artistic or intellectual creation, of a trip in the mountains and attendance at a concert? Moreover, what is a pleasure for one may seem a torture to another: one can either love or hate football, solitude, parties, reading or cabbage soup. How can positive and negative values be attributed to the same actions? Choices may also depend on whether they affect the short or the long term: is the trouble one takes in studying or athletic training worth the pleasure that will eventually result from it? Is the pleasure of feasting worth the tiredness of the next day? Finally, each person's preferences are always adaptive: if you cannot get what you want, you can always judge the grapes too sour, like the fox in the fable,[7] and the illusion of choice has to do more with a class *habitus* than with sovereign freedom.

(c) An action is good, Bentham says, if the sum of its consequences is better than that which would result from any other

---

Ideology, Chicago: Chicago University Press, 1977.

7. Bourdieu summed this up perfectly in the term *amor fati*: that is, the adjustment of expectations to the objective possibility or probability of fulfilment. Making a virtue of necessity implies a kind of love of necessity. Pierre Bourdieu, *Pascalian Meditations*, Stanford CA: Stanford University Press, 2000 (1979), p. 143.

action.[8] Although the principle is clear, its implementation poses serious problems: first, unless one is omniscient, it is impossible to gauge all the possible consequences of an action; second, it is even more difficult to know all the consequences of other possible actions. So, accepting that individuals calculate, it needs to be asked how they can calculate rightly.[9] Not only is this virtually impossible in practice; it forces us to put moral principles to one side. For one can no longer say: 'I am doing this because I promised to.'

(d) 'When we say that anything is in harmony with the utility of interest of an individual, we mean that it tends to augment the sum total of his well-being. When we say that anything is in harmony with the utility of interest of a community, we mean that it tends to augment the sum total of the well-being of the individuals of which the community is composed.'[10] Are these two applications of the utility principle compatible?[11] Undoubtedly not.[12] Nor do they tell us anything about the distribution of 'utility' (or happiness): it may be that an uneven distribution of individual happiness leads to a sum total of happiness greater than if it were equally distributed.[13] To escape the dilemma, we

8. Bentham's 'act utilitarianism' has been contrasted to John Stuart Mill's 'rule utilitarianism', which recognizes the prior existence of social norms.

9. 'If a man makes an ill reckoning, it is not arithmetic which is to blame, it is himself.' *Principles of Legislation*, p. 23.

10. Ibid., p. 4. We should note that, to underline his individualist (non-holistic) standpoint, Bentham does not say 'well-being (or happiness) of the community' but 'well-being of the individuals of which the community is composed'.

11. A wide debate has developed over the interpretation of Bentham's utilitarianism. The differing positions of Jean-Pierre Dupuy and Alain Caillé may be found in *Revue du MAUSS* 6, 1995.

12. 'It should already be clear from Leibniz that double maximization – that is, the maximization of two mathematical functions at once – is a logical impossibility. One can maximize the number of those who have a greater happiness than a certain prescribed threshold; one can maximize the sum of happiness among the population as a whole, or any other growing function of the individual happinesses. But it has no meaning to maximize both the happiness and the number.' Jean-Pierre Dupuy, 'Sur la formation du radicalisme philosophique d'Elie Halévy', *Revue du MAUSS* 6, 1995, p. 74. So, out goes the famous 'greatest happiness of the greatest number'.

13. See Gunnar Myrdal, *The Political Element in the Development of Economic Theory*,

must either presuppose a harmony of interests (the 'economic' version of utilitarianism), or give the task of creating it to an enlightened legislator (a kind of supreme calculator), or rely upon a form of 'altruistic egoism' (since happiness can also be found in willing the good of others, rejoicing over their happiness or empathizing with their misfortune), or compel some to sacrifice themselves to increase the collective happiness. Bentham aspired to be both educator and legislator, and so it is not clear that he made individual egoism the sole foundation of morality; he tended, rather, to identify individual happiness and collective happiness. Nevertheless, in the debate on the role of self-regarding interest against an artificial 'junction of interests' by the legislator, each side can find arguments in Bentham's works.[14]

(e) If it is held that the pleasures of life lie in consumption, the conclusion must be that 'the utility that the wage permits is paid for by the *disutility* of work',[15] even if some take more pleasure in earning money than in spending it.

HOW TO DEFINE UTILITY?

At first sight the utility principle – everyone tends to seek happiness and to shun pain – appears self-evident. Yet it raises a number of questions, especially as it is difficult to give the concept of utility an unambiguous meaning. At the level of common usage, the *Petit Robert* dictionary proposes as synonyms: good, profitable, indispensable, necessary. So expenditure may be useful because indispensable, or not useful because superfluous; some animals are useful, while others are considered harmful; advice that one follows is useful, otherwise serves no purpose. These few

London: Routledge, 1990 (1930), p. 41. The same problem arises with the Pareto optimum.

14. Alain Caillé, 'Les mystères de l'histoire des idées. Remarques à propos du cas Bentham', *Revue du MAUSS*, 6, 1995, pp. 125–46.

15. 'Work as "Disutility" and Money as "Happiness": Cultural Origins of a Basic Market Error', *Journal of Socio-Economics* 21(1), Spring 1992, pp. 43–64; retranslated.

examples show clearly that this way of conceiving utility rests upon a moral judgement liable to fluctuate from one individual to another, or even according to circumstances. Hence Georges Bataille's sense of desperation:

> Every time the meaning of a discussion depends on the fundamental value of the word *useful* – in other words, every time the essential question touching on the life of human societies is raised, no matter who intervenes and what opinions are expressed – it is possible to affirm that the debate is necessarily warped and that the fundamental question is eluded. In fact, given the more or less divergent collection of present ideas, there is nothing that permits one to define what is useful to man.[16]

Bataille is evidently right if we situate ourselves within the Benthamite tradition, for which the aim is to define what brings the greatest happiness not only to the individual but to the community of which he or she is part, and therefore to judge ('approve' or 'disapprove', as Bentham puts it) the effects of a particular action or the pleasures that a particular good may afford. This brings up all the problems inherent in such judgement, since the arithmetic of pleasure and pain – or of the ultimate consequences of an action – is impossible.

To anchor economic value in utility, the economists therefore faced two major problems: they had to define utility in a 'non-moral' way (so that it did not depend upon a value judgement), and they had to find a way of accounting for rational choice. Both conditions were necessary in order to establish uniform and constant 'laws'.

Jean-Baptiste Say was the first to redefine utility in a way that freed it from the variability from which it suffers in common parlance. Against those who claimed that certain things could have value without being really useful (a ring or an artificial flower, for example), he wrote:

16. Georges Bataille, 'The Notion of Expenditure', in *Visions of Excess: Selected Writings, 1927–1939*, Minneapolis: University of Minnesota Press, 1985, p. 116.

> You do not discover the utility of these products because you call only *useful* that which is so to the eye of reason, but you ought to understand by that word whatever is capable of satisfying the wants and desires of man such as he is. His vanity and his passions are to him wants, sometimes as imperious as hunger. He is the sole judge of the importance that things are of to him, and of the want he has of them. We cannot judge of it but by the price he puts on them. The value of things is the sole measure of their utility to man. It is enough for us to give them utility *in his eyes* in order to give them a value.[17]

This definitional 'power grab' removes utility from moral judgement – which in a way identifies it with what has 'utilitarian' value – and baldly asserts that things are useful if they are *desirable* to a certain individual at a certain moment and have an exchange value. Utility, then, depends not on the object as such but on the judgement we make of it and the price we are willing to pay to obtain it. But this subjective theory of utility rests on a tautology: if a thing is both useful and scarce, the economists say, it must have a price (an exchange value); but they immediately add that this price is the measure of utility (and scarcity). This amounts to saying that A = A, which hardly takes the definition further.[18]

---

17. Jean-Baptiste Say, *Catechism of Political Economy* (1815), London: Sherwood, Neely & Jones, 1816, pp. 6–7. This is not a long way from Condillac: 'We say that a thing is useful when it serves some of our needs; and that it is useless when it serves none of them, or when we can do nothing with it. Its utility is therefore based on the need we have of it. In accordance with this utility, we value it more or less highly: that is, we judge that it is more or less fit for the uses for which we wish to employ it. And this estimation is what we call value. To say that a thing is valuable is to say that it is good for some use, or that we consider it to be so. The value of things is therefore based on their utility – or, what comes to the same thing, on the need we have of it; or, what again comes to the same thing, on the use we can make of it.' Étienne Bonnot (abbé) de Condillac, *Le Commerce et le gouvernement considérés relativement l'un à l'autre*, Amsterdam and Paris: Jombert et Cellot, 1776, pp. 9–10. As if echoing this, Auguste Walras clarified: 'There is therefore this difference between morality and political economy: the former calls useful only those objects which satisfy needs admitted by reason; the latter gives that name to all objects that man may desire, whether in the interests of self-preservation or as a result of his passions and caprices.' *De la nature de la richesse et de l'origine de la valeur* (1832), quoted in Jean-Claude Liaudet, *Le Complexe d'Ubu ou la névrose libérale*, Paris: Fayard, 2004, p. 119.

18. José Manuel Naredo, *La Economía en evolución. Historia y perspectivas de las categorías básicas del pensamiento económico*, Madrid: Siglo XXI, 2003, pp. 214–15.

This change or reversal of meaning radically separated economics from social morality. Whereas classical economics (Smith, Ricardo, Marx) distinguished use value from exchange value – and conceived of utility in a common normative sense – neoclassical economic 'science' would base itself on the exuberance of solvent individual desires. As Léon Walras later said in a famous example, it may be that the same substance may be sought after by a doctor to cure a patient and by a murderer to poison his family, but in each case it may be described as useful – perhaps even more in the second than the first, since the murderer will be willing to pay more to obtain it. It is a deliberately cynical apology, designed to show that (economic) utility depends solely on the intensity of desire, so that the (morally) non-utilitarian can be brought under the category of the useful and therefore into the system of economics![19] To increase profit, economics therefore sets itself the task of liberating desires (technically termed 'preferences'), so that everyone can have unfettered enjoyment.

A further consequence of the subjective definition of value is that it makes money the unit of account in an 'arithmetic of pleasure and pain'. Since everyone chooses by price, it is price that measures the intensity of desire and 'sums up' the calculation that permits the maximization of pleasure and the minimization of pain.[20] This gives rise to a strange reversal: whereas calculation was supposed to define the utility of a good[21] for each consumer and

---

19. Walras, *Elements of Pure Economics*, p. 65. It is therefore only from a moral (not economic) point of view that one can criticize the multiplication of (by definition useless) gadgets or the 'tyranny of fashion', which imposes its marks of distinction. Cf. Jean-Jacques Goux, 'L'utilité: équivoque et démoralisation', *Revue du MAUSS* 6, 1995, pp. 106–24.

20. This was already Bentham's position: 'The only common measure involved in the nature of things is money. How much money would you give to buy this pleasure? … Those not satisfied with the exactitude of this instrument should find another, or say farewell to politics and morality.' Fragments of a manuscript published under the title 'Le calcul des plaisirs et des peines' (1782), *Revue du MAUSS* 5, 1989, pp. 75–6; retranslated.

21. In economic terms, the consumer prioritizes his preferences, which are then taken as transitive (fixed): if I prefer A to B and B to C, I must necessarily prefer A to C. The theory also assumes that preferences are independent of circumstances and of the choices made

thereby explain the formation of its price, the movement now is from price to utility. 'If the consumer desired a certain quantity of a good at a particular price, it is precisely because he needed it in that proportion.'[22] We should also note that this way of posing the problem assumes an 'acquisitive passion', so that the resulting pleasure depends on the quantity of goods that can be appropriated through market exchange.[23] But we cannot rule out the case in which lesser consumption allows increased satisfaction!

Finally, this redefinition of utility conjures away any explicit promotion of 'the greatest happiness of the greatest number'.[24] The Benthamite legislator has stepped aside, and all that remains is a postulated harmony of interests which, in Léon Walras and Pareto, finds expression in a theory of general equilibrium that is impossible to demonstrate.

This adds up to a real 'subjectivist revolution', which frees economic theory from any consideration of social values and leaves only the self-interested, calculating individual face to face with his coveted objects. Of course, certain assumptions lie behind this.

REDUCTIONIST ASSUMPTIONS

The first assumption is that human behaviour is entirely determined by self-interest, or rather the calculation of self-interest, and that such behaviour can be attributed to everyone. In other words, to borrow the terminology of Max Weber, the human subject knows only goal-oriented (*zweckrational*) rationality, which

---

by other players; each chooses for himself, without concerning himself about others. However, this is only a hypothesis, since there is actually no proof that the consumer does not hesitate, that his order of preferences is constant, or that he does not also decide in the light of other people's choices.

22. Caillé, 'Les mystères de l'histoire des idées', p. 143.

23. As economists define it, utility only concerns market goods and services. In big cities, pure air is both scarce and useful, but since it has no exchange value it escapes the attention of economics. See Naredo, *La Economía en evolución*, pp. 210–11.

24. Actual practice shows that the poorest usually have to be sacrificed to ensure the greatest happiness of the richest.

involves maximizing his 'utilities' or satisfaction and ignores the value-oriented (*wertrational*) rationality that respects certain norms of action. This claim may certainly be regarded as excessive.

Next, the theory claims that since individuals calculate, and since self-interest (not passion or morality) is their only motive for acting as they do, this necessarily leads them to make a rational choice. The only problem is that we do not really know how individuals calculate, and it cannot be excluded that they will make mistakes! The theory is therefore reduced to explaining behaviour *a posteriori*, on the assumption that everyone has made what seemed the best choice in light of the information at their disposal. Whether they preferred to buy a large rather than a small car, jewellery rather than clothing, or a gadget rather than bread, and whether or not they take masochistic pleasure in suffering, all their choices are considered rational – where this means simply that they had a greater 'interest' in one thing than in another. It seems clear, however, that a theory which claims to explain everything by a single 'reason' or cause fails in the end to explain anything at all; it merely registers what has been 'chosen' (that is, paid for) by asserting without proof that the choice was rational. As Say put it, 'we cannot judge of it but by the price', which is the sole measure of utility. He might have added that money is the most useful good of all, since it is totally removed from symbolization (from shared values) and allows us to buy anything so long as we have enough of it.[25]

Economists pretend to believe (and try to make us believe) that subjective reason coincides with objective reason. And they postulate that each individual's pursuit of self-interest, rationally enlightened by cost–benefit calculation, will ensure optimum

25. 'The utility of money is infinite, whereas the utility of a good is finite. ... With money, what counts is no longer the quality of the thing we possess but the fact of possessing it, intransitively. In the form of money, ownership becomes an end in itself. The enjoyment is in the possession, no longer in the object possessed.' Liaudet, *Le Complexe d'Ubu*, pp. 178–9.

functioning of the market and maximum satisfaction for all. This sounds reassuring, because it corresponds to the doctrine that justifies the market order to which we are subject.[26] But it does not correspond to any necessity of a universal or transhistorical 'human nature': it stems from the nineteenth-century power grab by neoclassical economists, who sought to roll uncontrollable passions into self-interested calculation and to make utility coincide with individual desires (so long as these were solvent!). Karl Polanyi put his finger on this reductionism:

> Single out whatever motive you please, and organize production in such a manner as to make that motive the individual's incentive to produce, and you will have induced a picture of man as altogether absorbed by that particular motive. ... The particular motive selected will represent 'real' man. ... For once society expects a definite behaviour on the part of its members, and prevailing institutions become roughly capable of enforcing that behaviour, opinions on human nature will tend to mirror the ideal whether it resembles actuality or not.[27]

Transmogrified though the concept of utility was in the hands of the classical economists, one is still surprised by their inconsistencies when they tried to shake off the symbolic dimension of goods and to reduce the subject to self-interested calculation. For, even if it is accepted that the 'desirability' (and hence 'utility') of a good depends solely on the desire of the person who seeks to acquire it, he or she cannot decide in a social vacuum, taking no account of the symbolic value that society attaches to various goods. In other words, the consumer's choice is never left entirely up to the individual: it is always overdetermined by affiliation to a social group that has already given value or meaning to

26. Game theory, on the other hand, shows that the pursuit of self-interest by everyone concerned does not lead to an optimum outcome.

27. Karl Polanyi, 'Our Obsolete Market Mentality', in *Primitive, Archaic, and Modern Economies: Essays of Karl Polanyi*, ed. George Dalton, Boston MA: Beacon Press, 1968, pp. 68–9. The term 'motive' should here be taken to mean 'central value of existence'.

certain goods rather than others. Marshall Sahlins refers to this as 'cultural reason':

> The reason Americans deem dogs inedible and cattle 'food' is no more perceptible to the senses than is the price of meat. Likewise, what stamps trousers as masculine and skirts as feminine has no necessary connection with their physical properties or the relations arising therefrom. … This understood, the rationality of the market and of bourgeois society is put in another light. The famous logic of maximization is only the manifest appearance of another Reason, for the most part unnoticed and of an entirely different kind.[28]

This little anthropological detour has marked the limitations of an 'unworldly' economic theory that claims to base itself on timeless and universal principles rooted in 'nature' or 'reason'. Whereas the natural sciences constantly test their hypotheses and are extremely attentive to data that might challenge their models, standard economic 'science' shuts itself up in an ideal system – that is, one which belongs to the world of ideas – without bothering about its compatibility with social practices often amply described by other disciplines. This makes it turn without gripping, so to speak.[29] The fact that sociology, psychology (not to speak of psychoanalysis) and anthropology have long questioned the rationality of the human subject does not seem to trouble economists, who simply describe as 'non-economic' the facts they prefer to ignore. In this they resemble a gardener who decrees

---

28. Marshall Sahlins, *Culture and Practical Reason*, Chicago: University of Chicago Press, 1976, pp. 169–70. Sahlins continues with a now classical example. Since there is more steak than tongue in an animal, and since both have the same nutritive value, steak ought to cost less than tongue. In fact, as we know, the opposite is true. Say would doubtless have explained the price difference by the fact that steak is more 'desirable' than tongue. However, these things depend not on individual taste but on the symbolic value that society attaches to 'superior' meats. In a different context, it is known that the Beti of Cameroon (and elsewhere in Africa) consider a chicken's head to be the daintiest morsel, reserving it for the head of the family or a guest they wish to honour. Marie-Pierre Essimi-Nguina, 'Ni têtes ni pattes: les vrais-faux poulets du supermarché', *Prétextes anthropologiques V, Itinéraires* 62, Geneva: IUED, 2002, pp. 49–58.

29. Even the 'non-economic' social sciences, which do not claim the same scientific status as economics, enable us to understand (and sometimes predict) human behaviour better than do all the models dreamed up by economists.

that any flower outside his little garden belongs to the class of 'non-flowers'. Economics exists only where economists have decided that it exists. Or, as Jacob Viner neatly put it, 'economics is what economists do'.

CHAPTER 7

EQUILIBRIUM

Equilibrium is unquestionably one of the keywords of economic 'science'.[1] Accounts (budget, foreign trade) have to 'balance' – otherwise there is a 'surplus' or a 'deficit'. Losses have to be 'offset' by gains, and the market must find an 'equilibrium price' satisfactory to all. What could be more reassuring? The harmony reigning in this enchanted world, which reminds one of the harmony of the spheres in antiquity,[2] is evidently steeped in Newtonian mechanics, with its belief in the reversibility of time and its ignorance of the entropy growth resulting from the use (and hence destruction) of natural resources in the production process.

1. 'The success of the concept of equilibrium in economics relates to the analysis of market prices. Equilibrium is an authorizing category, which makes price and quantity variation the hard core of "economic reality", involving an appreciation for the virtues of competition, market mechanisms and economic dynamism. ... The concept of equilibrium considers the "free prices" of "free markets" to be normal and therefore (economically) legitimate – which expresses well the fundamental theorem of the equivalence between equilibrium and optimum.' Lebaron, *La Croyance économique*, pp. 136–7.

2. The harmony of spheres – a theory of Pythagorean origin – is based on the idea that the universe is constructed in accordance with harmonious numerical relationships, such that the distances between the planets – in the geocentric picture of the universe: Moon, Mercury, Venus, Sun, Mars, Jupiter and Saturn – correspond to musical intervals.

THE WALRASIAN MODEL

Economists admit that the model of general equilibrium, first put forward by Léon Walras in 1874, is a *fiction* that does not describe how goods and services are actually exchanged yet offers a normative representation of how markets *should* behave to achieve an optimum. Walras said as much himself.[3] Being one of the first to use mathematics in economics, he eventually tried to demonstrate the 'theorem' of Adam Smith's invisible hand: if demand matches supply for a given set of goods in all markets, everyone will derive the greatest possible benefit from it. His proof for this general proposition – which, in a nutshell, was inspired by the French stock market – was as follows:

—consumers (buyers) and producers are 'rational': that is, they seek to maximize their satisfaction through exchanges that secure them some gain or profit;
—a single price, set for each good by a 'valuer' (obviously notional), prevents haggling, so that a consumer cannot acquire a good by paying more than another consumer because it has greater 'utility' for him;[4]
—there is a complete system of markets for all goods and services, both present and to come, which makes time disappear and

3. Cf. Émile Durkheim's view: 'The famous law of supply and demand, for example, has never been inductively established, as should be the case with a law referring to economic reality. No experiment or systematic comparison has ever been undertaken for the purpose of establishing that, in fact, economic relations do conform to this law. All that these economists could do, and actually did do, was to demonstrate by dialectics that, in order properly to promote their interests, individuals ought to proceed according to this law' (*Rules of Sociological Method*, p. 26). And Ricardo: 'The opinion that the price of commodities depends solely on the proportion of supply to demand, or demand to supply, has become almost an axiom in political economy, and has been the source of much error in that science' (*Principles of Political Economy and Taxation*, p. 260). See Bernard Maris, *Lettre ouverte aux gourous de l'économie qui nous prennent pour des imbéciles*, Paris: Seuil, 2003, pp. 24f. Aristotle (and later Karl Polanyi) stated that the value of exchange goods is equal or proportional to the value (or social status) of the parties to the exchange. This supports the position in Paul Jorion, 'Déterminants sociaux de la formation des prix du marché; l'exemple de la pêche artisanale', *Revue du MAUSS* 9, 1990, pp. 71–105.

4. The players (consumers and producers) are then said to be 'price takers'.

means that real uncertainty about future prices is of little or no significance;

—consumer demand and producer supply for each good are treated as two aggregates, which the valuer compares by means of a 'quoted price';

—if the quoted price cannot satisfy everyone concerned, the valuer keeps proposing new prices until – by a process of trial and error – all the demand and all the supply level out in an equilibrium price, but no exchange can take place until the equilibrium price is reached;[5]

—the situation is then declared optimal (the 'Pareto optimum'), since it is no longer possible to increase the satisfaction of one player without decreasing that of another;

—general equilibrium is achieved when all the markets (for each good) are in equilibrium.

This scenario further implies a set of hypotheses (apart from the fact that each player is 'rational'), which correspond to pure and perfect competition:

—no player has a dominant position that allows him to falsify the market results (atomicity);

—all producers offer the same product (there is only one kind of car or one model of trousers) and differ only in their prices (homogeneity of goods);

—all players are free to enter or leave the market;

—the means of production (capital and labour) can move freely from one firm to another or from one market to another;

5. This trial and error (Walras's *tâtonnements*) is characteristic of mechanistic thinking. In the manner of a pendulum, prices oscillate with less and less force until they settle at an 'equilibrium' point, when nothing moves any longer. It does not matter how long this takes: time does not exist.

—everyone knows all the prices (spot and future), thanks to the valuer, without having to do any research (free and perfect information);[6]

—externalities (that is, positive or negative consequences) generated by the economic process are not taken into account.

The task of neoclassical economics, in this case, is to show that there is an equilibrium price that may be defined by means of a set of equations.[7] Without considering technical problems that the model would have to solve to establish the sought-after optimum (sometimes called the 'most efficient state'), we can nevertheless make a number of remarks.

First of all, there is the highly peculiar nature of the approach. Instead of formulating a set of hypotheses and seeking to verify them in practice, it starts from the conclusion that it wishes to obtain (equilibrium exists and is positive) and then builds a set of hypotheses to 'verify' the predicted result.[8]

---

6. Jacques Sapir (*Les Trous noirs de la science économique. Essai sur l'impossibilité de penser le temps et l'argent*, Paris: Albin Michel, 2000, pp. 56ff.) lists twelve basic hypotheses that need to be simultaneously valid for the model to work. In practice, the system would have to be already in equilibrium before the valuer posted his 'correct' prices. The assumption of 'perfect information' is nowadays conveyed by the concept of market 'transparency', in the language of the international institutions. In reality, however, the markets are characterized more by their opaqueness. 'If everything were known about everything (if "transparency" existed), no one would make a profit. Profits exist, especially in the stock market, only because people never know what others will do: they anticipate it – which is not the same thing' (Maris, *Lettre ouverte aux gourous de l'économie*, p. 75).

7. Along with general equilibrium there is also a model of partial equilibrium – proposed by Alfred Marshall – which covers a single goods market (not all markets). It takes over the hypothesis of pure and perfect competition, adding a further assumption that price variations balancing the market in question bring no price changes on other markets. This gives a major role to the 'other things being equal' formula. Again it is a fiction with which economic 'science' feels comfortable.

8. This approach, already dreamed up by Cournot in 1838, involves the following: 'First, one discovers an equilibrium; second, one assumes (axiomatically) that agents (or their behaviour) will find themselves at that equilibrium; lastly, one demonstrates that, once at that equilibrium, any small perturbations are incapable of creating centrifugal forces able to dislodge self-interested behaviour from the discovered equilibrium.' Christian Arnsperger and Yanis Varoufakis, 'Neoclassical Economics: Three Identifying Features', in Edward Fullbrook, ed., *Pluralist Economics*, London: Zed Books, 2008, p. 18.

An unrealistic theory

It is evident that the conditions assumed in the model are never satisfied. Human agents are not always rational, some have greater economic weight than others, goods are not homogenous (think of all the 'models' of cars, watches or skirts), an automobile factory cannot switch overnight to planes or bicycles if demand falls off, a plumber cannot easily morph into a baker or computer programmer, the labour market has 'rigidities' not allowed for in the model, and price comparisons not only cost time and money but cannot take in much of the future. Everyone – even Léon Walras – agrees about that. The lack of realism flows from the initial hypotheses. However, what the model claims to describe is not reality but the world as it should (or could) be. A model, to be sure, is only a simplified presentation of particular circumstances as they are conceived by its designer; any criticism of it should therefore logically bear on the conclusions to which it leads – while respecting the conventions it assumes – and not imagine what it might be like if it had been constructed differently. Nevertheless, Walras's way of stacking up the initial hypotheses to 'confirm' the expected result is rather odd, to say the least. For the theory to be verified (and the market to become socially desirable), it is necessary to eliminate all markets dominated by a small number of sellers, to give up the advantages of mass production, to accept the absence of externalities, and to assume that information is perfect. That takes us a long way from the real world.

According to the theory, there should be only a single equilibrium – which means that, once it is attained, we are in a stationary or timeless situation. This is built into the hypothesis of perfect knowledge of present and future prices (which eliminates time) and into the mechanistic assumptions of neoclassical theory (for which time is reversible). But it also excludes any possibility of economic growth or innovation – which comes from making the firm more dynamic in anticipation of a possible new equilibrium – since no one will seek to increase their satisfaction. In this perspective, the market really does appear as the 'end of history'.

Walras's valuer is a very strange figure. He embodies the 'invisible hand', adjusting prices to quantities and supply to demand so that the miracle of the free market can come to pass. Of course, Walras's aim is to show that the market spontaneously achieves optimum allocation of resources.[9] But his valuer is an exact replica of the chief planner in a centralized economy (the Stalinist Gosplan).

> The discourses relating to market economics refer back to this Walrasian vision. But, if this were verified in actual practice, central planning should have won out against the market. The paradox is so great that a majority of economists have chosen to ignore it: the standard, and dominant, discourse on the market is incapable of conceptualizing the market.[10]

We should note that money plays no role in Walras's theory, except as a counterpart allowing goods and services to be obtained at the quoted price[11] (hypothesis of the neutrality of money, which actually plays a central role in modern economies). Nor can there

---

9. Léon Walras said that he was a socialist and sought to show scientifically how the market could be favourable to all. It is evidently reductionist to consider only the *Elements of Pure Economics*, since he also published *Études d'économie sociale. Théorie de la répartition de la richesse sociale* (1896) and *Études d'économie politique appliquée. Théorie de la production de la richesse sociale* (1898) [see *Studies in Applied Economics: Theory of the Production of Social Wealth* (London: Routledge, 2005)]. To his mind, pure, social and applied economics formed a whole. See Jean Weiller and Bruno Carrier, *L'Économie non conformiste en France au XXe siècle*, Paris: PUF, 1994, pp. 26ff.

10. Jacques Sapir, *Les Trous noirs de la science économique*, p. 21. See Bernard Maris (*Lettre ouverte aux gourous de l'économie*, p. 30): 'A first-year student knows that a perfect market system and a perfect planned system are equivalent.' Of course, this theoretical similarity rests on the (fictional) existence of a valuer, who does no more than match supply and demand without deciding on the appropriateness of producing one good rather than another.

11. According to Philip H. Wicksteed ('The Scope and Method of Political Economy', *The Economic Journal* 24, 1914, pp. 1–25), it is characteristic of economics that it requires a counterpart in the framework of exchange. What is obtained 'freely' from nature (or in the form of a gift) would therefore lie outside economics. See José Manuel Naredo, *La Economía en evolución*, pp. 222–3.

be any unemployment or overproduction – except 'frictional' – since any unused factor would bring a fall in the equilibrium price.

In any event, Walras himself did not manage to demonstrate his hypothesis, since it required a mathematical formalization that was not available to him.[12] The 'pseudo-demonstration' was supplied by Kenneth Arrow and Gérard Debreu in 1954; it earned a so-called 'Nobel prize' for Arrow in 1972 and Debreu in 1983. Their fine construction later fell to pieces, however, for several reasons.

An implausible optimum

Walrasian theory claimed to achieve the Pareto optimum (or 'efficient state'): that is, the best situation for society, in which it was impossible to increase anyone's satisfaction without undermining at least one other person's. However, not only is this not necessarily the optimum situation;[13] it has been shown that there is not only one possible equilibrium but a number of unstable ones.[14] Furthermore, as the initial resource endowment of the exchange partners is unequal, the only possible outcome – by trial and error – is growing inequalities. In other words, if left to itself, the market cannot improve its functioning and gradually arrive at

12. Contrary to what Walras thought, there is not just one solution for a system of *n* equations with *n* unknowns.

13. If one person owns everything and all others nothing, that is also a 'Pareto optimum'. Or, if one person's minimal loss entails a major gain for others, that goes against Pareto's optimum – which suggests that the 'optimum' has nothing to do with social justice. In practice, the market tends to concentrate wealth in the hands of a minority and to 'adjust' at the expense of the poor. We should also note that, according to the theory, all the decisions and actions of the players are supposed to bring them additional satisfaction, but that this leaves out of account the externalities (the positive or negative consequences) that they have for other players. By ignoring externalities, the Pareto optimum operates in a social vacuum.

14. This demonstration, known by the name of the Sonnenschein (or Sonnenschein, Mantel, Debreu) theorem, was carried out in 1974. It represents a fundamental challenge to the 'Arrow–Debreu theorem' of 1954, which was meant to show the possibility of a single equilibrium of all markets.

an equilibrium satisfactory to all: on the contrary, the imbalances will grow and the system will become more and more unstable. Worse, 'the Nash equilibrium demonstrates that, in a case more general than Walras's, the market gives the worst solution in a strategic universe.'[15]

The theory of general equilibrium and perfect competition, which supposedly justifies the benefits of the market, therefore clearly results in an impasse, yet it remains one of the main references in the discourse of economics.[16] Disturbingly, economists do not want to know: they persist in acting as if, despite everything, Walras-style liberalism provides the basis for policies capable of leading to collective well-being.[17] Since economists generally agree that most of the hypotheses in Walrasian general equilibrium theory are unrealistic (while considering them necessary if there is to be any hope of a mathematical solution to the problem), the trick is to make us believe that what is possible in the mathematical universe can be transposed to the real world (as if reality could conform to the results of 'science') and, worse still, that criticisms

15. The term 'strategic' here refers to game theory, in which the players are not simply maximizers ignorant of other people's decisions but anticipate reactions to their own decisions (Maris, *Lettre ouverte aux gourous de l'économie*, p. 30). See the end of the chapter on exchange.

16. 'So, here is a theory that claims to be capable of totally explaining the economy and society, a theory that pervades more than three-quarters of publications in the discipline and some ninety per cent of speeches. Yet scientifically it is a manifest failure.' Sapir, *Les Trous noirs de la science économique*, p. 74. Cf. Maris, *Lettre ouverte aux gourous de l'économie*, p. 19: in economic science, '99 per cent of what is taught, and 99 per cent of what underpins "research", is neither Marx nor Keynes but Walras.'

17. Sapir (*Les Trous noirs de la science économique*, pp. 65f.) shows that, in giving up the hypothesis of a complete market system, economists who follow Milton Friedman's view that rational anticipations lead to equilibrium cannot explain how people actually anticipate when there are several possible equilibria. Moreover, since rational anticipations imply taking externalities into account (what effect will my decision have on other people?), it is not possible to bring about the Pareto optimum (which is closed to externalities). 'It is not just *difficult* to demonstrate that a system of theoretical markets will generate an equilibrium in each market, on the basis of rational acts on behalf of buyers and sellers; rather, it is *impossible*!' (Arnsperger and Varoufakis, 'Neoclassical Economics', p. 19; emphases in original). 'The only honest solution is to admit that neoclassical economics is pure mathematical speculation, without any reference to the real world' (Sapir, *Les Trous noirs de la science économique*, p. 68).

and actual refutations of the model can be simply disregarded. Never mind that the theory is wrong, since what it claimed to show is as seductive as ever![18]

Of course, whether we prefer walking or riding a bike, or think the earth is round or flat, we still have to make exactly the same movements to go from A to B. In this case, theory has no influence on practice. We continue to say that the sun 'rises' or 'goes down', even if we know that these are only metaphors. On the other hand, when we try to fit reality into a theory – in this case, to achieve the greatest satisfaction for all, with theoretical premises that consider the competitive market as the optimum solution – it would seem right to ensure that the theory is valid and that its social consequences do not conflict with the end in view. But economists have no time for that. For them, the 'perfect' market is still the ideal, even though everyone knows that it is impossible to attain and, more important, that there can be no such thing. This leads them to propose absurd measures that contradict their stated intentions, because equilibrium theory assumes a closed system without the energy dissipation that actually occurs in the economic process. In fact, instead of achieving equilibrium, their measures disturb the system and, through the play of circular and cumulative causalities, result in crises which even the hardiest defenders of liberalism eventually call on the state to unravel.[19] Thinking to spread general prosperity and a market-induced social (Pareto) optimum, they end up increasing

18. 'By collapsing time into a form of product differentiation and assuming that agents have a complete knowledge of production and consumption possibilities, Arrow–Debreu makes it difficult to think about what happens outside of equilibrium when agents have only partial and incomplete information. The Arrow–Debreu framework sets too easy a task for economics.' Marglin, *The Dismal Science*, p. 167.

19. The 'subprime' crisis, which eventually triggered the near-bankruptcy of large banks in America and Europe and sent stock markets crashing in September 2008, offers a sorry example of this. In the end, it was national states that had to take over the banks and inject billions of dollars to underpin interbank loans and save the system. Having long preached that 'the markets are always right', economists had to revise their theory in the space of a fortnight.

poverty and social inequality.[20] It is not their intentions that are at issue but their ignorance and training, which stops them asking whether the model corresponds to reality. As the sociologist Terry Shinn pointed out, with reference to France's École Nationale de la Statistique et de l'Administration Économique,

> professors and students ... look at the world through a rigid, tightly controlled filter, whose structure guarantees a clear and perfectly integrated picture of people and things. ... One sees the world and comments on it in accordance with a set of axioms and general normative principles that politics, programmes and life's details have to follow.[21]

Beyond strictly economic considerations, we may conclude by noting that the concept of (stable) equilibrium has a highly positive connotation, and that it comes from mechanistic physics and shares its reversibility of time. It is therefore alien to the world of living beings, in which unstable equilibrium is the norm; a living creature must dispose of a supply of energy to maintain a certain equilibrium amid the constraints of its surroundings. The point here is not to import elements of the living order into the social domain – we have already warned against the dangers of such a procedure. But nor should we overlook the fact that economic processes have a temporal (or sequential) dimension and unfold in a context (the biosphere being the widest of all) in which energy issues are decisive, since its unstable equilibrium depends not only on the sun but on human activity. To be sure, 'nothing is created and nothing is lost', but 'everything changes form'. That is true of the planet too. Although it is unstable, its equilibrium is not threatened per se. But this might establish itself at a different level from that which we know today, endangering the survival of the

20. 'If you believe that a free market system will naturally tend towards equilibrium – and also that equilibrium embodies the highest possible welfare for the highest number – then ipso facto any system other than a complete free market will produce disequilibrium and reduce welfare. ... Most economists genuinely believe that their policy positions are informed by scientific knowledge, rather than by personal bias or religious-style dogma.' Keen, *Debunking Economics*, p. 163.

21. Quoted in Lebaron, *La Croyance économique*, p. 98.

human species. This is why the proposal of economic 'science' to reduce energy to its market cost – including, at best, the cost of related pollution – is far from addressing all the long-term consequences resulting from its use.

CHAPTER 8

THE GROWTH OBSESSION

We must start by asking why economic growth has become such a fetish. Numerous economists have amply shown that the usual way of calculating it suffers from patent defects and contradictions, and that it demonstrates neither 'good health' of the system nor the well-being that it is supposed to secure. Nevertheless, growth continues to be presented as an indispensable requirement on which the solution of all social problems depends – from those relating to employment, consumption and public services to those connected with foreign trade, pensions or public debt.[1] Just as economists freely admit that the figure of *Homo oeconomicus* is a reductionist fiction yet continue to act as if it were true, they recognize that the pursuit of growth is ecologically impossible yet persist in considering it necessary. What is the point of sticking to concepts that lead to a dead end? No doubt the natural inclination of our societies is to prefer comforting illusions to disturbing truths.

1. The report submitted by Jacques Attali to President Sarkozy in 2008, 'Freeing Growth', leaves one feeling stunned, not only because Attali (together with Marc Guillaume) had written a whole chapter on 'the theoretical critique of economic growth' in *Anti-économique* (Paris: PUF, 1975 [1974], pp. 97ff.), but also because most of the measures he now advocates threaten to have dire social and environmental consequences.

WHAT ECONOMIC 'SCIENCE' HAS CHOSEN TO EXCLUDE

Let us say at once that growth is not part of the vocabulary of classical economics. In those days, economists concerned themselves with 'the wealth of nations', 'the natural progress of opulence' or even ways of spreading 'abundance among the different classes of society', to speak the language of Adam Smith. On a close reading, one sometimes feels that Smith himself was surprised by the prospects of enrichment that the division of labour, trade and commerce held out, even if, in the end, he believed it was all part of the 'natural order'. But his optimism was not shared by Malthus or Ricardo (or later by John Stuart Mill), who thought that, under the impact of population growth and the natural limits of agricultural production, society would sooner or later grind to a halt despite rising productivity and the advantages resulting from foreign trade.[2]

That said, the way in which the early economists defined wealth posed a number of questions as a result of their determination to construct their discipline 'scientifically', on the basis of measurable quantities. Thus, in his *Principles of Political Economy* (1820), Thomas Malthus rejected Lord Lauderdale's broad definition of wealth as 'all that man desires as useful and delightful to him', on the grounds that this

> obviously includes every thing whether material or intellectual, whether tangible or otherwise, which contributes to the advantage or pleasure of mankind, and of course includes the benefits and gratifications derived from *religion*, from morals, from political and civil liberty, from oratory, from instructive and agreeable conversation, from music, dancing, acting, and all personal qualities and services.[3]

---

2. It is nevertheless remarkable that these authors regarded stasis as the outcome of demographic and 'ecological' factors bound up with the finite availability of land for agricultural use.

3. Thomas Robert Malthus, *Principles of Political Economy Considered with a View to Their Practical Application*, 2nd edn, London: W. Pickering, 1836, p. 23.

Of course, although this list is not exhaustive, it might be thought an excellent description of 'the good life' made up of 'material and intellectual' pleasures, as common sense would suggest. But, Malthus remarks, it is not serviceable because it does not allow us to measure 'intangibles' such as a doctor's services, the talents of a singer or the charms of conversation. Above all, how would we evaluate the growth or decline of a country's wealth by such criteria? The economic definition of wealth continued to preoccupy Malthus, who concluded:

> If then we wish, with M. Say, to make political economy a *positive science*, founded on experience, and capable of making known its results, we must be particularly careful in defining its principal term, to embrace only those objects, the increase or decrease of which is capable of being estimated; and the line which it seems most natural and useful to draw, is that which separates material from immaterial objects.[4]

This text is remarkable because it shows that, in its aspiration to 'positive' knowledge', economic 'science' limited itself early on to objects 'capable of being estimated': that is, to material resources that could be bought or sold on a market. What is more, it stresses the importance of the 'increase or decrease' of these objects for the estimation of wealth:

> A country will therefore be rich or poor, according to the abundance or scarcity with which these material objects are supplied, compared with the extent of territory; and the people will be rich or poor, according to the abundance or scarcity with which they are supplied, compared with the population.[5]

These definitions, which herald the advent of national accounting, help us to understand not only what economic 'science' includes in its object of study, but also what it *excludes*, for want of being able to evaluate it in an 'objective' manner – as if it were enough

4. Ibid., p. 33. In his *Definitions in Political Economy* (London: John Murray, 1827, p. 234), Malthus defined wealth as 'the material objects necessary, useful or agreeable to man, which have required some portion of human exertion to appropriate or produce'.

5. *Principles of Political Economy*, p. 34.

to consider that what escapes calculation does not exist. Malthus clearly saw the problem, when he wrote that 'to estimate the value of Newton's discoveries, or the delight communicated by Shakespeare and Milton, by the price at which their works have sold, would be but a poor measure of the degree in which they have elevated and enchanted their country.'[6] But, since this 'degree of elevation and enchantment' is strictly 'inestimable', it should be left out of account. In other words, certain things unquestionably have a value, but as they have no price they elude economic 'science' because of its very construction.[7]

It is mostly agreed that 'the economy dominates everything', but one would do well to ponder on all the things that economics deliberately omits, and that are the ultimate foundation of the charms of life.

NATIONAL ACCOUNTING AND THE INVENTION OF GDP

National accounting techniques came into general use only in the 1940s. This led to the concept of gross domestic product (GDP), whose annual variations made it possible to calculate the growth rate that ostensibly measured the success or failure of various 'national economies'. What is involved here? GDP is a statistical aggregate that annually records the total value produced within a country by adding together the monetary value-added[8] resulting

6. Ibid., p. 49. Today we might add that an author's worth is most often measured by the number of his books sold or the size of his royalties; what Malthus refused to contemplate (market evaluation of 'unproductive' labour) has become reality!

7. This joins up with what Lord Kelvin said in 1883: 'When you can measure what you are speaking about, and express it in numbers, you know something about it: but when you cannot measure it, when you cannot express it in numbers, your knowledge is of a meagre and unsatisfactory kind.' Quoted in Marglin, *The Dismal Science*, p. 309, n3.

8. Each firm adds value to the goods it transforms. To take the simple case of a baker, GDP will not include the flour he uses (because it has already been taken into account in what the farmer produced and the miller ground), but only the value of his labour that made it possible for the flour to turn into bread.

from all productive activity and the cost of public services (state expenditure, civil service salaries, social benefits, etc.). The growth rate, on which all eyes are generally fixed, represents the (positive or negative) variation in GDP from one year to the next.

This definition calls for a number of remarks:

(a) 'Non-market transactions' (domestic tasks, mutual services, voluntary work, undeclared work, the informal economy, etc.) do not feature in the national accounts.[9] Thus, in a substantive perspective the 'true wealth' of a country (natural heritage, disinterested exchange, etc.) is devoid of value, since it lies outside the realm of the market: what really counts is not taken into account.

(b) The costs involved in 'repair' activities (car repairs or hospital expenses following a road accident, the cleaning of polluted rivers or industrial sites, protective installations such as noise barriers along motorways, handling the aftermath of oil spills, etc.) are treated as *positive* values because they stimulate activity, as is the employment of extra policemen, security guards or judges to tackle rising crime.[10]

(c) Real nuisances for which no monetary compensation is paid (air pollution, airport noise, soil contamination, environmental degradation, etc.) do not enter the reckoning and constitute 'negative externalities'.[11]

(d) GDP does not take into account the 'cost' of the destruction of goods 'provided freely' by nature. So, the price of petrol, high

---

9. It has been estimated that such transactions correspond to roughly three-quarters of GDP in France. We also need to add legacies and presents within or between households. 'Non-market' plus gift-related benefits thus exceed in value those included in GDP. See Ahmet Insel, 'La part du don, esquisse d'évaluation', *Ce que donner veut dire. Don et intérêt*, Paris: La Découverte/MAUSS, 1993, pp. 221–35.

10. As Frédéric Bastiat (1801–1850) pointed out in his 'parable of the broken window', the glassmaker gets richer by repairing the damage, but the homeowner who bears the cost could otherwise have spent the money on a good that would have brought him greater satisfaction.

11. In a way, the cost of negative externalities is loaded onto those who are its victims, since their medical bills increase in step with the pollution to which they are exposed.

though it is, does not reflect the fact that the resource is extracted in order to be irreversibly destroyed, with an impoverishing effect on the common heritage.

(e) By itself, annual GDP variation tells us nothing about how wealth is distributed within a country, and nothing permits a judgement that all profit from it equally. The national accounts ought to be examined closely from this point of view – although that is rarely done.

(f) GDP figures evidently involve no judgement about the quality (or social desirability) of market activities: they could refer just as well to potatoes or weapons, narcotics or medicine, music lessons, advertising or prostitution. This amoralism is made possible by the monetary homogenization of all goods and services. Good resource management, however, should make decisions on what to produce (or not produce) depend on politics rather than the market.

This definition therefore rests upon a number of conventions established by economists and statisticians, in line with their own objectives. But a problem arises once the media, for example, make GDP the barometer of collective prosperity, since, as we noted above, it lumps together disparate elements and takes no account of factors that give life much of its charm, beginning with the maintenance of a home and the workings of generosity. Economists will immediately retort that that is not what GDP is for. And they are surely right. A rise or fall in GDP records no more than a variation in the volume of market activity; it does not indicate whether collective well-being is enhanced or diminished as a result – unless, that is, a tax increase is used to fund better public services or benefits (which involves a rise in GDP). Nevertheless, economics pundits continually invoke the growth rate to inform consumers, producers and financiers of favourable or unfavourable trends in the economy, and to alert them to the consequences these might have for their welfare.

This is more than a 'slippage'; it is a real change of meaning based on a *confusion between quantity and quality*: the assumption is that *more* (more activity and production involving market exchange) necessarily means *better*. In other words, it is suggested that the growing commodification of nature and social relations (biodiversity patenting, for example, or the transfer of childcare from grandparents to crèches) is always a mark of progress that deserves to be celebrated.

This is why a Californian research team inspired by Herman Daly and John Cobb have developed a Genuine Progress Indicator (GPI) to make up for the inconsistencies of GDP. The chief conclusion is that income per head in the United States (calculated from GDP) virtually doubled between 1975 and 2000, while GPI stagnated throughout those twenty-five years.[12] This is further evidence, if it were needed, that social wealth cannot be measured by GDP. What counts in the GDP statistics are not the results of production (or the benefits from it) but the obligatory *process* of growth.

THE GROWTH OBLIGATION AND ITS CONSEQUENCES

Except in international comparisons of the 'wealth of nations', as viewed by economic 'analysts', pundits and gurus, the key statistic is not GDP as such but its rate of annual growth. Hence the endless estimates of how fast a country will grow this year or next – as if everyone's life depended on it.

12. The Genuine Progress Indicator takes into account the value of household labour and the informal economy (considerably underestimating their value, in our view), as well as inequalities in income distribution, and subtracts everything that concerns the cost of accidents, crime (losses due to theft and murder, prison expenditure), defence spending, air and water pollution, soil degradation, and so on. For a more detailed definition, see John Talberth, Clifford Cobb and Noah Slattery, *The Genuine Progress Indicator 2006*, www.rprogress.org. Cf. Douthwaite, *The Growth Illusion*.

But in fact the indicator is important for the survival of *the system*, rather than of the people within it. A firm that stops growing – that is, no longer accumulates profit – is soon excluded from the market, in keeping with the principle of social Darwinism: grow or perish. Why this obligation to grow? The main theoretical reason, which is too often ignored, has to do with the institution of property.[13]

We need to distinguish between conditions for the use of something (enjoyment or 'possession') and property rights. In the case of real estate – a field, to take the simplest example – the rules of *possession* include access, farming possibilities, management (deciding what to grow), exclusion of those who do not have these rights, or even the transfer of these rights to others (by contract or bequest). These rules may vary from one society to another, but in essence they define which person or persons are authorized to use a particular resource. *Property rights* include all the rights of possession (enjoyment or use) but, in addition, they involve the power to sell the resource (real estate) for a sum of capital, or to mortgage it for monetary resources so long as one is able to pay the interest and to repay the loan over a fixed period of time. The property right – the fundamental institution in the system – therefore permits special access to financial capital through various kinds of contract: sales (giving up the rights attached to ownership and enjoyment), rental (transferring enjoyment while retaining ownership) and mortgage (retaining enjoyment while alienating the property in whole or in part).[14]

---

13. For the following considerations I am indebted to Rolf Steppacher, and particularly his article 'Property, Mineral Resources and "Sustainable Development"', in Otto Steiger, ed., *Property Economics. Property Rights, Creditor's Money and the Foundations of the Economy*, Marburg: Metropolis Verlag, 2008, pp. 323–54. Steppacher leans in turn on Gunnar Heinsohn and Otto Steiger, *Eigentumsökonomik*, Marburg: Metropolis Verlag, 2006. I have summarized the argument to make it more accessible, while being aware that this does not always do justice to the complexities of the subject.

14. The ease with which US banks gave capital to homeowners, and the disastrous management of loan guarantees, were at the origin of the subprime crisis of 2008–09.

When rules governing use (enjoyment or 'possession') are transformed into legal property rights, the holders of those rights gain increased access to monetary resources without the need to save them up. But, above all, the credit relationship involved in the mortgage mechanism radically changes the evaluation of the resources in play, since those resources now have to produce enough to cover the interest and to repay the loan over a certain period.[15]

> It is not only that a property-based economy 'allows', 'seduces' and 'pushes' for growth, it also imposes growth as a result of the conditions of credit.... [Hence there is a] *specific economic pressure* that prevails in property-based economies: the pressure for exponential growth imposed by interest, the proverbial time pressure imposed by the period for which the credit is granted, the pressure to improve cost–benefit conditions in order to be able to refund.[16]

So, a farmer who used to have enjoyment of a field and grew wheat or potatoes on it, and who then became its property owner[17] and mortgaged it for a capital sum, finds himself faced with the new problem of how to farm the field in the most 'profitable' way, so that he can meet his new obligations. Since his traditional crops threaten to be insufficient, it will be preferable to rent out the field or to build something on it; not only will the resource be allocated to different uses, but these will now be determined by the logic of profit.

---

15. 'The credit relationship creates four things: money, a debt, an obligation to repay the debt with interest, and therefore an obligation to produce more than one has received. Repayment with interest introduces the necessity of growth , as well as a whole number of corresponding obligations.' Rolf Steppacher, 'La petite différence et ses grandes conséquences: possession et propriété', *Nouveaux Cahiers de l'IUED* 14, Paris: PUF/ Geneva: IUED, 2003, pp. 184–5.

16. Steppacher, 'Property, Mineral Resources and "Sustainable Development"', pp. 335–6.

17. This corresponds to the situation of many farmers in the South – but also in the North after the French Revolution – who acquired property rights on land over which they had previously enjoyed only use rights. It also explains why certain countries – Switzerland among them – disallow speculation on certain categories of 'agricultural land': the plots are certainly someone's 'property', but that person cannot choose the use to which he puts them.

This logic applies to the whole economic system.[18] Firms must borrow investment capital from banks to keep their means of production up to date, and they must make enough profit not only to cover input costs and pay their workforce (and shareholders!) but above all to pay the bank interest and amortize their investment. Rapid changes in technology accelerate this renewal process and increase the need for new investment: one need only think of the built-in obsolescence of computer systems, the assembly-line changes necessary for each new automobile model, or the plethora of corporate mergers and takeovers – truly it is necessary to grow to stay alive! The system may thus be compared to a cyclist, who has to move forward to keep his balance. Or, as Marshall Sahlins put it, 'that sentence of "life at hard labour" was passed uniquely upon us [Westerners]',[19] because of our obsession with economic growth. 'This is why the liberal economist is forced to accept the postulate of indefinite growth – not at all because it *can* be indefinite (nothing proves that, everything suggests the opposite) but because it *has to be* indefinite.'[20] 'Economic reason' presupposes the obligation of limitless – and boundless – growth, and transforms society into a mere profit-making association.[21]

It is impossible to escape the logic of the system – that is, of the market – without radically challenging it. As things stand, the question posed to all economic agents is 'how to grow?', or 'how to increase my profit?' There are not so many ways of doing this.

---

18. The stock market turmoil of October 2008 amply demonstrated this, since the drying up of interbank loans threatened the whole system with paralysis and compelled governments to intervene on a massive scale.

19. *Stone Age Economics*, p. 4.

20. François Partant, *Que la crise s'aggrave*, Paris: Solin, 1978, p. 95.

21. Indeed, capitalism defines itself as 'a requirement of limitless capital accumulation by formally peaceful means. It ceaselessly brings capital into play in the economic circuit in order to derive a profit from it – that is, to increase the capital for reinvestment, which is the primal mark of capitalism.' Luc Boltanski and Ève Chiapello, *Le Nouvel Esprit du capitalisme*, Paris: Gallimard, 1999, p. 37.

The first and simplest is to bank on increased demand for one's goods and services: if the population rises, there will be a need for more wheat, cars and electrical energy. Hence the farmer will sow new ground, the car manufacturer will produce more vehicles, and large industrial groups will bring more nuclear power stations or wind farms into service. However, in the industrial countries a rising population only offers the prospect of marginal profits, so long as unemployment does not climb too much and soluble demand increases.

The second, more promising, solution is the one that has largely prevailed until now: to transform nature and social relations into commodities,[22] so that everything has a price and is up for sale. It began with private appropriation of the land and water, then moved on to the buying of labour power (generalization of wage labour), and continues today with the patenting of seeds, the charging of fees in higher education and trafficking in bodily organs (kidneys, eyes, liver),[23] not to speak of the constant injunction that everyone must learn to 'sell themselves'.

The third solution, linked to innovation and productivity gains, is to launch new products in the hope that they will become necessities (refrigerators, cars, televisions, iPhones and iPads), and to produce them more cheaply than one's competitors, perhaps through industrial location. 'Creative destruction', as Schumpeter

22. This commodification of nature is the 'economic side' of Descartes's programme, which, to avoid 'sinning against the law which obliges us to procure, as much as in us lies, the general good of all mankind', recommends that we deploy all our new knowledge 'to make ourselves, as it were, the masters and possessors of nature'. 'Discourse on the Method of Rightly Conducting the Reason and Seeking for the Truth in the Sciences' (1637), in *The Philosophical Works*, vol. 1, London: Cambridge University Press, 1968, p. 119.

23. It is said in justification of this that everyone owns their own body and is free to do with it what they wish – which implies that 'the whole of the visible and invisible world is a commodity' (Sapir, *Les Trous noirs de la science économique*, p. 94). Nor should we forget the 'childbearing market' – one can 'hire out a belly' for anything between 60,000 and 140,000 dollars in the United States (*Tribune de Genève*, 28 June 2008) – or the 'commodification of the human' through new and more subtle forms of wage control, which tend to do away with the boundary between work and private life. See Marie-Dominique Perrot et al., eds, *Ordres et désordres de l'esprit gestionnaire*, Lausanne: Réalités sociales, 2006.

saw, makes former cutting-edge objects obsolete: the computer replaces the typewriter, WiFi eliminates wired devices, and new software versions make older ones unusable. The tradition of 'novelty' condemns still operational sectors and replaces them with more 'modern' ones that induce new behaviour which no one has dreamed of before. It is not certain that this increases collective happiness, but it does boost the profits of those who succeed in anticipating (or creating) 'needs' and making consumers more and more market-dependent.

The fourth and last solution is to exploit profitable 'niches' where every extravagance is permissible. The successes of the luxury industry (jewellery, watches, fashion, etc.) are only the tip of the iceberg: since profit comes only from solvent demand, it is more worthwhile to produce drugs against obesity than against malaria, to invest in palaces rather than popular housing, to seduce the rich rather than to satisfy the poor. Economic logic therefore fuels inequalities: the most profitable market is necessarily geared to people with the greatest purchasing power and supposedly limitless 'needs'. The taste for pleasure and comfort is indeed limitless, and the trend is towards ever more wasteful 'conspicuous consumption'. This is true within the industrialized countries, but also at world level. What is the point of producing things for people who cannot afford to buy them? Paradoxically, this market segmentation can also serve to fuel economic growth: since envy is at the heart of the system, one can always hope that today's luxury will become more 'democratic' through a mimetic effect, and that markets will thus open up to new buyers, as has often been the case in history (examples include the motor car, refrigeration and air travel). Then the task will be to invent more niches symbolizing membership of the 'happy few' – perhaps the enjoyment of clean air, walking on specially designed prairie footpaths instead of garden lawn, or candlelit dinners in a zone inaccessible to mobile phone waves…

But the growth obligation is not to be criticized only because it entails greater inequality and creeping commodification of nature and social life, however much these offend against our moral sense. Limitless growth, as everyone now admits, is quite simply impossible.[24] For it essentially draws upon non-renewable resources (coal, gas, oil) and endangers the whole ecosystem through pollution linked to industrial production (ozone hole, greenhouse effect, soil degradation, desertification, scarcity of drinking water, greater frequency of cyclones, higher sea levels, release of carbon dioxide due to heating of the permafrost, etc.). All these phenomena have been public knowledge for at least thirty years.[25] The law of entropy growth, based on a principle of thermodynamics, has nothing to do with the growth that economic 'science' has made obligatory. The balance between these two 'exigencies' is uneven. The first belongs to the realm of nature and will continue to operate whatever happens; the other, rooted in the market organization of society, was invented two centuries ago and cannot survive the unrealistic promises it has made and is incapable of fulfilling.[26] Mainstream economic 'science', but also international organizations, politicians and the media, continue to ignore this by advocating growth as the panacea for all the ills of society. As is all too often the case, the problem is passed off as a solution.

We can agree that it is hard to shake off this view of the world; we have been incorporating it for too long. You've got to be pushy, we are told. Be one of the winners, if not actually

---

24. In a way this involves a generalization of the 'tragedy of the commons' (see Chapter 5, note 31 above).

25. We need only mention the report to the Club of Rome (Donella H. and Dennis L Meadows, Jørgen Rander and William W. Behrens III, eds, *The Limits to Growth*, New York: Universe Books, 1972), and Nicholas Georgescu-Roegen, *The Entropy Law and the Economic Process*, Cambridge MA: Harvard University Press, 1971.

26. 'The price of fossil fuels was (and is) set at the cost of getting them out of the ground, which is about as sensible as valuing the money one withdraws from the bank at the cost of the bus fare to go and get it.' Douthwaite, *The Growth Illusion*, p. 42.

top dog. Profit from what life can offer, starting with what you can get out of your job or the money you have invested. Always try to maximize your satisfaction.

This is a kind of involuntary servitude, 'which constricts us from outside but is also, inseparably, an inner reality that constricts us from within'.[27] Such is indeed the force of mainstream economics: it has managed over time to impose what was originally only a norm to which few people conformed. Human beings are not 'naturally' rational and do not necessarily pursue their own interests. But, if placed in a competitive context that punishes those who refuse to play the game, they end up conforming to the expectations of the system and thereby vindicate the theory on which it is based. A first way of distancing ourselves from obsession with growth and acquisitiveness is to pay less attention to what we have won and more to what we have lost (collectively and individually). In order to survive, or even to hope for a 'good life', we must change our direction and way of thinking. The scale of the task is obvious. In criticizing economic liberalism, Durkheim remarked long ago: 'If we had to break with it, we would have to recast the whole of our social organization as well.'[28] What if that really is the issue?

---

27. Alain Accardo, *De notre servitude involontaire. Lettre à mes camarades de gauche*, Marseilles: Agone, 2001, p. 17.

28. Émile Durkheim, *La Science sociale et l'action (articles publiés entre 1888 et 1908)*, Paris: PUF, 1990 (1987), p. 265; quoted in Marie Auffray-Seguette, *Les Biens de ce monde, L'économie vue comme espace de recomposition de la religion dans la modernité*, Paris: EHESS, 2008, p. 394.

CHAPTER 9

GROWTH OBJECTION

Why is enough never enough?[1]

Without repeating what we have said elsewhere, let us nevertheless recall some essential points.[2] First, the term 'degrowth' or 'downscaling' (*décroissance* in French) was hurled as a slogan (or 'grenade', Paul Ariès said) at a conference organized in 2002 by Rocade, the Network for Post-Development Growth Objectors. Since infinite growth is not possible in a finite world, this struck participants as a sensible (if not very original) solution; the famous report to the Club of Rome had been called in French *Halte à la croissance?*,[3] and more than thirty years ago, in 1975, the Hammarskjöld Foundation in Uppsala had published a report in which it had proposed either 'zero growth' or a growth pause in the industrial countries, together with the adoption of a more sober, less fuel-intensive lifestyle.[4] Jacques Grinevald had even used the word *décroissance* in the title of a work devoted to Nicholas

1. Title of Chapter 11 of Marglin, *The Dismal Science*, p. 199.

2. Rist, *The History of Development*, pp. 240ff.

3. Meadows, et al., eds, *The Limits to Growth*. The question mark in the French title probably reflected the difficulty of condemning growth at the end of the post-war Golden Age.

4. *What Now: The 1975 Dag Hammarskjöld Report, prepared on the occasion of the Seventh Special Session of the United Nations General Assembly, 1975*, special issue of the Hammarskjöld Foundation journal *Development Dialogue*, 1975.

Georgescu-Roegen.[5] However, the concept had been hit by a kind of collective amnesia – which shows that it sometimes takes a long time for ideas to penetrate people's minds, before they bubble up again with sudden force. Certainly there has been no shortage of publications on the theme in recent years, whether to promote it[6] or to discredit it.[7]

Of course, it is impossible to tease out any consensus among participants in the debate, since those who consider themselves 'growth objectors' range from libertarian anarchists to others generally thought of as being on the far right. The approaches within this loose conglomeration are often contradictory, and the exchanges sometimes heated. A closer typology, based on the various practices in question, might include:

---

5. Nicholas Georgescu-Roegen, *Demain la décroissance. Entropie, écologie, économie*, Preface and translation by Ivo Rens and Jacques Grinevald, Lausanne: Pierre-Marcel Favre/Paris: Sang de la terre, 1995 (1979). The title has recently been 'pirated' by the philosopher of the French New Right, Alain de Benoist!

6. *Défaire le développement, refaire le monde*, Paris: Parangon, L'Aventurine, 2003; Michel Bernard, Vincent Cheynet and Bruno Clémentin, eds, *Objectif décroissance. Vers une société harmonieuse*, Lyons/Paris: Silence et Parangon, 2003; Serge Latouche, *Survivre au développement*, Paris: Mille et une nuits, 2004; Jean-Paul Besset, *Comment ne plus être progressiste… sans devenir réactionnaire*, Paris: Fayard, 2005; Paul Ariès, *Décroissance ou barbarie*, Villeurbanne: Golias, 2005; Jean-Claude Besson-Girard, *Decrescendo cantabile*, Paris: Parangon, 2005; Bernard Guibert and Serge Latouche, eds, *Antiproductivisme, altermondialisme, décroissance*, Lyons: Parangon/Vs, 2006; Serge Latouche, *Le Pari de la décroissance*, Paris: Fayard, 2006; Jean-Pierre Tertrais, *Du développement à la décroissance. De la nécessité de sortir de l'impasse suicidaire du capitalisme*, Saint-Georges d'Oléron: Éditions libertaires, 2006; Nicolas Ridoux, *La Décroissance pour tous*, Lyons: Parangon/Vs, 2006; Serge Latouche, *Petit traité de la décroissance sereine*, Paris: Mille et une nuits, 2007; Alain de Benoist, *Demain la décroissance! Penser l'écologie jusqu'au bout*, Paris: Edite, 2007; Baptiste Mylondo, ed., *Pour une politique de la décroissance*, Villeurbanne: Golias, 2007; Vincent Cheynet, *Le Choc de la décroissance*, Paris: Seuil, 2008; Stéphane Lavignotte, *La décroissance est-elle souhaitable?*, Paris: Textuel, 2008; Serge Latouche, *Farewell to Growth*, Cambridge: Polity Press, 2009; Serge Latouche and Didier Harpagès, *Le Temps de la décroissance,* Paris: Thierry Manier, 2010. The sites: www.decroissance.org/, www.decroissance.info, www.lalignedhorizon. The journals: *Silence! et Entropia* and *La Décroissance*.

7. ATTAC, *Le Développement a-t-il un avenir? Pour une société économe et solidaire*, Paris: Mille et une nuits, 2004; Christian Comeliau, *La Croissance ou le progrès. Croissance, décroissance, développement durable*, Paris: Seuil, 2006; Jean Jacob, *L'Anti-mondialisation. Aspects méconnus d'une nébuleuse*, Paris: Berg international éditeurs, 2006; Cyril di Méo, *La Face cachée de la décroissance*, Paris: L'Harmattan, 2006; René Riesel and Jaime Semprun, *Catastrophisme, administration du désastre et soumission durable*, Paris: Encyclopédie des nuisances, 2008.

—consistent and resolute growth objectors who try to live outside the world of commodities, practising self-provision, eco-friendly construction and new anti-systemic lifestyles designed to establish 'spaces of degrowth';[8]

—political (or democratic) growth objectors who expect the state to impose rules on the national and international market that save resources and redistribute wealth, ban nuclear power stations, genetically modified foods and new superstores, promote recycling and economic decentralization, and put the local neighbourhood at the centre of a new conception of society;

—anarchist growth objectors who condemn the state's subordination to the market and growth, considering these inimical to their goal of autonomy and self-management;

—forced growth objectors who, faced with unemployment or job insecurity, have no choice but to reduce their consumption, without necessarily feeling that people can live better with less;

—pragmatic growth objectors who challenge consumption models, worry about their ecological footprint and try to live in a deliberately sober and frugal manner;

—voluntary-sector growth objectors who, convinced that a start must be made somewhere, put a lot of effort into local initiatives such as the Associations pour le maintien d'une agriculture paysanne (AMAP), Local Exchange Trading Systems (LETS), voluntary gardening and other part-time activity;

—utopian growth objectors who, in the name of conviviality and social ties, campaign for a change in values and reject 'imperialist culture' or the lie that economics must dominate everything.[9]

---

8. Camille Madelain, 'Pratiques de la décroissance', *Notes et travaux* 76, Geneva: IUED, 2005.

9. See, for example, the site ceremovi.org, Centre de recherches sur les modes de vie.

This list – which does not cover the whole spectrum – simply shows that for now the slogan of 'degrowth' allows us to group together, but also to oppose ideologically, many individual or collective practices that seek to escape the market system by devising alternative lifestyles and addressing the ecological dangers we face.

But a slogan is not a worked-out conception – as we should know by now. We should also remember Paul Watzlawick's point that, in trying to change a given situation, it is often dangerous to advocate the exact opposite, since what has to be changed is the 'system's structure' itself; otherwise 'the attempted solution *is* the problem'.[10] In opposing 'degrowth' to the 'growth requirement', one agrees in advance to fight on the terrain of economic 'science', with the enemy's choice of weapons. Serge Latouche can insist that 'the slogan of "degrowth" is primarily designed to make it perfectly clear that we must abandon the goal of exponential growth', and that 'degrowth is not the same thing as negative growth'.[11] But this has largely gone unheard. Worse, some opponents of degrowth have gone so far as to claim that growth objectors seek to promote linear economic degrowth – to which they reply that, just as indefinite growth is impossible, it is neither possible nor desirable to organize 'indefinite degrowth' of the global economy.[12] In reality, of course, no growth objector has ever envisaged 'indefinite degrowth': that is, the eventual ending of production, which would be absurd.

ACTUALLY OCCURRING 'DEGROWTH'

To clarify matters, we should first distinguish between two separate phenomena: those that are part of the 'economic' sphere

10. Paul Watzlawick, John H. Weakland and Richard Fisch, *Change: Principles of Problem Formation and Problem Resolution*, New York: Norton, 1974, p. 57 .

11. Latouche, *Farewell to Growth*, pp. 3–4.

12. Comeliau, *La croissance ou le progrès*, pp. 10, 226–7, 265.

and those that fall within the province of nature. Although the 'objects' may sometimes be the same (natural resources, means of production, consumer goods, labour power, etc.), they are either apprehended within an economic *discourse* that assigns them a role, and a price, as commodities, or else treated as *elements of the ecosystem*. In the first case, we have a set of commodities that are exchanged for other commodities (by means of a 'fictitious commodity', money); in the second case, we are speaking of a collective heritage, productive and partly renewable, which must be both deployed and preserved.

From an economic point of view growth is a programme (an objective and a necessity[13]), while from the point of view of the ecosystem – and before it is a slogan – 'degrowth' is an actual reality: that is, it means the programmed end of cheap oil, soil degradation and desertification, freshwater shortages, deforestation, air pollution, exhausting of fish stocks, decreased biodiversity, and so on. Although based on different 'points of view' (different ways of observing and understanding the world), the two phenomena develop in parallel: indefinite economic growth, carried along by the programme of thermo-industrial society, is at the origin of an accelerated 'degrowth' of resources that threatens collective well-being.

We may well wonder why people do not find this more worrying, or, as Jean-Pierre Dupuy puts it, 'why we do not believe what we know'.[14] To begin with, 'actually occurring degrowth' is often imperceptible, because the phenomena that testify to it, even real and present dangers, may not be immediately obvious to either

13. A 'programme' is, in a primary sense, 'that which is written in advance' (a concert programme lists the works to be performed), but in the computer world, for example, a complex programme is 'self-programming and developing: it evidently "works" to achieve the goal set for it, but it can choose the means to that end, without being completely controlled by the human programmer.' Marie-Dominique Perrot, Fabrizio Sabelli and Gilbert Rist, *La Mythologie programmée. L'économie des croyances dans la société moderne*, Paris: PUF, 1992, pp. 52–3.

14. Jean-Pierre Dupuy, *Pour un catastrophisme éclairé. Quand l'impossible est certain*, Paris: Seuil, 2002, pp. 84, 142–3.

the senses or the social imagination.[15] They therefore have to be identified by scientists, whose estimates and predictions are based on very sophisticated models. However, people whose interests are negatively affected by the scientific reports often deliberately cast doubt on their reliability and argue that no action is necessary – that growth can go on as if nothing were amiss. Furthermore, the extreme consequences of such phenomena will only be felt in the future, so that the difficulty of looking ahead in time stands in the way of a challenge to present habits. This also explains why politicians, whose time frame is dictated by the electoral calendar, do not rush into measures that might be deemed 'unpopular' and lose them votes. Finally, the financially prosperous classes in the industrial countries know that any disasters resulting from their lifestyle will first affect the poor in faraway lands, and they can hope to mitigate the troubles ahead by agreeing to pay a higher price to compensate for them.[16] These prevarications or denials cannot hide the fact that 'actually occurring degrowth' seriously threatens the collective well-being of the inhabitants of the planet, even if some may hope in the short term to escape its effects. This is why it is urgent to reverse the trend and to advocate a kind of 'degrowth' at the level of social practices, which should not be confused with a simple economic recession.

---

15. Those who go on living near Chernobyl are not aware, individually and in the short term, of the effects of the radioactivity. The diminished ozone layer (which no one can personally 'notice') causes an increase in skin cancers. PCBs (polychlorobiphenyls) are one of the persistent organic pollutants (POPs), which do not break down easily and accumulate in the food chain. Ubiquitous in the environment, they are ingested daily in small quantities in our food and are another of the dangers we cannot directly experience.

16. Europeans will not witness (except on television) either the disappearance of the Tuvalu islands, or the flooding of Bangladesh, or the desertification of farming areas in Africa. Their petrol and water will become more expensive, but will not run out on them. They will pay more for wheat and fish, but will not go completely without them.

AVOIDING THE ECONOMIC TRAP

We should recognize, however, that the 'degrowth' slogan is full of ambiguities. How can one combat economic growth while claiming to stand outside the constraints imposed by the framework of economic 'science'? How can one speak of degrowth while arguing that it does not mean the opposite of growth but something different?[17] There is also the problem of communication between languages. It may be that French plays some tricks here, especially because it allows us to use the same noun, *décroissance* (which is, of course, derived from the verb *décroître*, to decrease), for two different things: a phenomenon that is actually occurring (as described above) and a will to do away with the cult of growth (a slogan). Although English-speakers seem to have recently come to accept the neologism 'degrowth' – and, for this and other reasons, we have also decided to use it here – they are more at ease with the term 'downscaling', with its connotation of greater simplicity and a move away from luxuries to more accessible objects. Although the word is polysemic – it can also suggest switching the scale of forecasting from the global to the local – it has the advantage of not immediately connoting an economic phenomenon. As for German – whose capacity to form compound nouns is virtually limitless – no colleague has yet found a satisfactory equivalent for *décroissance*, precisely because the terms that first spring to mind, such as *Wachstumsabnahme*, *Wachstumsschrumpfung* or *Wachstumsbeschränkung*, all refer to the idea of reducing the growth rate measured by GDP, whereas growth objectors have something else in view, which it is probably impossible to define in economic terms, and which is more akin to terms like 'deconstruction' or 'detoxification'.[18]

17. Conscious of these ambiguities, Serge Latouche argues that 'we should be talking at the theoretical level of "a-growth", in the sense in which we speak of "a-theism", rather than of "de-growth". And we do indeed have to abandon ... the irrational and quasi-idolatrous cult of growth for growth's sake.' *Farewell to Growth*, p. 8.

18. See Vincent Cheynet, *Le Choc de la décroissance*, Paris: Seuil, 2008, p. 80.

In other words, the problem has to be thought about in terms that go outside the models of mainstream economic 'science'. What should decrease or not grow are the flows of energy–matter which enter into production and consumption, turning into waste and high entropy (that is, unusable energy). What should decrease is the bingeing of a system based on the 'more' (more profit) principle, which cannot be cured of it without imploding. The point, then, is to challenge the structural obligation of indefinite growth, which merely increases social inequalities and is driving the planet towards catastrophes that are impervious to economic forecasting.[19] 'Growth objectors', then, do not place themselves on the same ground as economists: they concern themselves with perfectly real phenomena that lie outside the discourse of economic 'science', and they radically question the founding assumptions of that 'science'. The debate is not just about ideas but about a fundamental question.

Growth objectors do not advocate the opposite of economic growth or hope for recession, but consider that the system established by economic 'science' (produce and consume more because more = better) is full of danger. It was created at a time when today's questions were unimaginable, and so there can be no question of blaming the founding fathers of the 'science'; they did not know what was unknown to them, and believed that nature in its bounty would dispense inexhaustible, and therefore free, resources. But the world has changed, even if economists pretend not to know it and ignore other scientists who base themselves on proven facts and draw our attention to the catastrophes ahead. 'Actually occurring degrowth', as we have defined it above, is a fact that economists cannot take into account, because their

19. The constant refrain that economic growth is necessary to create jobs is contradicted by the facts. In France the unemployment rate was 6.2 per cent in 1980 and 9 per cent in 2006. During the same period, the GDP increased by 56 per cent. Jean-Luc Pasquinet, 'Développer l'esprit critique', in Baptiste Mylondo, ed., *Pour une politique de la décroissance*, Villeurbanne: Golias, 2008, p. 54.

'science' only reacts to short-term events and naively judges that an increase in prices will be enough to deflate demand and restore a hypothetical equilibrium. But it is the long term that counts, and at that level economic 'science' offers no help ('in the long term we are all dead', Keynes famously quipped). We must therefore heed the warnings of scientists, rather than a theory that is taking us straight to disaster.

In addition to the ecological concerns that affect the whole of humanity, other considerations refer to the exceptional position of the countries of the North, whose material comfort is largely based on the tapping of resources that belong to all. This scandal has long lain hidden beneath the mad hope that the 'underdeveloped' countries will one day catch up with the standard of living of the 'developed' countries. But that delusion, which consisted in taking the exception for the rule, has now fallen apart, linger though it does in the minds of many, especially in the countries of the South.[20] This cannot fail to raise a daunting ethical and political problem. Can one really continue to act as if the imbalance did not exist, and get used to a state of lopsided coexistence? Since the material prosperity of the thermo-industrial mode of production cannot be spread worldwide, should we not be exploring a different path?

The first task is to change how we look at 'poverty', which is too often confused with the scandalous plight to which mainstream economic 'science' has condemned most people in the South.[21] Far from Rousseau's vision of the 'noble savage', we need to ask how most societies in the past managed to live on a little,

---

20. As Majid Rahnema points out, 'most [people in the South] *would like to believe* that they or their children will one day enjoy all the supposed benefits of technology and the facilities and comforts of so-called modern life. Having spurned any return to tradition for themselves, many poor people in the rich countries, and both rich and poor in the poor countries, *would like to believe* that the path to modernity is open to them individually and collectively.' Majid Rahnema and Jean Robert, *La Puissance des pauvres*, Arles: Actes Sud, 2008, p. 283; emphases in the original.

21. Majid Rahnema, *Quand la misère chasse la pauvreté*, Paris/Arles: Fayard/Actes Sud, 2003.

while inventing not only marvellous symbolic systems – whose architectural traces often still compel our admiration – but also social forms of reciprocity that allowed them to confront the necessities of life in a collective manner. Without falling into a binary opposition between 'paradise lost' and 'present hell', or into a form of tropical romanticism, how can we fail to notice that those who seem to 'want for everything' (in comparison with the innumerable technological protheses that have become indispensable in the industrialized world) show proof of a social wealth and, dare we say it, a *joie de vivre* rarely encountered in countries that think of themselves as rich? This assertion may well seem extravagant, or even unseemly. It obviously applies not to those who live in utter destitution, but to those who, from our point of view, are 'poor' simply because they neither know nor wish for the comfort to which we are accustomed, and who make up the majority of people in the countries of the South. Conversely, is it not significant that, when they spend some time in our part of the world, they are surprised and pained by the dehumanized spectacle that our societies offer? To be sure, the complex hierarchical relations that characterize so-called 'traditional' societies conflict with our egalitarian and individualist perspective based on 'human rights'. The mutual dependence involved in manifold social networks sometimes appears in our eyes as clientelism or a Mafia-like clan structure. Yet these are social logics (not lacking in self-interest!) which enable people to forge ties with one another, to accumulate in order to redistribute, and to avoid a situation where some are poor or 'socially orphaned', without anyone to turn to for help.[22]

The point of these remarks is not at all to suggest adopting here social models, each very different from the other, which assure 'have-nots' a difficult but decent life, so long as it is not devastated

22. Emmanuel Seyni Ndione, *Dynamique urbaine d'une société en grappe: un cas*, Dakar: ENDA, 1987, p. 154.

by war, political troubles or invasive market mechanisms. Rather, the point is to ask a question that takes account of the world situation, to place the idea of 'the good life' within a broader context, to refuse to take the West as the model, and to reflect upon the way in which social bonds can procure goods that are unavailable if everything is left to the market. The question is not whether the lifestyle to which Western societies have grown accustomed of late can be preserved, but whether it should not be radically changed so that it (again) resembles what was ordinary in all societies that preceded ours and still make up the vast majority of humanity. Could a proliferation of social ties make up for a decrease in the goods on which we have become dependent?

'SUSTAINABLE DEVELOPMENT' OR ANOTHER MODEL?

In fact, a large fringe of those concerned about environmental issues are content to show that our habitual comforts would not be eroded if we simply consumed less or differently. They therefore seek, rightly, to reduce or even eliminate the vast waste resulting from the 'growth at all costs' obsession (passenger and freight transport, tons and tons of packaging, bottled water, advertising, and so on). To this end they propose making production (especially of food) geographically closer to the point of consumption;[23] transforming intensive agricultural systems and doing away with fertilizers and pesticides that damage the soil, water tables and people's health; considerably reducing energy consumption (already a possibility with greater eco-efficiency[24]);

23. The change of course may be 'synthesized into a "virtuous circle" of eight R's: re-evaluate, reconceptualize, restructure, redistribute, relocalize, reduce, re-use and recycle. These eight interdependent goals can trigger a process of de-growth that will be serene, convivial and sustainable.' Latouche, *Farewell to Growth*, p. 33.

24. On the other hand, a 'rebound effect' can reduce (or even cancel out) the possible economies: for example, modern light bulbs consume less energy, but people leave them on longer.

developing renewable energy sources, heat insulation of buildings, and so on. Measures along these lines feature in the undoubtedly well-intentioned 'sustainable development' programme – a deceptive expression that yokes together two contradictory concepts, and that continues to be hijacked by its fiercest opponents.[25]

All this is certainly useful, but it diverts attention from the real debate by pretending that the task is not so much to do (or produce) less as to put forward a different model of society, a different mode of production and consumption. Unfortunately, even among growth objectors, it is common to argue about means (on the basis of ideological convictions) without asking about ends. Some want to act right now, either by practising a kind of economic autonomy in rural regions, or, more modestly, by reducing the ecological footprint of their daily activities, in the hope that this will persuade others to follow suit (when the aim is not simply to salve their own conscience). Others denounce 'energy-guzzlers' or those who fail to pose the problems at a political level. And still others argue that any state compulsion amounts to 'eco-fascism', since bureaucrats will engage in no more than 'disaster management' by seeking to make capitalism and ecology compatible.[26] The first group make action the priority, even if this means acting alone; the second maintain that social choices are up to society as a whole and that individual action is meaningless; the third call for a radical social critique that will put an end to both capitalism and the state. As we said before, these

---

25. The www.decroissance.org site contains an anthology of statements by politicians and businessmen that press the concept of 'sustainable development' into the service of growth. Sadly, it is also true that this ambiguity was present in the Brundtland report that launched the oxymoron in 1987.

26. In the eyes of some 'anarcho-situationists', who insist that catastrophe lies just around the corner, official action is merely preparing people for a new kind of submission to capitalism. But, although it is right to denounce (preventively?) 'barracks ecologism' and to question the effectiveness of bureaucracy in warding off disaster, a simple anti-state and anti-industry posture is not a sufficient alternative. See René Riesel and Jaime Semprun, *Catastrophisme, administration du désastre et soumission durable*, Paris: Encyclopédie des nuisances, 2008.

positions are theoretically and politically incompatible, even if they are all based on denunciation of an 'unsustainable' system.

The real task for growth objectors is not to preach austerity but to understand (and to convince others) that the growth obsession is counterproductive; that we can continue to produce but must do so differently, by changing the context and setting different goals for collective life; and that there are ecological *and* social limits which, as psychoanalysis teaches, are a structuring factor in genuine freedom. It is not a question of nostalgia for the past, of wanting to 'turn the clock back', which would anyway be completely devoid of meaning. Rather, there is a wish expressed in practice to put an end to an absurd system, and above all to reveal the wealth that lies outside the market and is often greater than the market can ever procure. This is also the perspective in the recent Jackson Report, entitled *Prosperity without Growth?* Although it considers that degrowth is liable to bring economic 'instability', it convincingly attacks the obsession with growth and identifies ways in which everyone's well-being might be improved without it.[27]

This is why growth objection should not be thought of as a movement preoccupied with restrictions, renunciation or rationing. Rather, its main focus is on the new possibilities that would open up for a society freed from the obligation to sacrifice everything to growth and profit. All sacrifice presupposes a victim, and we might say that in market society it is the 'invisible hand' which holds the blade. In reality, however, everyone is potentially both administrator and victim of sacrifice, both polluter and polluted,

27. Tim Jackson, *Prosperity without Growth? The Transition to a Sustainable Economy*, London: Sustainable Development Commission, 2009. This critique of growth – which sees it as both necessary and dangerous for the survival of the system – is still largely constructed within the framework of mainstream economics. It does note some of its defects, but one would like to have seen a rather more radical challenge. Jackson has clearly opted to be 'reasonable' in order to convince the greatest possible number of readers, even if his recommendations will undoubtedly offend the 'economic consensus' and sometimes appear as pious wishes. But, of course, there are more ways than one of instilling doubt in the minds of mainstream economists.

engaged body and soul in economic and social competition but at risk of being crushed by its effects, forced to work ever harder for goods and services that used to be free,[28] or for 'new' products whose built-in obsolescence will soon render them useless. What would it be like to live in a society that refused to sacrifice nature and an ever larger number of its members? We are not thinking of a life where people 'go without' (electricity, telephones, medicine, etc.) but of a different way of living. Thus, to combat the market-driven squandering of energy in the global shipment of various goods for the consumption of the rich (meat, vegetables, fish, flowers, etc.), local currencies that are legal tender in only limited areas have the virtue of encouraging geographic proximity between producers and consumers – a simple (and free!) way of 'relocalizing' the economy and stimulating local wealth, in direct opposition to the perverse effects of international currencies.[29] Growth objectors do not aim to found a 'republic of wise men' that would lay down the rules of the 'good life' for all. Their first concern is to ask questions, but also to explore new paths to autonomy from the constraints of the system, using nature without abusing it,[30] and rediscovering non-competitive ways of relating to other people. Between an (always dangerous) utopianism and (often derisory) practical recipes, there is room for questioning and invention. If society cured itself of its obsession with economic

28. Living in an unpolluted neighbourhood, bathing on a clean beach, leaving one's children in a crèche during working hours, and so on.

29. Though not widely known, communal, complementary or alternative experiments with local currencies go back quite a long way. In Switzerland the WIR (or *Wirtschaftsring*) system has been in existence since 1934. According to Christophe Place (*Community Currency for Local Economy: A Grassroots Innovation for Prosperity through Democracy*, Paris: HEC, 2010), there were more than 2,600 local currencies in 2007. They tend to flourish in periods of crisis: in 2002 in Argentina, for instance, the *Red argentina de trueque* created *patacons* that were widely used in parallel to the devalued peso. The best-known examples in Britain are the Lewes Pound (Sussex) and the Totnes Pound (Devon), the latter linked to the Transition Towns initiative that aims to break dependence on petrol.

30. Does the Cartesian project of making ourselves 'masters and possessors of nature' not remind one of the main characteristic of 'property right' in ancient Roman law: that is, the power to use and abuse.

growth, which practices would become possible and which would come to appear obsolete?[31]

In this connection, we should note all those things since the time of Malthus which have escaped market accountability yet been central to the charms of individual and social existence. Many things have value to each one of us without having a price (since they are not exchanged on the market): for example, the pleasure we take in social relationships, our happiness in regaining some freedom from market circuits, our closeness to others who share a more frugal lifestyle, the attachments that arise when (contrary to Adam Smith's preaching) we rely on other people's goodwill, not only on their self-interest. This may all sound 'idealistic' in a world given over to competition, and of course it cannot be claimed that 'fewer goods' *necessarily* means 'stronger ties'. But once again we are outside the realm of economic 'science'.[32] And it would be quite out of place for it to decree that such things are of no importance because it is incapable of giving an account of them.[33]

WHAT ABOUT THE WELL-BEING OF THE SOUTH?

That leaves a final point, which keeps recurring in debate. Although it is not so difficult to imagine the industrial countries organizing

31. The annual worldwide advertising budget has been estimated at $500 billion (Jean Gadrey, *La décroissance: idées fortes, terme ambigu*, http://alternatives-economiques.fr/blogs/gadrey/2009/10/08).

32. Much else besides eludes economic calculation: air or water quality, deforestation effects, ozone layer shrinkage, dwindling biodiversity, the social costs of migration or social exclusion, the melting of glaciers and polar ice caps, and so on. But these doleful modern concerns were evidently unknown to the classical economists.

33. During the oil price crisis of 1973, Switzerland introduced a number of 'motor-free Sundays', when only ambulances, public transport and police vehicles were allowed to circulate. 'Economic constraint' then expressed itself in a kind of new freedom of speech, as people rejoiced at being able to approach others (on foot, or on a bicycle, scooter or bus) in ways that would have been unthinkable if they had been shut up in a car. How can one evaluate the pleasure we suddenly take in speaking to a stranger (something that is the rule in 'traditional' societies)?

themselves differently, so that they no longer place all their hopes in growth but are less greedy with energy, more respectful of the ecosystem and more inclined to share their wealth, should the countries of the South also be deprived of growth, given that their 'needs' are far from satisfied and their aspirations for greater well-being are legitimate? Is more growth not needed to fund more schools, medical centres, infrastructure and water supplies? Many do think that is the answer: growth deceleration in the North, growth acceleration in the South.[34] Evidently this is based on fine sentiments, but it involves a hazardous distinction between (capitalist) economic growth and (good) 'development' and forgets the experience of the twentieth century. Unfortunately, sixty years of 'development' – which took many different forms and rested on all kinds of theories, including in self-styled socialist countries – ended in failure,[35] for the very simple reason that the pursuit of 'development' was always primarily the pursuit of growth. Measured in terms of GDP, growth was often sustained or even rapid, but it did not produce the desired effects, except in certain countries of Southeast Asia with authoritarian regimes. As the United Nations Development Programme recognized, 'Just as economic growth is necessary for human development, human development is critical to economic growth.'[36] A development somehow uncoupled from growth is no more than a figment of the imagination, for it is completely illusory to hope that 'development' can take place without all the counterproductive effects of economic growth. Should the countries of the South therefore be left in their existing plight? Certainly not. First of all, they will continue to produce (as they have always done), but they could produce for themselves and ensure their food independence and sovereignty, but, instead of joining the race dictated by the

34. ATTAC, *Le Développement a-t-il un avenir?*, pp. 171–221.

35. See Rist, *The History of Development*.

36. UNDP, *Human Development Report 1991*, Oxford: Oxford University Press, 1991, p. 2.

international organizations to export not only raw materials but flowers, fruit and vegetables, cotton, wood or soya animal feed to the rich countries, they could produce for themselves and ensure their food independence. They could also redistribute the large sums extorted by a minority, and pull out of the international arms trade that allows governments to wage war on their own people. In other words, solutions exist for the countries of the South to break out of the vicious circle of economic growth in which 'development' has confined and impoverished them while claiming to bring them happiness. Finally, it is in the countries of the South that the baneful consequences of economic growth are most clearly visible, since it has been able to work itself out more freely there than in the North, favouring weak or corrupt regimes and driven by the economic dictates of former colonial powers or international financial institutions.[37] The results are well known. It certainly takes a lot of naivety – or blindness – to think that growth should be kept up, in the name of 'development' no less.

The 'degrowth' current appeared at a time when ecological concerns came together with a critique of 'development'. This original confluence partly explains the character of the debates among 'growth objectors', since some are mainly sensitive to the threats weighing on the environment, while others base their stand on exposures of economic growth masquerading as 'development'. This difference in emphasis is naturally reinforced by divergent, sometimes irreconcilable, ideological and political approaches; there is no reason to be surprised at this, or even to deplore it, since over the last decade a new awareness has gradually spread, by various routes, to an ever larger section of public opinion, as a succession of ecological, financial and food crises have shaken the

37. For those who think that on balance growth has reduced the numbers of 'the absolute poor', especially in Asia, we might point out that it has considerably increased the gap between the poorest and the richest. The very poor are a little less poor than before, but the richest have become super-rich.

world. It is understandable that some try to retain the privileges that the present system offers them. But the system seems to be rapidly approaching its limits, and that is why a different one needs to be invented. Although growth objection takes many forms, they are all sounding the tocsin and challenging the main cause of the problems in store for us. They are like emergency medicine, which deals with the most urgent matters without troubling to make a complete clinical assessment of the patient first, but they imply a critique of the foundations on which economic 'science' has been based for two centuries, preparing people's minds for the necessity of radically new ones.

We should bear in mind that the classical school treated the 'stationary economy' scenario with a certain detachment: it did not imply for them a frozen equilibrium, still less the cessation of economic activity, but pointed ahead to a time when it would become impossible to increase agricultural output any further (and food prices would therefore rise), so that profits would have to be entirely steered into wages and the amortisement of existing capital investment. In other words, the stationary economy corresponds to the cessation of growth rather than of the economic process per se (which is not the same thing at all).[38] We may ask ourselves whether the hypothetical situation imagined by the classical economists is not in danger of coming true, as the result of a general shortage of raw materials rather than a decline in agricultural output. So long as the distribution of profit is not done at the expense of the workers!

Be this as it may, since the race for growth and the quest for profit are two sides of the same phenomenon that upsets the natural environment and life in society, we can see why John Stuart Mill sincerely hoped that a stationary economy would

38. See Paul Fabra, *L'Anticapitalisme. Essai de réhabilitation de l'économie politique*, Paris: Flammarion, 1979, p. 268.

be preferred to it. His remarks would not seem amiss to today's growth objectors:

> I confess I am not charmed with the ideal of life held out by those who think that the normal state of human beings is that of struggling to get on; that the trampling, crushing, elbowing, and treading on each other's heels, which form the existing type of social life, are the most desirable lot of human kind, or anything but the disagreeable symptoms of one of the phases of industrial progress. ... Nor is there much satisfaction in contemplating the world with nothing left to the spontaneous activity of nature; with every rood of land brought into cultivation, which is capable of growing food for human beings; every flowery waste or natural pasture ploughed up, all quadrupeds or birds which are not domesticated for man's use exterminated as his rivals for food, every hedgerow or superfluous tree rooted out, and scarcely a place left where a wild shrub or flower could grow without being eradicated as a weed in the name of improved agriculture. If the earth must lose that great portion of its pleasantness which it owes to things that the unlimited increase of wealth and population would extirpate from it, for the mere purpose of enabling it to support a larger, but not a better or a happier population, I sincerely hope, for the sake of posterity, that they will be content to be stationary, long before necessity compels them to it.[39]

39. John Stuart Mill, *Principles of Political Economy* (1848), Book Four, Ch. 6, §2, London: Longmans, Green & Co., 1921, pp. 748, 750.

CHAPTER 10

ECONOMIC 'SCIENCE' AS RELIGION

Throughout this study of the assumptions of economic 'science', we have seen that most of them rest on nothing certain: the present dominance of market exchange is a form of reductionism, the universal of *Homo oeconomicus* is a figment of the imagination, primal scarcity is a fable that does not stand up to anthropological scrutiny, the definition of utility is tautologous, the scientific pretensions of standard economics are based on an obsolete mechanics incapable of grasping irreversible ecological phenomena, the equilibrium theory of neoclassical fame has been definitively refuted by economists themselves, and economic growth, which is necessary only for the system's survival, has led to a dead end. Nevertheless, these false ideas continue to be taught as truths. This is a mystery that we must now try to clear up.

FROM ÉMILE DURKHEIM TO LOUIS DUMONT

'If a ubiquitous statement presented as rational or scientific shows itself unjustified as such, there is a strong chance that it was imposed by another type of consistency and can be identified as one outcrop, as it were, of the underlying ideological network.'[1]

1. Dumont, *From Mandeville to Marx*, p. 22.

This seems a promising trail, but before we pick it up we should dispel a possible semantic confusion. What Louis Dumont considers ideology is 'the totality of values and ideas common to a society'[2] or, in other words, a set of shared social representations or images, and not one of the various interpretations of social or political reality (liberal, Marxist, social-democratic, etc.) to be found in an 'open society'. Although legitimate, this definition of ideology might lead to misunderstandings, and that is why for present purposes I prefer Durkheim's concept of 'religion', which refers to obligatory beliefs or rituals (that is, 'truths' which, unlike political ideologies, appear beyond dispute within a society and impose themselves on all its members). Religion, he writes, is 'the way in which the special being that is society thinks about the things of its own experience'.[3] In this sense, it has nothing in common with inmost personal conviction or a supernatural realm or any divine figure; it condenses everything people 'should' believe in a given society, simply because it is believed that everyone believes it.[4]

Louis Dumont's thesis suggests that, if the falsities of standard economic theory are held to be 'rational and scientific', it is because they are part of a wider system of representations, categories or interpretive grids that confer upon them a kind of 'immunity' from overly thorough investigations of their validity. The dominant concepts are thus protected by their participation in the banality of ordinary speech.[5] Despite the impression it often

2. Ibid., p. 7.

3. Durkheim, *The Elementary Forms of Religious Life*, p. 436.

4. The thesis that a disguised 'secular religion' underlies shared beliefs and obligatory behaviour in modern societies has been extensively developed in Perrot, Sabelli and Rist, *La Mythologie programmée*, 1992.

5. This confirms the position of Marx and Engels that 'the ideas of the ruling class are in every epoch the ruling ideas, i.e. the class which is the ruling material force of society, is at the same time its ruling intellectual force.' *The German Ideology* (1845), London: Lawrence & Wishart, 1965, p. 61. In addition, a symbolic power is exerted on the dominated classes to make them accept – as if by 'social magic' – the same principles of knowledge and evaluation of the world and to bring about their adherence to the established order

gives of building itself up outside social realities – or of haughtily ignoring them – economic 'science' cannot escape the spirit or *episteme* of the age, which dictates the conditions of possibility for the deciphering of the world. For there are nomadic ideas or concepts that jump across disciplines and pass from scholarly language into ordinary thinking; they fertilize different orders of discourse by changing their meanings, and end up generating pseudo-truths that are piously recorded in the common stock of spontaneous popular knowledge.

Growth is a prime example. In the Western tradition, it first saw the light of day with Aristotle, who considered it 'natural' since everything worthy of scientific consideration (not only plants or animals but also the state) is born, grows, matures and dies.[6] 'Growth' then went through a long biological detour[7] before becoming one of the keywords of economics. The details will have to be omitted here, but we should note that the positive character that attaches to economic growth has its roots in both Aristotle and biological discourse (for both of which, by the way, infinite growth is an impossibility!). Obviously one cannot be 'against' growth if it is considered part of nature, but everyone should know that it is never right to claim that what is true in the natural order is also true in the social order.

Similar points apply to *equilibrium* and *utility*, two terms with definite positive connotations in the collective imagination, and also to *need* (sometimes converted into 'preferences'), about which there is usually agreement, even if it is never clearly defined. What is more deserving of admiration than to reach and maintain equilibrium, whether static in the case of a child's building blocks,

---

(Bourdieu, *Pascalian Meditations*, pp. 169, 177ff.). This links up with Louis Dumont's idea of an 'underlying ideological network'.

6. The Greek verb φύω ('to grow') gave the noun φύσις (which means 'nature' and is the etymology of 'physics'). For Aristotle, that which is 'natural' or 'physical' is what 'develops' or 'grows'. See Rist, *The History of Development*, pp. 29f.

7. Pierre Achard, Antoinette Chauvenet, Élisabeth Lage, Françoise Lentin, Patricia Neve and Georges Vignaux, *Discours biologique et ordre social*, Paris: Seuil, 1977.

or dynamic in the case of a cyclist, or psychological in an adult going through a difficult period? No matter that the word varies from one situation to another, it always expresses the same kind of satisfaction. What is worse than to suffer from an equilibrium disorder, or to realize that your budget – or your neighbour's – does not balance? So, why blame economists for constructing a theory to show that 'general equilibrium' corresponds to the best of possible worlds? As for 'utility', is it not one of the main criteria for our everyday choices? Neoclassical economists may have divested the term of all moral content and reduced it to no more than the 'desirability' of an object (and therefore the price one agrees to pay for it), but they are still speaking of utility, even if their definition strays from the ordinary meaning. Are we not bound to prefer the useful to the useless, futile or harmful, and to prioritize our choices, like Crusoe on his island, in order to satisfy our wants and assert our interests?

Although economic discourse does its best to be 'scientific', it often uses everyday language, whose very ordinariness helps to make it more acceptable. Unlike other sciences, in which researchers have gradually created distinctive concepts for objects they observe (or whose existence they suspect, as in particle physics), economics is happy to stick with ordinary language, doing no more than surreptitiously changing the meaning of words.[8] This calls to mind Louis Dumont's remark that errors in an ostensibly 'rational and scientific' statement may be disguised by 'a different kind of coherence' belonging to an order in which the statement is considered true. Economic 'science', then, ensures its dominance by inscribing its discourse within common sense (that is, a body of shared truths), to establish a coincidence between what it asserts (through the words it uses) and what everyone believes. This does not happen without a certain confusion between the 'scientific'

8. Léon Walras tried to impose the term 'ophelimity' to underline the special meaning he gave to utility, but this did not catch on.

vocabulary and ordinary language – a confusion that has to do with what is implicit in the discourse. The social consensus (or 'religion', as Durkheim would say) that is established around everything that goes without saying – that is, the positive, necessary and desirable[9] character of growth, equilibrium, utility, and so on – is then transposed into the domain of economic 'science', ensuring its legitimacy and removing its basic concepts and its results from critical scrutiny (since their truth is guaranteed *a priori* by a higher religious body that is not open to question). The errors that a serious analysis might uncover are therefore excluded from discussion, since to demonstrate and denounce them would be to challenge a set of shared beliefs that have an irresistible force conferred on them by the whole society. We may certainly measure the efficacy of belief by the importance of the things it makes people believe, but we may also measure it by everything it prevents people from believing as it consigns any fact that contradicts it to the realm of the false and the absurd.[10]

NATURALIST DOGMAS

This 'truth transfer', which draws on implicit beliefs to bolster the validity of economic theories, may doubtless also operate in reverse. As we have seen, economic 'science' is as normative as it is descriptive:[11] it sets out what should be the case and does not merely draw conclusions from the data it gathers. More, it

9. Marie-Dominique Perrot, 'Passager clandestin et indispensable du discours: le présupposé', in Gilbert Rist and Fabrizio Sabelli, eds, *Il était une fois le développement…*, Lausanne: Éditions d'En Bas, 1986, pp. 71–91.

10. Heliocentrism and Earth's rotation around its own axis were first condemned on religious rather scientific grounds. Closer to our own day, Darwinian evolutionism is challenged in the name of a belief in 'creationism' or 'intelligent design'.

11. 'The economic reasoning is often obscured by the fact that normative principles are not introduced explicitly, but in the shape of general "concepts". … The basic concepts are frequently charged with normative implications. … The perpetual game of hide-and-seek in economics consists in concealing the norm in the concept.' Myrdal, *The Political Element in the Development of Economic Theory*, p. 192.

involves a performative aspect that enables it to bring what it asserts into existence. For instance, it can decree that there is a 'market' where there is none – which follows the interpretation of 'traditional' exchanges in formalist economic anthropology, and chimes with the Public Choice claim to reduce conjugal relations to a series of cost–benefit negotiations. Economic 'science' can also induce behaviour that conforms to it, as if that proved it was true, or make people believe that scarcity is a constitutive part of human experience or life in society, even if what it really does is make scarcity appear in the course of the 'economic process'.[12] In other words, economic 'science' has so established itself in the contemporary mind that no one can escape the kinds of reasoning it has popularized, especially as life itself is more and more reduced to 'management' of its economic side. Conventional wisdom therefore largely rests on snippets from the economists' bible: 'it's expensive because it's scarce', or the opposite, 'nothing is free', 'everyone follows their interests', and so on. Alongside 'real life' – the colour of the sky, a neighbour's moods, the taste of fruits, the rigours of work, the fertility of the earth, the passing of time, the ravages of disease – one must also 'reckon' with 'economic realities', which overhang the whole of social life and allow no one to escape them. In a paradoxical reversal, a 'science' built itself up without checking its models against the realities they were supposed to describe; its hypotheses were either fragile (that is, true only in certain precise circumstances) or false;[13] and it nevertheless claimed to rule the world through the voice of its self-proclaimed experts. It is as if the closure to reality characteristic

12. This is especially true of stock markets, which live on self-fulfilling prophecies.

13. 'In the theory of refutation, the test that really counts is not the one designed to prove a conjecture but the one designed to falsify it. Well, precisely, conjectures about the behaviour of agents – the only ones really testable in Popper's sense – have all been falsified in rigorous experiments since the second half of the 1970s. Yet standard economists drone on with their preference theory as if none of this had happened.' Sapir, *Les Trous noirs de la science économique*, p. 97.

of the discipline was the prerequisite for it to issue judgements, or orders, in the name of the 'reality principle'![14]

Has religion gone over to the side of economic theories? The polemical point has been made in the past that there is little to choose between standard economic 'science' and theology.[15] But there is more. In a recent thesis, Marie Auffray-Seguette argues that economics has become the new religion of our time:[16] the 'illusion of heterodetermination', as she calls it, means that society projects onto another world what it has itself instituted, making it seem that the 'laws' governing it come from a realm beyond (nature or science). This connects with Clément Rosset's conclusion: 'Naturalistic ideology may thus be regarded as religious ideology come of age, for which the idea of nature confirms and consolidates its basic assumptions.'[17] This is the issue: where is 'reality'? Does it lie in social practices, where everyone goes about their business, works, wins or loses, gives and receives, hopes or despairs? Or does it lie in the economic theories that claim to speak the truth and impose conduct they deem necessary and 'in-

14. To repeat: economic 'science' is eminently normative; it prescribes what ought to be the case. Over time it has penetrated the collective imagination so deeply that everyone now behaves as if what it stated were true: one must always win, grow and pursue one's self-interest. This evidently reinforces the scientific pretensions of economics: the fact that everyone conforms willy-nilly to what it asserts is proof that it must be right!

15. 'The mainstream economic thinking that serves as the reference for government figures and top media economists is therefore nothing other than theology.' Sapir, *Les trous noirs…*, p. 97. And Serge Latouche, after pointing out that economists have always been incapable of predicting crises or stock market crashes, concluded: 'Priests are sometimes unworthy, but religion remains unassailable' (*L'Économie dévoilée*, p. 27). See also Lebaron, *La Croyance économique*, Paris: Seuil, 2000; François Gauthier, 'La religion de la "société de marché"', *Entropia* 5, Autumn 2008, pp. 93–107; and, even more polemical, Paul Lafargue, *La religion du Capital* (1886), which parodies the Lord's Prayer and the Creed and turns the Ave Maria into Ave miseria…

16. Marie Auffray-Seguette, *Les Biens de ce monde. L'économie vue comme espace de recomposition de la religion dans la modernité*, Paris: EHESS, 2008.

17. Clément Rosset, *L'Anti-nature. Éléments pour une philosophie tragique*, Paris: PUF, 1986 (1973), p. 35. And he continues: 'At least one philosopher in the eighteenth century considered that critiques of religion in the name of nature amounted to a return of religion in force and a restoration of the eternal foundations of religious ideology: David Hume, in the *Dialogues on Natural Religion*. The central theme of these dialogues is that the deepest religiosity lies not in the idea of God but in the idea of Nature' (ibid., p. 39).

escapable' because it is part of a reality inscribed in nature? What should we believe? That human behaviour varies, now generous or altruistic, now self-interested or egoistic; or that everyone pursues only their own interest at all times? That our time is always precious; that it belongs only to God or that it is also at our disposal? That nature is miserly or generous? That everything is scarce, or that a sense of plenty is possible so long as we do not give in to all the enticements of the market? In fact, a belief in the existence of these 'realities' or economic 'constraints' (which seem to fall from the sky, uncreated by anyone) is a further sign of the illusion of heterodetermination, which blinds us and inscribes economic doctrines within the field of religiosity. Hence Steve Keen's remark: 'Even some of the most committed economists have conceded that, if economics is to become less of a religion and more of a science, then the foundations of economics should be torn down and replaced.'[18]

In other words, it is difficult to know whether religion – condensed in the certainties of conventional wisdom, which everyone is required to believe – justifies the assertions of a standard economic 'science' that borrows much of its terminology, or whether, on the contrary, economics has captured the former space of religion, by claiming to define the norms (or 'constraints') that society must obey. Frédéric Lebaron favours the second option: he points out that the field of economists has become closer to the field of religiosity (where 'collective beliefs are produced and reproduced'), since 'a piece of social magic, which owes much of its force to the "modern" belief in science and mathematics, places it outside the world; … the dominance of neoliberal economics since the late 1970s is thus only the historical manifestation of a deeper process of *conversion*, which has rooted belief in the autonomy of the economic sphere and turned economics into

18. Keen, *Debunking Economics*, p. 19.

a collective illusion resting on the belief in science.'[19] Belief is therefore always present – which society could forgo it without dissolving its own founding imaginary? It is now in the service of new ruling classes, as Marx once suggested, but it is also in the service of a system that includes everyone, even its slaves.[20]

A further parallel with religion is the intransigence that the most orthodox version of neoliberalism shares with religious fundamentalism. As the psychoanalyst Thierry de Saussure pointed out, 'the essentially cognitive dimension through which fundamentalist discourse is formulated, often very dogmatically, reflects its claim to possess the truth or, at least, to have privileged links to it.'[21] Is this not exactly what we find among zealots of the dominant theory? Not only do they 'claim to possess the truth'; they also have a sense of belonging to a fraternity that guarantees their personal (and professional) security and spares them the anguish of being confronted with divergent opinions. 'Since I hold the truth', they think, 'I don't need to listen to others.' The manifestations of religious fundamentalism (which are most often seen on the margins of the three 'religions of the Book') are today widely criticized or condemned. Is it not equally urgent to keep a check on economic fundamentalism, which is at least as dangerous as other kinds for society as a whole?

Whichever solution one chooses, the conclusion is much the same: economic 'science' owes all its credit or reputation (the faith people have in it[22]) to its insertion within the religious field, and hence to the pre-eminent place it occupies in the collective consciousness. This gives it the privilege to issue 'truths' (most often, merely plausible assertions) that are capable of shaping the

---

19. Lebaron, *La croyance économique*, p. 244; emphasis in the original.

20. In traditional societies, religion (or myth) plays a founding, structuring role whereby certain practices are defined as either compulsory or forbidden. In modern society, belief serves the system by making it socially acceptable.

21. Thierry de Saussure, *L'Inconscient, nos croyances et la foi chrétienne. Etudes psychanalytiques et bibliques*, Paris: Le Cerf, 2009, p. 193.

22. Benveniste, *Indo-European Language and Society*, pp. 99ff.

course of society and the lives of millions of people, with an assurance and pretension not a whit inferior to the magisterium of the Roman Catholic Church.[23]

THE SELF-IMMUNIZATION OF ECONOMIC RELIGION

Now, this insertion of economic 'science' into the religious sphere is not a simple fact to which we must resign ourselves by accepting that 'if reality is economics why not conform to it?' For all religion is characterized by its *immunity defence*: criticisms cannot touch it. You say the market doesn't keep its promise to allocate resources in an optimum way? That's because the market is not yet perfect. Doesn't growth only benefit the rich? That's because the poor don't take sufficient part in it. Isn't the economic process gradually destroying natural resources? That's because the right price hasn't yet been found for them. One is constantly reminded of the immunity of religious truths from any challenge: if God has not answered a mother's prayer for her child to be cured, it is not because the existence of God is doubtful but because she did not pray long enough or with sufficient faith; if the witch arrested by the Inquisition does not confess even under torture, it is because the devil has possessed her and given her the superhuman strength to resist (which is one more reason to burn her at the stake); if an Azande does not get the answer he wants by consulting his oracle, it is not because the procedure is open to question but because the poison used was of bad quality or the person in charge of the ceremony lacked experience;[24] in

23. The only difference is that Catholics probably accept the Vatican's injunctions less than the 'truths' issued by economic 'science'. 'As a former student at the ENSAE [École nationale de la statistique et de l'administration] remarked, macroeconomics is not personalized but presented as an 'indisputable truth', which, like mathematics, has no need of references to particular authors' (Lebaron, *La croyance économique*, p. 115).

24. Before taking an important decision, the Azande people resorted to all manner of magical practices, the best known of which was to inject poison in a chicken and say: 'If I

the former Soviet Union bad harvests were always blamed on inadequate planning, never on the planning system itself. What religion holds to be true *necessarily* eludes debate: social cohesion always depends on a shared imaginary that cannot be shaken by an encounter with the real world.[25]

Although economic 'science' is a social construct with a historical origin – opinions differ about the precise date – this does not alter the fact that its basic axioms now present themselves as dogmas to which every economist must subscribe on pain of excommunication.[26] Similarly, although the field of economics is criss-crossed by struggles among competing schools to impose their own orthodoxy, this does not weaken its affinity with the religious field:[27] all the 'churches' – that is, all sets of shared beliefs and rituals – experience internal rivalry and disputes about the interpretation of particular doctrinal points, as well as reform currents that seek to purify practices or return to the origins of the faith. The history of the Christian Church demonstrates – if that is necessary – that the seemingly sharpest quarrels do not weaken the institution but actually strengthen it, by defining more and

---

should do this [marry such-and-such a woman, build a hut in a particular place, etc.] may the chicken survive; if I shouldn't do it may the chicken die.' If he got the 'wrong' answer, he could always 'appeal' by using a different poison (the 'king's poison' was considered the best) or by turning to another soothsayer. See Edward Evan Evans-Pritchard, *Witchcraft, Oracles and Magic among the Azande* (1937), Oxford: Oxford University Press, 1976; and Gilbert Rist, 'Le concept de "développement" est-il rationnel? Un concept occidental à l'épreuve de la démarche interculturelle', in Fernand Ouellet, ed., *Pluralisme et École*, Quebec: Institut québécois de recherche sur la culture, 1988, pp. 57–83.

25. 'Ideology (or religion) does not define the content of belief (which is always perishable) but rather the *mode* of belief (which is imperishable). This means that, whatever "tissue" it is given, religion is able to find in it the traces of a prior order that made its existence possible.' Rosset, *L'Anti-nature*, p. 41.

26. 'It should be obvious that there is nothing like an economy out there, unless and until men construct such an object.' Dumont, *From Mandeville to Marx*, p. 24.

27. 'Even if the producers of economic belief are divided by what are sometimes reduced to opposite "ideologies" (neoliberalism, Keynesianism, socialism, Marxism, etc.), they are all part of the same universe and try to impose their own economic beliefs upon it. Caught up in a struggle to impose particular economic beliefs, they all contribute unconsciously to recognition of the legitimacy of economic belief.' Lebaron, *La croyance économique*, p. 154.

more precisely what is and what is not acceptable (or believable), and above all by restating what is considered to be indisputably true. This evidently poses a difficult question about the boundaries between tolerated heterodoxy and condemned heresy.

CHAPTER II

TOWARDS A NEW PARADIGM?

> The difficulty lies, not in the new ideas, but in escaping from the old ones, which ramify, for those brought up as most of us have been, into every corner of our minds.
>
> *John Maynard Keynes*[1]

The crisis that shook the world economy from summer 2007 is what we have to thank (if that is the right word) for the redoubled intensity of the critiques of economic 'science'. These were varied in character, and although they did not fall into completely separate groups it is possible to distinguish two types: on the one hand, an internal or scholarly critique put forward by dissident economists, whose voices had trouble making themselves heard amid the prevalent din of 'orthodoxy'; on the other hand, a 'militant' critique, which holds mainstream economics responsible for the numerous ills afflicting the planet, and which has recently aroused greater public resonance through the activity of the 'alternative globalization' movement and, to a lesser extent, that of the growth objectors. However, these various critiques were not enough to break down the neoliberal certitudes, whose champions also believe that their remedies serve the common good.

---

1. John Maynard Keynes, *The General Theory of Employment, Interest and Money*, London: Macmillan, 1961, p. viii (from the Preface to the 1936 edition).

So, what other forms of critique are available? Who should the debate be opened up to? Certainly to historians and anthropologists, who have often featured in the preceding chapters. An interdisciplinary approach is just what is now needed to call the basic axioms of economic 'science' into question, by continuing the work begun twenty-five years ago by the Mouvement anti-utilitariste dans les sciences sociales (MAUSS).

HETERODOXY AS THE SOLUTION?

How should we evaluate the various critiques? The unorthodox stream, which consists of many currents, ought to be the most promising, since it involves recognized economists with often prestigious positions, who might be thought to exercise considerable influence on the mainstream.[2] Before going on to discuss contemporary debates, Pascale Combemale noted:

> The three great unorthodox economists were, in chronological order, Marx (1818–1883), Keynes (1883–1946) and Schumpeter (1883–1950). None of them, however, managed to found a true heterodoxy: that is, an overall alternative economic discourse with scientific pretensions. Part of their work was translated into the language of professionals and absorbed into the mainstream; the other part, more literary, seemingly more rigorous and certainly less susceptible to formalization, scattered to the winds of history, rejected by economists as the pre-scientific errors of misshapen theories.[3]

In Combemale's view, the same is true of present-day heterodoxies, such as the Regulation and 'Convention Economics' schools, which – despite their efforts to rethink the place of the market and money, to recontextualize economic activity in the life of society,

2. It is perhaps to be regretted, however, that many critiques of economic 'science' propose no more than to moralize or humanize it (without explaining how this is to be done), or else pass the buck to 'politics' and 'reasonable' democratic decisions (as if the political field can be independent of the economic).

3. Pascal Combemale, 'L'hétérodoxie: une stratégie vouée à l'échec?', in Latouche, ed., *L'Économie dévoilée*, p. 163.

to introduce radical uncertainty into decisions, and to take account of the irreversibility of time – have not constituted an 'overall alternative to the mainstream' because they are prisoners of 'the epistemological and methodological constraints that are the rules of the game imposed on all economists'.[4] Heterodoxy, then, can only be defined in terms of the orthodoxy it questions: it can at most take a distance from that orthodoxy, add or subtract certain elements and clarify its conditions of validity, but it cannot mount a fundamental challenge. More, the *internal* critique of economics must preferably express itself in the language of mathematics in order to participate in academic debate, so that in a way the orthodox model is able to swallow up or 'phagocytose' theoretical innovations.[5] Finally, in the unlikely event that a theory now regarded as heterodox managed to supplant the dominant orthodoxy, it must be asked what would be gained by the exchange of one verity for another. This is why a pluralist economics is needed: one which draws upon various sources (including anthropology) to account for the full range of economic practices, which can only appear through the filter of multiple theories.

A formula of Serge Latouche's, which is often repeated by his epigones, insists that we need to 'decolonize our imaginaries' in order to break our attachment to the dominant theory. The idea behind this is clear, but perhaps the metaphor is not so well chosen. Is decolonization sufficient? In fact, Latouche is as well placed as others to know that in many cases decolonization

---

4. Ibid., p. 175.

5. 'Sooner or later, orthodoxy generally succeeds in feeding off internal critiques, as we can see in the efforts to treat the problems of expectations, costs, asymmetrical or deficient information, different kinds of rationality, different types of market, organizations, state intervention, the internationalization of ecology, and so on.' Ibid., p. 164. In another article, however ('L'hétérodoxie encore: continuer le combat mais lequel?', *Revue du MAUSS* 30, 2007, pp. 56–67), Combemale also stresses the plasticity of the orthodox current, which evolves in response to empirical refutations: the Washington Consensus, for example, and the 'shock therapy' imposed on ex-Communist countries in the 1990s were abandoned after the damage they were causing was realized; the 'free market' cannot serve as a panacea regardless of the institutional context.

scarcely altered the relations between colonizers and colonized, and above all that it scarcely altered the minds of the colonized, however much certain African dictators laid claim to 'authenticity'. The imaginary of the standard model continues to dominate people's minds, and that is why some do not hesitate to propose a straightforward 'exit' from the economy.[6]

Let us be clear about the words we are using. It is unthinkable to 'exit from the economy' if that means we no longer produce, consume, invest and exchange, for in that sense, which Karl Polanyi calls 'substantive', the economy is inseparable from human life; 'men, like all other living beings, cannot exist for any length of time without a physical environment that sustains them.'[7] Polanyi spelled this out in another text: 'The fount of the substantive concept is the empirical economy. It can be briefly ... defined as an instituted process of interaction between man and his environment, which results in a continual supply of want-satisfying material means.'[8] Although one might discuss – and criticize – this recourse to the naturalistic concept of 'needs', the point is clearly made that the 'substantive economy' prioritizes the relations of human beings among themselves and with their environment, and that these are shaped by institutions. This contrasts with the formal economy (or formalist economics), which 'refers to a situation of choice that arises out of an insufficiency of means. This is the so-called scarcity postulate. It requires, first, insufficiency of means; second, that choice be induced by that insufficiency.'[9] This is indeed the approach from which extrication is necessary. How?

6. See, for example, the *Sortir de l'économie* bulletin at http://sortirdeleconomie.ouvaton.org and other texts available online.

7. Karl Polanyi, *The Livelihood of Man*, New York: Academic Press, 1977, p. 19.

8. Karl Polanyi, 'The Economy as Instituted Process' (1957), in *Primitive, Archaic and Modern Economies: Essays of Karl Polanyi*, p. 145.

9. Ibid., p. 143.

THE DIVERSITY OF ECONOMIC FORMS

Karl Polanyi's reference to the 'empirical' economy is a first avenue worth exploring.[10] For, if the conclusions of economic anthropology[11] differ so radically from the postulates of standard economic 'science', is it not because the two disciplines rest upon opposite conceptions of knowledge and methodological principles? Whereas economic 'science' adopts a normative position, basing general 'laws' on a postulate of primal scarcity and a behaviourally uniform human nature, economic anthropology mainly concerns itself with human practices and ways of acting. So, 'the economy' (production systems, rules of exchange and distribution, the division of labour, etc.) may take very different forms, depending not only on the ecological milieu (forest, savannah, coastal region, high plateau) but above all on history, culture, traditions and the distribution of power: in short, on *institutions*.[12] There is not one economy resting on a few universal principles, but *economic forms* (or types of exchange) that vary with the society, environment and 'institutional arrangements'.[13]

---

10. It is significant that Polanyi here places 'empirical' between inverted commas. He is not proposing that economics be constituted as an 'empirical science' founded only on naive observation of human practices, for, as we know, 'facts do not speak for themselves'; a theoretical viewpoint is always necessary to define the object of study. The point, rather, is simply to understand the economic process beyond the single market form, which is based on the scarcity postulate and the matching of (scarce) means with mutually exclusive ends.

11. With the obvious exception of the now-discredited formalist current (Melville Herskovits, Raymond Firth).

12. 'The task of economic science is to observe and describe empirical social reality and to analyse and explain causal relations between economic facts.... But the proposition that one state of society, actual or imagined, is politically preferable to another can never be inferred from the results of scientific work.' Myrdal, *The Political Element of Economic Theory*, p. 1. This echoes Thorstein Veblen's critique of the naturalism of economic 'science' (which ignores preference changes induced by social transformations) and his insistence that economics should stick to observed practices and, above all else, play a useful or 'serviceable' role in guiding decisions.

13. Here especially 'convention economics' differs from standard economic 'science', in that it recognizes the existence of different norms ('conventions') in different 'cities' (or institutional arrangements), which define behaviour that departs from the mere pursuit of individual self-interest. As Stephen Marglin argues, 'much of the apparatus of mainstream

This proposition obviously sticks in the throat of the champions of standard economic 'science', who reject such diversity and claim to find the same postulates everywhere (or try to squeeze the life of all societies into their theoretical model, hoping to prove its universal validity). The other social sciences, however – so long as they do not espouse methodological individualism – adjust their theories and reach different results in the light of their object of study. Not without reason has sociology or psychology gradually become more specialized, since different 'worlds' (work, countryside, suburbs, etc.) or lifetime situations (child, adolescent, migrant, etc.) cannot be understood in the same way. Not only the approaches but also the conclusions are different. It would clearly be absurd to suggest that sociology or psychology is 'unscientific' because it shows that men behave differently from women, that an urbanized European does not reason in the same way as an African villager, or that a traditionalist (Protestant or Catholic, Jew or Muslim) does not share the same values as an agnostic libertarian. Standard economic 'science' is therefore a very special case, since it is the only social (or human) science that refuses to engage with its 'field' – that is, actual social practices – and devotes itself instead to the construction of formal models whose validity rests only on solutions to a set of equations. But what if, to change paradigms, the first necessity was to stop accepting the false claim of economic 'science' to generalize its underlying model?

Nevertheless, to admit that there is a diversity of *economic forms* does not just mean accepting that each one's validity is restricted to a certain geographical area, on the grounds that savages do not behave like civilized people. For, whatever neoliberal economists may think, the market is far from being the only possible form

---

economics is totally unnecessary if all we are interested in is describing the world. ... In short, if the normative agenda were absent, I believe economics would be different from what it actually is' (*The Dismal Science*, p. 292).

of exchange, nor is it ubiquitous even in societies that seem most subject to it. An already quite old study shows that gift-giving

> in contemporary French society has a total value roughly equal to three-quarters of GDP, not counting cash gifts between households, ritual or spontaneous gifts within and between households, 'helping hands' or blood and organ donation. ... If these were included, it is quite possible that the 'market' value of goods and services exchanged within gift and return-gift relations would be higher than GDP.[14]

This calculation, however problematic, clearly shows the gap between normative economic theory – which would have us believe in the hegemony of the market – and empirical study of social reality, which produces quite different results and prevents a conclusion that the gift is purely a relic of bygone practices.[15] Because of its methodological refusal to base its conclusions or 'laws' on an examination of social practices, economic 'science' therefore suffers from an incorrigible reductionism. It describes only the enchanted world of the market, while scorning the reality of society.

It may well be asked whether it is legitimate to speak of a 'gift economy', since the importance of gift-giving does not depend on the quantities exchanged but on the quality of the social bond maintained through the exchange.[16] But this objection may be overcome in two ways: first, nothing obliges us to apply the term 'gift economy' to all the transactions carried out in a given society, since in fact it everywhere *coexists* with the market form of exchange; and second, the persistence of gifts and return gifts in all societies clearly shows that the axiomatics of self-interest,

---

14. Ahmet Insel, 'La part du don. Esquisse d'évaluation', *Ce que donner veut dire. Don et intérêt*, Paris: MAUSS/La Découverte, 1993, p. 234.

15. Other examples may be found in Jacques T. Godbout, *Ce qui circule entre nous. Donner, recevoir, rendre*, Paris: Seuil, 2007, pp. 94ff.

16. 'But if the term "gift economy" is meant to designate societies where public forms of gratitude take effect through ceremonial gift-giving practices, then it is based on a real misconception. For it turns that practice into an economic act, which is not what it is.' Marcel Hénaff, 'De la philosophie à l'anthropologie. Comment interpréter le don?', *Esprit* 282, February 2002, p. 141.

which determines the behaviour of *Homo oeconomicus*, is never the one and only reason for exchange. Moreover, when Marcel Mauss, in the concluding chapter of *The Gift*, evokes the world of social insurance, mutual benefit systems, co-operatives and the English Friendly Societies, he does not hesitate to affirm: 'We can and we should return to the archaic.'[17] Today he would doubtless mention the inclusive social economy, which combines market-procured resources with others that derive from state redistribution and reciprocity. If we also bear in mind its joint management structures, which put social ties before profit, could we not say that it is based on a series of 'archaic' elements?[18] Thanks to the web of social networks, there really is a life outside – or alongside – the market. Thus, reciprocity and generosity are just as much part of the 'substantive' economy as is self-interested exchange. But whereas economic 'science' manages to explain the latter, it is quite incapable of interpreting the former.

THE NEWTONIAN IMPASSE

This attention to the diversity of exchange is not intended only to open up economic theory to the gains of the social sciences and the complexity of human behaviour, so that the fiction of the maximizing automaton (who has never existed anywhere and never will) can finally be laid to rest. A much more fundamental issue is to reconsider the link that economic 'science' established from the start with the natural sciences, then dominated by Newtonian mechanics. In the name of their 'science', economists ought to recognize that their conceptual framework is today out of date and that, in order to understand the economic process,

17. Mauss, *The Gift*, p. 67; translation modified.

18. Following on from Mauss, health, education and personal safety should be considered 'public goods', to be funded by the state and made freely available to citizens. But the exact opposite is happening today: the state has stopped playing the role of a countervailing power to the market.

it is necessary to take into account not only the first law of thermodynamics (the conservation of energy and matter) but also the second law concerning the irreversible degradation of energy. A purely mechanistic base prevents economic calculation from including the harmful effects of human activity on the environment[19] and sustains the (equally harmful) belief in infinite progress and economic growth.[20] So, the economic paradigm shift does not merely involve leaving the empyrean of abstraction to which immoderate use of mathematical formalization leads; it also means understanding the world as it is and as it is changing. The credibility of economic 'science' therefore depends on its capacity to evolve hand in hand in scientific discoveries – which, at the moment, is far from being the case.

The detour via economic anthropology may also open up other perspectives not unrelated to the previous point. One characteristic of many 'traditional' economies is the 'partitioning' of markets (though the term 'market' is not really appropriate here). This means that not every good can be exchanged for any other; that there is a hierarchy such that the circulation of prestige goods obeys different rules from those that govern the exchange of subsistence goods.[21] Without going into the details of these practices, which may be found in both Africa and Melanesia, let

19. Of course, 'standard' economics calculates the cost of 'negative externalities' in the hope that, if everyone's property rights to disputed resources are clearly defined and if transaction costs are close to zero, exchange will permit an optimum allocation of resources, the state intervening only to recognize property rights and to lower transaction costs (Coase theorem). But, although this method makes it possible to resolve conflicts of interest, it does not do away with the actual pollution!

20. Naredo, *La Economía en evolución*, p. 72.

21. 'Among the Siane of New Guinea too, goods were divided into heterogeneous categories: subsistence goods (products of agriculture, gathering and crafts); luxury goods (tobacco, palm oil, salt, pandanus fruit); precious goods (seashells, bird of paradise feathers, ornamental axes, pigs used for ritual consumption at weddings, initiations, peace treaties and religious festivals). Each category had its own form of circulation.' Maurice Godelier, 'Formes non marchandes de circulation du produit social', in J. Copans, S. Tornay, M. Godelier and C. Backès-Clément, eds, *L'Anthropologie: science des sociétés primitives?*, Paris: Éditions E.P., 1971, pp. 225–37, republished in *Socio-Anthropologie* 7, 2000, http://socioanthropologie.revues.org.

us simply note that in this form of economy no money can serve as a common denominator or general equivalent among various categories of goods, and that these are classified according to their origin and destination. This may seem complicated to us, but its logic is perfectly clear: different goods are not worth the same and cannot be exchanged for just anything.[22]

This way of seeing is evidently scandalous for mainstream economics, since it radically challenges the use of money as *general* equivalent. The dogma we are asked to sign up to is that everything can be bought and everything can be sold. But we might mention certain exceptions, which do not go all the way back to the ban on simony (the selling of spiritual goods as indulgences or ecclesiastical benefices). For example, there is the public ban on trading in blood and human organs (which doesn't prevent illegal trafficking, of course[23]), or the personal 'de-marketization' of objects such as the 'priceless' Louis XVI commode I inherited from my Aunt Louise, or family jewellery whose value is more symbolic than monetary. Not everything is for sale, then – for various reasons to do with sentiment or the social order, which converge in the idea that unique, *non-reproducible objects have a special status*.

When economic 'science' first took shape in the early nineteenth century, the illusion of the infinite bounty of nature impeded any awareness of the finitude (or non-reproducibility) of natural resources. Ricardo, quoting Say, mentioned 'the original and indestructible powers of the land' alongside 'other gifts of nature which exist in boundless quantity', such that 'no one would pay for [its] use when there was an abundant quantity not

22. Another way of 'partitioning' markets is to use local currencies (see Chapter 9, note 29 above). In that case, goods differ from one another only by their origin: local or non-local.

23. According to the World Health Organization, the trade in human organs, 'which flourishes on corruption and gaps in the law, accounted for approximately ten per cent of kidney transplants in the world in 2005'. 'Mobilisation contre le "tourisme de transplantation"', *Le Monde*, 23 August 2008, p. 7.

yet appropriated, and, therefore, at the disposal of whosoever might choose to cultivate it'.[24] How times have changed! We may therefore rightly ask whether such a perspective is still pertinent today, and whether – given what we know about ecological limits – non-reproducible resources (or stocks)[25] should not be excluded from the 'law' of the market, which grants those with money a wrongful power over 'common goods'.[26] This would simply take us back to Ricardo's old rule, which included in political economy 'such commodities only as can be increased in quantity by the exertion of human industry',[27] thereby avoiding the confusion that the spread of the market has created among categories of goods with different origins. Is it not more sensible to take seriously the unavoidable finitude of certain resources than to get involved in a struggle against imaginary (because socially constructed) scarcity that is lost in advance?

It now remains to define how such goods would be administered if they were excluded from the market. The first question concerns the property regime under which non-renewable resources would be placed, since neither private nor public property solves the problem of equitable access (including for future generations) to

24. Ricardo, *Principles of Political Economy and Taxation*, p. 34. This implies – for Ricardo and Say – that such free ('priceless') goods fall outside the market. On the other hand, in his *Essay on the Principle of Population*, Malthus cast serious doubt on the infinite bounty of nature.

25. The present trend, on the contrary, is to 'commodify' such goods a little more, in the hope that the 'law' of the market, reacting to decreased supply, will increase the price of the resources and therefore make them less attractive except for those with the income to absorb the price rise.

26. The definition of 'global public goods' is far from assured. The UN Charter of Economic Rights and Duties of States (General Assembly Resolution XXIX: 3281, 12 December 1974, Art. 29) stated that 'the sea-bed and ocean floor and the subsoil thereof, beyond the limits of national jurisdiction as well as the resources of the area, are the common heritage of mankind.' This definition – which might have been promising, since it concerned non-renewable resources – was abandoned in favour of an inventory that includes 'goods' such as culture, knowledge, the environment, peace, prosperity, security, international economic stability, and so on. This is evidently not the perspective we would favour. See François Constantin, ed., *Les Biens publics mondiaux. Un mythe légitimateur pour l'action collective?*, Paris: L'Harmattan, 2002, p. 26.

27. Ricardo, *Principles of Political Economy and Taxation*, p. 6.

goods located in specific geographical areas that benefit from an excessive situational rent, and which therefore involve a kind of 'ecological colonialism'.[28] The only theoretically plausible solution – which would evidently face considerable political obstacles! – would be to bring non-renewable resources under an international authority that regulated access to them, in accordance with their intended use and its ecological consequences.[29] In addition, one might imagine that non-renewable resources could be obtained only in exchange for special accounting units (or non-convertible currency), reflecting 'values' based on the actual exchanges with the environment.[30] Utopian, no doubt, but it forces us to think at last about the relationship between economic growth and the use of reserves, and about the consequences of granting property rights over goods that no one has created.

The preceding remarks suggest that economic 'science' should be made more attentive to the diversity of forms of exchange, and that stocks (or non-renewable resources) should have a *special status* that takes account of the entropic process linked to their use. Does this amount to a 'comprehensive alternative to the dominant current' or the basis for a new economic theory (which would also have to flow out of a new political programme)? It would be fanciful to think so.

---

28. Naredo, *La Economía en evolución*, p. 52.

29. This is the solution envisaged by Joseph E. Stiglitz: 'To remedy the problem of the global commons ..., the only sensible and workable remedy is some form of global public management of global natural resources', a set of regulations concerning uses and actions that cause 'negative externalities' (*Making Globalization Work*, London: Penguin, 2007, p. 165). The Montreal Protocol (1987) and the Kyoto Protocol (2005) are a first timid approach to the problem. In creating carbon emission rights, Kyoto paves the way for a 'carbon currency' to exist alongside the 'normal' currency (the dollar), much as a 'butter coupon' is required as well as money to buy butter in periods of rationing. See Matthieu Calame, *La Tourmente alimentaire. Pour une politique agricole mondiale*, Paris: Ed. Charles Léopold Mayer, 2008, pp. 177–87.

30. It is absurd that the monetary standard (the dollar) has a purely self-referential and tautological (as well as fluctuating) value. Since the ending of its gold convertibility in 1971, one dollar is simply worth... one dollar. We should also ask serious questions about the role of money in equating the value of human labour with that of a barrel of petrol or a hectare of forest. See Calame, *La Tourmente alimentaire*, p. 187.

Let us imagine for a moment how one might rid economic theory of its unrealistic or clearly false assumptions and make it capable of grasping what it has (intentionally or unintentionally) ignored, especially the depletion of natural resources and a series of environmental problems.[31] The question, in other words, is how economics might become an art rather than a science – useful for understanding fundamental issues (not only the market) that underlie production, consumption and exchange. Returned to its old meaning of 'good administration of household affairs', economics would then – like any good head of a family – begin by drawing up an inventory of available resources, clearly distinguishing stocks and funds, assessing the risks of overuse or wastage and listing the available sources of energy – and, in addition, redefine the collective rights linked to particular resources.[32] Next it would identify the many possible kinds of circulation of goods and services (through the market, redistribution, production for self-consumption, gift-giving), basing its criteria on relations among the agents themselves (which are not always self-interested but also sometimes passionate) and on the intended use of the goods. The economic approach would therefore be essentially descriptive. It would first focus on the general operational conditions, so as to make an intelligent and reasonable (rather than 'rational'!) choice to produce this or that good for a particular purpose, estimating not only the short-term gains but also the long-term losses, and taking into account all the social and ecological implications.

31. Of course, since the success of 'sustainable development', there are now many authors who write about 'environmental economics', but this is mainly concerned with 'market stimuli', the internalization of externalities, the 'pricing' of natural elements such as water, air or landscape, and public policy; it does not break with the rules of 'standard' economics or take account of the entropy inseparable from thermo-industrial production.

32. Beyond the distinction between stocks and funds, one might also consider use-related differences and ask, for example, whether it is legitimate to charge the tap water we drink at the same rate as the water used to fill a swimming pool; or whether different tariffs might not apply to electricity produced from renewable (water or wind) and non-renewable (fossil or nuclear) resources.

Such an economics would start from practices and energy-matter flows, in order to bring out what the production decision would inevitably destroy, to predict the likely effects, and to share the costs on an equitable basis. These are only avenues to explore, but they lead in directions very different from those characteristic of ordinary economics.

But perhaps, while waiting for a new paradigm, we should follow a more radical path and look again at Michel Foucault's thesis that, although 'in any given culture and at any given moment there is always only one *episteme* that defines the conditions of possibility of all knowledge',[33] there are some epochs when that very culture imperceptibly challenges its founding codes and laws that it hitherto considered part of a legitimate order. There comes a time 'when it frees itself sufficiently to realize that these orders are perhaps not the only possible ones or the best ones'.[34] In other words, we can perceive key historical moments when what used to be thinkable suddenly becomes *unthinkable* (or vice versa). Foucault's 'archaeological' work shows that such a break occurred around the turn of the nineteenth century, with the shift from the study of wealth to the 'discovery' of political economy. The question that needs to be asked is whether we are approaching a comparable moment, in which a new turnaround in people's thinking will make today's certainties appear obsolete. Of course, it is always presumptuous to imagine that one is at a turning point in history. But if we consider the major changes that have taken place in fields as different as physics, genetics, astrophysics and medicine,[35] can we reasonably believe that our conception of social life (and particularly economic theory) will not be affected? If Foucault was right that only one *episteme* overarching

33. Michel Foucault, *The Order of Things: An Archaeology of the Human Sciences* (1966), London: Routledge, 2001, p. 183.

34. Ibid., p. xxii.

35. This covers, more or less, the acronymic compound BANG (Bio-Atomic-Nano-Genetic).

all knowledge is possible in each epoch (and that it can change), how can we think that an imminent turnaround is impossible? The dominant economic paradigm, petrified in concepts derived from Newtonian mechanics, obstinately ignores the consequences of the inevitable entropy bound up with the laws of thermodynamics. Will it be able to escape challenge for much longer?

To be more specific, rather than being left to 'economics', should the description and interpretation of economic phenomena (production, consumption, exchange) not be 'embedded' in a multidisciplinary approach that takes all their various aspects into account? Against the general trend to specialization and fragmentation of knowledge, should there not be an expanded discipline that covers the constant interaction of social, biological, physical, energetic and ecological phenomena?

CONCLUSION

> The crisis consists precisely in the fact that the old is dying and the new cannot be born.
>
> *Antonio Gramsci*

> We can't solve problems by using the same kind of thinking we used when we created them.
>
> *Albert Einstein*

This book has investigated the theoretical foundations of mainstream economics and the reasons why, in its present state, that 'science' (or that representation of the world) is incapable of solving the main problems that face us today: the growth of social inequalities, both within and between nations, and the rise of ecological dangers. A critique of its core assumptions has brought out some of the unspoken or implicit elements in economic discourse, which are largely responsible for the errors and aberrations to which it leads. The conclusion we reached was that it is necessary to invent a new paradigm – one based on an approach to 'economic facts' that takes into account not only the diversity of 'economic forms' but also their relationship with ecology (especially with non-renewable resources), instead of proposing a normative, 'otherworldly' reduction of all human activities to their market dimension.

Should this thesis require confirmation, the crisis we are living through today provides – alas – remarkable supporting evidence. Although most of this book was written before Summer 2007, the tremors that then began to shake the capitalist system perfectly illustrated the dead end into which mainstream economics had strayed. There are two aggravating circumstances, moreover. The first has to do with the fact that no one (or almost no one) seriously foresaw the events. When Queen Elizabeth expressed surprise at this, during a visit to the London School of Economics in late 2008, a group of distinguished economists replied to her more than six months later that 'it was principally a failure of the collective imagination of many bright people'.[1] No doubt that was only part of the explanation, but it showed the degree of paralysis that affected a large section of the profession. The second reason for surprise is perhaps even graver. If the metaphor of a dead end is apposite, one can find a way out only by retracing one's steps, not by advancing into it even further; yet curiously that is just what was preferred. To be sure, 'crazy traders' were scapegoated, and some public figures prided themselves on wanting to 'moralize capitalism'; the G20 summit held in London on 2 April 2009 undertook, a little incautiously, 'to make sure that this crisis is the last'. But otherwise what was done except to inject billions of dollars, euros or pounds into the financial system? What for? To 'restore confidence' – which, in the language of today's decision-makers, has become the acceptable synonym for growth (which is now called 'green').

A LOOK BACK AT THE ORIGINS OF THE CRISIS

We cannot here consider in detail the reasons for the crisis, which has already given rise to numerous analyses, but we should at

1. Letter dated 22 July 2009. See Frédéric Lemaître, 'La crise remet en cause le savoir et le statut des économistes', *Le Monde*, 5 Septembre 2009.

least highlight a few key elements. We may start with the fact that, according to the OECD, the share of wages and salaries – compared with the share of capital – in national income (or in value-added within the national economy) has stagnated, or even fallen, since the 1980s.[2] This is why, in the United States, two ways were used to boost household consumption in the context of low pay: one was personal investment in the stock market, which contributed to the bubble and permitted rapid gains; the other was the lifting of restrictions on mortgage credit, which was justified on the spurious grounds that the value of real estate could only go up and would bring a profit in the event of resale. As a result, from 2006 on, many low-income households – which had been strongly encouraged to use their property as loan collateral – were unable to keep up repayments because of interest-rate rises (from 1 per cent in 2003 to 5.25 per cent in 2006), while in the meantime their loans had been 'securitized' in the banking market under various names and presented as both a safe and a highly profitable investment (a contradiction in terms, if one accepts that profitability is proportionate to risk!). As the value of these 'toxic assets' neared zero, the banks were therefore forced to take them off their balance sheets – with a total loss of more than 500 billion dollars, which the injection of fresh liquidity by central banks and sovereign funds did not manage to soak up. Savers became increasingly distrustful of the banks, which had lost them a lot of money, and intensified the crisis by withdrawing large sums from

2. We cannot enter here into the war of figures over the way in which macroeconomic statistics are constructed. According to Michel Husson ('La baisse tendancielle de la part salariale', 23 September 2007, published at www.attac.org), the share of wages and salaries fell by 8.6 per cent in Europe and 3.5 per cent in the United States between 1980 and 2005. It is true that their share was exceptionally high at the beginning of the 1980s – which, for some, casts doubt on the baseline. But although their share has remained more or less constant for the past ten years, it must be borne in mind that pay differentials have actually widened, since the excessive remuneration paid in the form of 'salaries' to a tiny minority of executives distorts the calculation and camouflages a real decline at the lower end of the pay scale. See also Frédéric Lordon, 'Le Paradoxe de la part salariale', www.blog.mondediplo.net.

their accounts. Finally, in Spring 2008, the British government was forced to nationalize the Northern Rock bank, and in September the US government, having already intervened to save the Freddy Mac and Fannie Mae federal mortgage associations, allowed the bankruptcy of Lehman Brothers to go ahead and endanger the whole of the banking system. The stock markets, already sharply down, lost another 20 per cent of their value in early October. Millions of Americans faced the loss of their homes; millions of savers found themselves fleeced.

Such, in broad outline, is the scenario that played itself out in the United States and rapidly spread to the rest of the industrialized world. But how are these events linked to the critique we have made of the dominant economic paradigm? Were they not merely a passing aberration due to many factors that might just as easily not have existed? What if US interest rates had not been so high? What if the credit-rating agencies had done their job properly? What if the financial 'whiz kids' had failed to disguise their toxic assets as structured products that no one understood the first thing about? Well, be this as it may, the problem runs much deeper.

POLANYI IS BACK

In this scenario, it is possible to identify three main 'actors': labour (paid less, despite higher productivity), land (in the form of real estate mortgages) and money (the value of which lost all contact with 'reality'); that is, the three 'fictitious commodities' which, in Karl Polanyi's account, serve an ostensibly self-regulating market.[3] In what sense are they fictitious? Quite simply, they have not been 'produced' to be bought and sold, because the value of human life has other criteria, nature was not created by anyone, and monetary tokens, which are first of all claims on the central bank,

3. Polanyi, *The Great Transformation*, pp. 68–76.

are liquid assets stemming from financial mechanisms. So, it was the spread of the market around the turn of the nineteenth century that converted into commodities that which had been previously 'embedded' in society and had no autonomous existence. From that time on, 'interest is the price for the use of money ...; rent is the price for the use of land ...; wages are the price for the use of labour power.'[4]

Polanyi was certainly convinced that this 'satanic mill' of total commodification would inevitably destroy society if it could reduce it to a mere appendage of the market, but he thought that the omnipotence of markets had collapsed for ever with the crises of the 1930s. Although his optimism proved largely unfounded, his analysis remains valid today, even if he could never have imagined the scale of the present crisis. Beyond the particular special circumstances we have briefly alluded to, it is clear that the three 'fictitious commodities' have literally 'gone crazy' over the last decade. Labour was remunerated more and more unreasonably, as 'poor workers' were reduced to near-destitution and middle-class disposable incomes were squeezed, while a tiny minority was paid wildly excessive sums; in a 'developed' society no one is 'worth' only a few dollars or euros an hour, and no one 'deserves' to earn several million (or tens of millions of) dollars a year. Land served only as a pretext to create money, with no regard for the guarantees that debtors are supposed to offer lenders, and financial speculation took care of the rest. But the more interconnected financial markets are, the greater is the risk from speculation. To borrow one of Keynes's numerous metaphors, we might say that speculators – who were well aware that everyone cannot be

4. Ibid., p. 69. That said, even outside the wages system or private property, the 'value' of labour or natural resources depends in all societies on their 'social use'. There are places where the services of a griot, a sorcerer or a hunter are more in demand than those of a 'mere' farmer; wind is 'worth' something only if one knows how to build mills or wind farms, and oil is 'interesting' only if technology is available to convert it into fuel. The environment does not exist without the human beings who inhabit it, but it has its own 'laws' that may turn against them if they put too many demands on it.

a winner – behaved as in a game of Black Peter, where everyone tries to pass the losing card on to someone else; the only difference is that the toxic assets fouled up the whole game. Polanyi was therefore wrong 'historically', but his analysis of the deep causes of crisis is still topical today.

As for the remedies, we know that they were essentially financial, since it was necessary to rescue the banks from the brink of disaster and to avoid a catastrophic loss of jobs. Hence the $5 thousand billion assigned to rebuild the reserves of the financial institutions, to recapitalize the banks and to eliminate the 'toxic assets'. Some have expressed surprise at this sudden doctrinal volte-face, which transformed the state into the saviour of a system that had previously considered it worse than useless. But that is to forget that the liberalization (or deregulation) at the origin of the crisis was largely unleashed by the state itself upon the decision-making centres of the economy.[5] On this point too, Polanyi was right to say of the crises of the nineteenth and early-twentieth centuries: '*Laissez-fare* was planned; planning was not.'[6] If today, after years of yielding to the sirens of neoliberalism, the various national states – and, ultimately, the taxpayers – have been forced to intervene massively (however far we still are from the 'planning' that Polanyi spoke of!), this is not because of an ideological about-turn, but simply in order to preserve 'the vital social interests affected by the expanding market mechanism' and to avoid a situation where 'the inherent absurdity of the idea of a self-regulating market … eventually destroyed society'.[7] 'For if market economy [is] a threat to the human and natural components of the social fabric, … what else would one expect

---

5. 'Even free trade and competition required [state] intervention to be workable.' Ibid., p. 150. The opposition between state and market is not as great as some claim: are they not tightly interwoven with each other and subject to the same relations of strength? 'Still more disturbing is the gradual privatization of the state over the last twenty years' (Jacques Généreux, *La Grande régression*, Paris: Seuil, 2010, p. 43).

6. Polanyi, *The Great Transformation*, p. 141.

7. Ibid., p. 145.

than an urge on the part of a great variety of people to press for some sort of protection … without any theoretical or intellectual preconceptions on their part, and irrespective of their attitudes towards the principles underlying a market economy.'[8]

CHANGING EVERYTHING SO THAT IT REMAINS THE SAME

Does this mean that the lessons of the crisis have been drawn? Nothing is less certain. The watchword remains as before: confidence must be restored and 'strong, sustainable and balanced world growth' must be promoted. Such was the essential message of the two G20 summits (London, 2 April 2009 and Pittsburgh, 25 September 2009).[9] This obsession with growth, which we have criticized at length, now reached its peak. Of course, to calm the anger of ordinary people, there were fleeting attacks on the 'excesses', 'recklessness' and 'irresponsibility' of securities dealers, and it was agreed not to top up the 'variable part' of their salary unless profits were being made. But these fine words remained a dead letter, since the bonuses paid by US banks in the third quarter of 2009 were higher than ever. The supposed justification was the large profits recorded over the year, but such measures, which were seen as real provocations, further deepened income inequality. They confirmed that the system had not changed: it was still geared entirely to profit, despite the occasional puffed-up talk of making it more moral.

The keyword, repeated in every tone of voice, remained 'growth': sometimes green, but above all 'sustainable'.[10] In the

8. Ibid., p. 150.

9. The respective communiqués may be consulted at www.wcoomd.org/files/1.%20Public%20files/PDFandDocuments/Highlights/G20_Final_London_Communique.pdf; and www.pittsburghsummit.gov/mediacenter/129639.htm.

10. The Statement of World Leaders in Pittsburgh used the word 'growth' twelve times in its preamble and twenty times in the first nine sections of the final text (without including the synonym 'recovery').

past, the adjective had been regularly attached to 'development', as a concession to environmental concerns following the famous Brundtland report *Our Common Future* (1987), although some evil tongues had already pointed out that the oxymoron risked being understood not as a type of development that respected ecological constraints but as 'sustained development'.[11] Today their fears appear amply justified. At a theoretical level (which has considerable practical implications), one of the gravest consequences of the present crisis is that ecological concerns have virtually disappeared from the thoughts of decision-makers; the failure of the Copenhagen conference on climate change showed this collective nonchalance about any long-term vision.[12]

One might have thought that the crisis would trigger a new burst of theoretical energy, a serious examination of its deep underlying causes. Had events not been worrying enough to prompt any questioning of the fundamental principles of economic 'science'? Could we not expect full-scale revisions after history delivered its damning verdict on the likes of Alan Greenspan and Larry Summers, who, in various formulations, had declared that the existence of a financial bubble was no more than a fairy tale, and that the real estate market was perfectly healthy? The only problem was that economic 'science' is not independent of the social forces that ensure its legitimacy.

For, although the crisis struck at millions of people's homes or jobs (or both),[13] it scarcely touched what went on in the minds of economists. How can one even seriously blame them, since they all did their thinking within the standard paradigm? Keynes's relative return to favour, after years of mockery from neoliberal

11. See Rist, *The History of Development*, pp. 178ff.

12. The Pittsburgh Statement referred to clean energy and climate change in only two of its fifty paragraphs (nos 31 and 32).

13. According to Paul Krugman ('How Did Economists Get It So Wrong?', *New York Times*, 6 September 2009), the financial bubble caused losses of $13 trillion to US households and wiped out 6 million jobs.

'freshwater economists',[14] does not change the picture, since it only involves a dispute between rival schools about the finer points of 'market efficiency'. It is also significant that those who are sometimes considered the most critical members of the profession, and who were commissioned by the French president to propose a new indicator of wealth to replace GDP,[15] contented themselves with a few relatively minor adjustments that do not challenge the basic model.[16]

So, at the economic and political levels, the crisis did not stimulate the right questions and dashed hopes in the possible emergence of a new paradigm. But history cannot be snubbed so easily. As Marx already knew, the capitalist system had always been subject to crises 'in which this contradiction of capital discharges itself in great thunderstorms which increasingly threaten it as the foundation of society and of production itself',[17] and he specifically linked them to the deviations of finance capital.[18] But, however recurrent, crises teach nothing (to economists). Without going back to the Crash of 1929 (which has been copiously analysed, in the fond belief that the disastrous response to it will never be repeated), we might mention others closer to the present day: 1973–4 (when stock markets plunged by 48 per cent), 1987, 1997–8 in Asia, and the 'Internet bubble' of 2000. None of these made any impact on the theory.[19]

---

14. 'Freshwater economists' (mainly based in lakeside Chicago) are often contrasted to the more or less Keynesian 'saltwater economists' of the East Coast. Krugman, ibid.

15. The Commission on the Measurement of Economic Performance and Social Progress was appointed in 2008 and delivered its report in the summer of 2009. It was jointly chaired by Joseph Stiglitz, Amartya Sen and Jean-Paul Fitoussi.

16. The Commission mainly added new indicators for income distribution, well-being, health and the collective heritage (stocks of human and physical capital) – a refinement of the Human Development Indicator (HDI) proposed by the UNDP in 1990, largely under the inspiration of Amartya Sen. In fact, this approach is not without its dangers, since it comes down to setting a price on things that cannot be valued in money terms and therefore expands the realm of the commodity a little further.

17. Karl Marx, *Grundrisse: Foundations of the Critique of Political Economy* (1857–8), London: Penguin/NLR, 1993, p. 411. It seems as if one is reading Karl Polanyi…

18. Karl Marx, *Capital*, Volume 3, London: Penguin/NLR, 1981, pp. 1046f.

19. The crisis of 1973–4 did put an end to the Fordist compromise and marked a return

Why so much persistence in denying reality? It is exactly as if the religious character of mainstream economic 'science' made it immune from all criticism. Paying no heed to actual social practices, seemingly unaware that *Homo oeconomicus* is only a fiction of its own creation, it lies there preserved in the aspic of its certainties, comforted by the elegance of the theorems it has devised to shape reality to the 'rationality' of its economic actors. The failure is manifest, yet no one seems to have drawn the consequences. Its most prestigious champions expect a 'return to normal': that is, to 'strong, sustainable and balanced growth', as the Pittsburgh Statement put it.

THE BLINDNESS OF ORDINARY ECONOMICS

Economics is a very strange 'science', whose resistance to historical facts recalls the obstinate defence of religious dogmas in the face of evidence to the contrary. So, a paradigm change cannot be expected to come from the mainstream loyalists, since even their often heated internal disputes scarcely affect the underlying assumptions that they all share.

As we have tried to show, what is needed is a *change of paradigm*. This does not mean denying the 'economic facts' (production, consumption and exchange of countless goods and services) but, rather, adopting a different approach from the one taken by ordinary economic 'science'. Karl Polanyi spoke of 're-embedding' those facts in society: that is, seeing them as phenomena whose existence is not separate from the rest of human life, but which are woven into the social fabric. For example, unemployment is not simply an 'adjustment variable' of the labour market, and price is not the only way of estimating the 'value' of a good. In the end, the 'utility' of things depends on the way we look at them, not on

---

to neoliberal economics, but the change took place within the capitalist paradigm.

the price we are willing to offer to obtain them. Without a doubt, therefore, the contribution of anthropology reveals not only ways of doing and exchanging, but also forms of social life that largely go outside the fictions of ordinary economic discourse.

We need to take Polanyi's approach further, by 're-embedding' the economy in global ecology and assessing the consequences of 'economic facts' for the whole of the Earth System (which include all kinds of pollution, energy supply and consumption, deforestation and the depletion of ocean resources, climate change and the erosion of biodiversity, to mention only the most important phenomena). To be sure, in treating land as a 'fictitious commodity', Polanyi showed an awareness of the special status of what is more generally called 'nature', which for a long time had been (and ought to be) outside the market. But the knowledge we have gained in recent decades has made a critique of market fundamentalism even more urgent than it was in his day. Social life is also life in nature: it is impossible to imagine one without the other, to concern oneself with society but fail to consider its biotope, or, conversely, to sanctify (or 'sanctuarize') nature but ignore those who live in it. True globalization is not what the economists talk about. To focus only on commodity and capital flows, rejoicing at the freedom with which they circulate and aspiring to make them still freer and more numerous, adds up to a very sorry picture of the world. The macroeconomics that claims to encompass everything ends up grasping almost nothing – and, in particular, leaves out what is essential. It is exactly as if, in judging the quality of a novel, one were to mention only the number of pages it has.

Ordinary economics, then, is a 'science' whose short-sightedness sometimes borders on blindness. It counts and re-counts everything the market registers, but forgets that the figures it plays with are far from reflecting the real world. You're wrong, someone might object: economists know perfectly well that they only deal with market exchange, and that there are other 'spheres' of activity or problematics which lie outside their compass, or which they have chosen to disregard for the sake of methodological rigour. Okay, let's accept that. But that is not the end of the story. For most economists are not content simply to describe: they never stop prescribing. It is on their advice that decisions are made as to whether interest rates should be raised or lowered, whether trade should be liberalized or made subject to public regulation, whether 'shareholder value' justifies relocation, whether the price of raw materials should be fixed on a spot market or reflect their inevitable scarcity in future, whether primal forest should be replaced with lucrative oil palms, whether investment should go into anti-obesity drugs or anti-malarials, whether the market of emerging economies will save the national automobile industry. In answer to each of these questions, 'serious', highly reputed, economists formulate a 'rational expectations hypothesis', which provides policymakers or businessmen with 'scientific' backing for their decisions.

However, these decisions in line with one economic theory or another are not only 'economic', nor can they be reduced to semi-scholarly considerations on the exchange of goods and services and the profit to be derived from it. For, if it is accepted that the economy is not an autonomous field disconnected from other dimensions of human life, some account must be taken of all the effects it is likely to have. Each 'economic' decision affects a considerable number of people and has implications for the biosphere, both predictable and unpredictable, that are of concern to us all. Of course, these social and ecological consequences do not enter into the highly sophisticated models of professional economists, most of whom, if accused of neglecting them, would snap back that no one can be expected to do the impossible. But the damage is done. And they should bear the main responsibility for it.

To look for a way out of the present crisis through 'strong, sustainable and balanced world growth' is therefore a total aberration, and the commitment at the G20 summit in London to 'prevent a crisis like this from recurring again' lacks all credibility. The sought-after 'recovery' (of solvent demand, that is) will only add to the problems and hasten the onset of even graver and less controllable crises associated with climate change, energy and food. It may be easy to create money and buy up banks that are 'too big to fail', but it will be much trickier to deal with the programmed depletion of oil reserves, rising sea levels or global warming.

HOPES OF CHANGE?

Whereas most neoliberal economists are largely immune from any challenge to their assumptions, the victims of the system are gradually coming to realize that it is possible to protect themselves from it, if not to escape it altogether. Their criticism is practical rather than theoretical, but it has the merit of going to the heart of the problem: growth.

Kenneth Boulding's aphorism is well known: 'Anyone who believes growth can be infinite in a finite world is either a madman or an economist.' And, since most people do not wish to be taken for either, we have seen the birth of a movement of 'growth objectors' and a new striving for simplicity that frowns on growth for its own sake, prefers public transport to private cars, rejects advertising, reduces meat consumption, recycles instead of throwing away, buys directly from farmers instead of in supermarkets, worries about ecological footprints, and so on. Chapter 9 stressed that these individual and collective initiatives are far from involving a significant change of trend in society as a whole. In a quite surprising way, however, they help to spread the idea that a different way of living is possible.

The diehards of growth at any price will argue that, when a crisis breaks out and causes real 'degrowth' (of GDP), as it did in 2009, the social and human costs are considerable. To this there are two closely related answers. First, a system based on the growth compulsion inevitably goes wrong when the compulsion remains but its satisfaction becomes impossible. Or, to use a comparison of which Serge Latouche is fond, society then resembles a drug addict suddenly deprived of his daily fix; the worst may happen, and the resulting mad rush is a threat to social protection and employment. Recent events are confirmation of this. The corollary is that a society based on sustainable degrowth, balanced, serene and harmonious (the reader can choose the adjective), is a *realistic and achievable project*,[20] but this requires a break with the conceptual schemas inculcated in us in the last few decades, and therefore a challenge to the economic dogmas.

A final counter-argument is that growth objection is only a posture on the part of the North's spoiled children, who can painlessly give up a certain degree of comfort and claim to be criticizing the system. Yet only recently Bolivia, on the initiative of President Morales (in office since 2006), set out in search of a way of organizing society different from the growth-oriented 'development' associated with economic liberalism. The main idea behind the National Development Plan is that everyone should 'have a good life' (*bien vivir*), in contrast to the Western idea of 'well-being' centred on the acquisition of material goods, which always threatens to be at the expense of nature and other people.

---

20. Serge Latouche, *Le Pari de la décroissance*, Paris: Fayard, 2006; *Petit traité de la décroissance sereine*, Paris: Mille et une nuits, 2007; and *Farewell to Growth*, Cambridge: Polity Press, 2009. These works by Latouche clearly demonstrate the possibility of such a society. Under the title *Contre-pouvoirs et décroissance*, the journal *Entropia* (no. 9, Autumn 2010) published a number of excellent articles on the originality and ambiguities of this Amerindian 'new way' opposed both to capitalism and to 'development'. Far from limited to Bolivia, this extends to Ecuador, Mexico (in the form of resistance to the established powers, outside Zapatista-controlled Chiapas) and elsewhere in the Americas, promoting the renewal of Amerindian cultures. In any event, the point is to question the centrality of economics in the conduct of political affairs.

'The "good life" means "living well together", [since] one cannot live well if others live badly. It means living as members of the community, under its protection and in harmony with nature.'[21] Or again: 'The "good life" rests on access to and enjoyment of material goods, and on the blossoming of everyone in their affective, subjective and spiritual life, in harmony with nature and the community of human beings.'[22] History will tell whether President Morales's goal is achieved or not, but that is not really the point. The simple fact that it exists signals that, in the South as well as the North, voices are being raised to criticize a system that has fetishized growth and should now be discarded.

Revolutions in how people think about the world, in their values and beliefs, do not happen from one day to the next. They may begin with speeches or actions, or with a rejection of behaviour that did not previously seem objectionable. They may come from the North or the South, from the rich or the impoverished. But such changes always spring from the realization that it is impossible to continue in the way that used to be considered the only one possible. Is Karl Polanyi's hoped-for 'great transformation' dawning on the horizon? It is too early to say, but things are certainly on the move. It will involve a change in people's practices – which is finally beginning – and a critical revision of the economic paradigm.

CRITIQUE AS THE PRECONDITION OF A NEW PARADIGM

A new economic paradigm is now necessary. According to Thomas Kuhn,

---

21. *Plan nacional de desarrollo: Bolivia digna, soberana, productiva y democrática para vivir bien, Lineamentos estratégicos, 2006–2011*, I.1.2, La Paz: Ministerio de Planificación del Desarrollo, 2006.

22. *Decreto supremo* 29279, Article 5, Clause 2.

> the transition from a paradigm in crisis to a new one from which a new tradition of normal science can emerge is far from a cumulative process, one achieved by an articulation or extension of the old paradigm. Rather it is a reconstruction of the field from new fundamentals, a reconstruction that changes some of the field's most elementary theoretical generalizations as well as many of its paradigm methods and applications.[23]

It is therefore pointless to 'tinker' with the old paradigm to make it fit reality, as some are trying to do today. The aim must be to start on a new footing: to address economic questions from the other end, as it were, or with an eye trained on everything that economic 'science' leaves in the dark (the reasons for growth and its ecological consequences, the persistence of 'irrational' behaviour and non-market exchange, the confusion that money introduces between different resources and goods, etc.). This new model cannot emerge in the laboratory of economists alone, both because it requires many kinds of knowledge ranging from history through global ecology to social anthropology, and because it must be part of a social movement against the effects of the present paradigm. The task is therefore interdisciplinary and social, geared to an understanding of the reasons for, and consequences of, human activities. The fortress of economic 'science' will be shaken as a result, since the economy (even in the form of 'infrastructure') cannot be thought of as a domain sealed off from changes in society and the natural environment.

This book makes no claim to offer a new economic theory. It aims simply to 'sound an alarm bell' and to raise a voice against the dead end into which standard economic 'science' has led us. Once again: the criticisms contained in it are not new, as the numerous references clearly show. Some points have been made within the field of economics, and are indebted to authors who are recognized by their peers. Others draw on the work of historians, sociologists or anthropologists, or even on politicians

23. Thomas Kuhn, *The Structure of Scientific Revolutions*, 2nd edn, Chicago: Chicago University Press, 1970, pp. 84–5.

whose way of looking at 'economic facts' gives them a different perspective from the one offered by the 'science' of the market. Economics is not confined to the things that standard economic 'science' would have us believe, and it is right that these voices should be heard.

Although polemic against economic 'science' as such, or against the hegemony it claims over the other social or human sciences, is an integral part of this book, there is no question of taking delight in the argument. Our concerns have been very different: the state of the planet, the rise of social inequalities, the consequences of indefinite economic growth, and the aberrations of a system that holds us captive. The general trend in mainstream economics is to carry on regardless. But that is no longer an option, and the task facing us has been to set out as simply as possible the reasons why it is necessary to formulate a new paradigm. What is at stake is the survival of humanity. It is no longer enough to believe in the future: we must also prepare for it and therefore get down to work.

BIBLIOGRAPHY

Accardo, Alain. *De notre servitude involontaire. Lettre à mes camarades de gauche*, Marseilles: Agone, 2001.

Achard, Pierre, Antoinette Chauvenet, Élisabeth Lage, Françoise Lentin, Patricia Neve and Georges Vignaux. *Discours biologique et ordre social*. Paris: Seuil, 1977.

Adjakly, Edo. *Pratique de la tradition religieuse et reproduction sociale chez les Guen/Mina du Sud-Est du Togo*. Geneva: Institut universitaire d'études du développement, coll. 'Itinéraires', 1985.

Akerlof, Georges A., and Janet L. Yellen. 'Can Small Deviations from Rationality Make Significant Differences to Economic Equilibria?'. *American Economic Review* 78, 1988, pp. 44–9.

Amselle, Jean-Loup. *Rétrovolutions, Essais sur les primitivismes contemporains*. Paris: Stock, 2010.

Arendt, Hannah. *The Human Condition*. Chicago: University of Chicago Press, 1958.

Ariès, Paul. *Décroissance ou barbarie*. Villeurbanne: Golias, 2005.

Arnsperger, Christian, and Yanis Varoufakis. 'Neoclassical Economics: Three Identifying Features'. In Edward Fullbrook, ed., *Pluralist Economics*. London: Zed Books, 2008, pp. 13–25.

ATTAC. *Le développement a-t-il un avenir? Pour une société économe et solidaire*. Paris: Mille et une nuits, 2004.

Attali, Jacques, and Marc Guillaume. *L'Anti-économique*. Paris: PUF, 1975 (1974).

Auffray-Seguette, Marie. *Les Biens de ce monde. L'économie vue comme espace de recomposition de la religion dans la modernité*. Paris: EHESS, 2008.

Ba, Amadou Hampaté. 'La notion de personne en Afrique noire'. *Colloques internationaux du CNRS* 544, n.d., pp. 181–92.

Barre, Raymond. *Économie politique*, vol. 1, 10th edn. Paris: PUF, 1975.

Bataille, Georges. 'The Notion of Expenditure'. In *Visions of Excess: Selected Writings, 1927–1939*. Minneapolis: University of Minnesota Press, 1985.

Baudrillard, Jean. *For a Critique of the Political Economy of the Sign*. St Louis: Telos Press, 1981 (1972).

Bayart, Jean-François, ed. *La Réinvention du capitalisme*. Paris: Karthala, 1994.

Bazin, Laurent, and Monique Selim, eds. *Motifs économiques en anthropologie*. Paris: L'Harmattan, 2001.

Benoist, Alain de. *Demain la décroissance! Penser l'écologie jusqu'au bout*. Paris: Edite, 2007.

Bentham, Jeremy. *Principles of Legislation* (trans. from the French abridgement of Étienne Dumont [1802]). London: Oxford University Press, 1914.

Bentham, Jeremy. 'Le calcul des plaisirs et des peines'. *Revue du MAUSS* 5, 1989, pp. 75–6 (fragments of a manuscript written about 1782).

Benveniste, Émile. *Indo-European Language and Society*. London: Faber, 1973.

Berthoud, Gérald. *Vers une anthropologie générale. Modernité et altérité*. Geneva: Droz, 1992.

Berthoud, Gérald. 'L'économie: un ordre généralisé? Les ambitions d'un prix Nobel'. *Revue du MAUSS* 3, 1994, pp. 42–60.

Berthoud, Gérald. 'Que nous dit l'économie?'. In Serge Latouche, ed., *L'Économie dévoilée. Du budget familial aux contraintes planétaires*. Paris: Autrement, 1995.

Besset, Jean-Paul. *Comment ne plus être progressiste… sans devenir réactionnaire*. Paris: Fayard, 2005.

Besson-Girard, Jean-Claude. *Decrescendo cantabile*. Paris: Parangon, 2005.

Boltanski, Luc, and Ève Chiapello. *Le Nouvel Esprit du capitalisme*. Paris: Gallimard, 1999.

Boudon, Raymond. *The Logic of Social Action: An Introduction to Sociological Analysis*. London: Routledge & Kegan Paul, 1981 (1979).

Boudon, Raymond. 'Individualisme ou holisme: un débat méthodologique fondamental'. In Henri Mendras and Michel Verret, eds, *Les Champs de la sociologie française*. Paris: Armand Colin, 1988, pp. 31–45.

Boudon, Raymond. 'L'individualisme méthodologique'. *Encyclopaedia universalis*, vol. 2: *Les Enjeux*. Paris, 1990, pp. 1134–8.

Boulding, Kenneth. 'Notes on a Theory of Philanthropy'. In Frank G. Dickinson, ed., *Philanthropy and Public Policy*. Cambridge MA: National Bureau of Economic Research, 1962, pp. 57–71.

Bourdieu, Pierre. *Pascalian Meditations*. Stanford CA: Stanford University Press, 2000 (1979).

Buchanan, James M. *Economics: Between Predictive Science and Moral Philosophy*. Austin: Texas A&M University Press, 1987.

Buckles, Kasey. 'Understanding the Returns to Delayed Childbearing for Working Women'. *American Economic Review* 98 (2), May 2008, pp. 403–7.

Caceres, Bruno. *Loisirs et travail du Moyen Âge à nos jours*. Paris: Seuil, 1973.

Caillé, Alain. 'Deux mythes modernes, la rareté et la rationalité économiques'. *Bulletin du MAUSS* 12, December 1984, pp. 9–35.

Caillé, Alain. 'Les mystères de l'histoire des idées. Remarques à propos du cas Bentham'. *Revue du MAUSS* 6, 1995, pp. 125–46.

Caillé, Alain. *Dé-penser l'économique. Contre le fatalisme*. Paris: La Découverte/MAUSS, 2005.

Calame, Matthieu. *La Tourmente alimentaire. Pour une politique agricole mondiale*. Paris: Charles Léopold Mayer, 2008.

Camerer, Colin F. 'Gifts as Economic Signals and Social Symbols'. *American Journal of Sociology* 94, 1988, pp. 180–214.

Cheynet, Vincent. *Le Choc de la décroissance*. Paris: Seuil, 2008.

Cheynet, Vincent, Michel Bernard and Bruno Clémentin, eds. *Objectif décroissance. Vers une société harmonieuse*. Lyons/Paris: Silence et Parangon, 2003.

Collectif. *Défaire le développement, refaire le monde*. Paris: Parangon, L'Aventurine, 2003.

Combemale, Pascal. 'Ce qui se sait vraiment en économie'. *Revue du MAUSS* 8, 1990, pp. 113–14.

Combemale, Pascal. 'L'hétérodoxie: une stratégie vouée à l'échec?'. In Serge Latouche, ed., *L'Économie dévoilée. Du budget familial aux contraintes planétaires*. Paris: Autrement, 1995.

Combemale, Pascal. 'L'hétérodoxie encore: continuer le combat mais lequel?'. *Revue du MAUSS* 30, 2007, pp. 56–67.

Comeliau, Christian. *La Croissance ou le progrès. Croissance, décroissance et développement durable*. Paris: Seuil, 2006.

Condillac, Étienne Bonnot, abbé de. *Le Commerce et le gouvernement considérés relativement l'un à l'autre*. Amsterdam and Paris: Jombert et Cellot, 1776.

Constant, Benjamin. *De l'esprit de conquête*. Lausanne: Pierre-Marcel Favre, 1980 (1814).

Constant, Benjamin. *Political Writings*. Cambridge: Cambridge University Press, 1988.

Constantin, François, ed., *Les Biens publics mondiaux. Un mythe légitimateur pour l'action collective?* Paris: L'Harmattan, 2002.

Cordonnier, Laurent. *Coopération et Réciprocité*. Paris: PUF, 1997.

Dag Hammarskjöld Foundation. *What Now: The 1975 Dag Hammarskjöld Report, prepared on the occasion of the Seventh Special Session of the United Nations General Assembly, 1975*. Special issue of the Hammarskjöld Foundation journal *Development Dialogue*, 1975.

Douthwaite, Richard. *The Growth Illusion: How Economic Growth Has Enriched the Few, Impoverished the Many and Endangered the Planet*. Totnes: Green Books, 1999 (1992).

Dumont, Louis. *From Mandeville to Marx: The Genesis and Triumph of Economic Ideology*. Chicago: Chicago University Press, 1977.

Dupuy, Jean-Pierre, and Jean Robert. *La Trahison de l'opulence*. Paris: PUF, 1976.

Dupuy, Jean-Pierre. 'Sur la formation du radicalisme philosophique d'Élie Halévy'. *Revue du MAUSS* 6, 1995, pp. 61–79.

Dupuy, Jean-Pierre. *Pour un catastrophisme éclairé. Quand l'impossible est certain.* Paris: Seuil, 2002.

Dupuy, Jean-Pierre. *La Panique.* Paris: Les Empêcheurs de penser en rond, 2003.

Durham, Jimmie. 'Eloheh or the Council of the Universe'. *Development* 3/4, 1981, SID, Rome, pp. 10–16.

Durkheim, Émile. *The Rules of Sociological Method.* New York: Free Press, 1962 (1895).

Durkheim, Émile. *La Science sociale et l'action (articles publiés entre 1888 et 1908).* Paris: PUF, 1987.

Durkheim, Émile. *Elementary Forms of Religious Life.* London: Routledge 1998 (1912).

Essimi-Nguina, Marie-Pierre. 'Ni têtes ni pattes: les vrais-faux poulets du supermarché'. *Prétextes anthropologiques* V (62), 2002, Geneva: Institut universitaire d'études du développement, pp. 49–58.

Evans-Pritchard, Edward Evan. *Witchcraft, Oracles and Magic among the Azande.* Oxford: Oxford University Press, 1976 (1937).

Fabra, Paul. *Capitalism versus Anti-Capitalism: The Triumph of Ricardian over Marxist Political Economy.* New Brunswick NJ: Transaction, 1993.

Fullbrook, Edward. 'De la domination néo-classique et des moyens d'en sortir', *L'Economie politique* 28, 2005, pp. 78–91.

Fullbrook, Edward, ed. *Pluralist Economics.* London: Zed Books, 2007.

Galbraith, John K. *The Economics of Innocent Fraud: Truth for Our Time.* Boston MA: Houghton Mifflin, 2004.

Gauchet, Marcel. *The Disenchantment of the World: A Political History of Religion.* Princeton NJ: Princeton University Press, 1997 (1985).

Gauthier, François. 'La religion de la "société de marché"'. *Entropia* 5, Autumn 2008, pp. 93–107.

Généreux, Jacques. *Les Vraies Lois de l'économie.* Paris: Seuil, 2005 (2001 and 2002).

Généreux, Jacques. *La Grande régression.* Paris: Seuil, 2010.

Georgescu-Roegen, Nicholas. *The Entropy Law and the Economic Process.* Cambridge MA: Harvard University Press, 1971.

Georgescu-Roegen, Nicholas. *Energy and Economic Myths: Institutional and Analytical Economic Essays.* New York: Pergamon Press, 1976.

Georgescu-Roegen, Nicholas. *Demain la décroissance. Entropie, écologie, économie.* Lausanne: Pierre-Marcel Favre, 1979; Paris: Le Sang de la Terre, 1995.

Giraud Pierre-Noël. *L'inégalité du monde. Economie du monde contemporain.* Paris: Gallimard, 1996.

Godbout, Jacques T. *Le Don, la dette et l'identité. Homo donator vs Homo oeconomicus.* Paris: La Découverte, 2000.

Godbout, Jacques T. *Ce qui circule entre nous. Donner, recevoir, rendre.* Paris: Seuil, 2007.

Godbout, Jacques T., and Caillé, Alain. *The World of the Gift*. Montreal: McGill–Queen's University Press, 2000 (1992).

Godelier, Maurice. 'Formes non marchandes de circulation du produit social'. In Jean Copans, Serge Tornay, Maurice Godelier and Catherine Backès-Clément, eds, *L'Anthropologie: science des sociétés primitives?* Paris: Éditions E.P., 1971, pp. 225–37.

Goux, Jean-Jacques. 'L'utilité: équivoque et démoralisation'. *Revue du MAUSS* 6, 1995, pp. 106–24.

Grinevald, Jacques. 'Le sens bioéconomique du développement humain: l'affaire Nicholas Georgescu-Roegen'. *Revue européenne des sciences sociales* 13 (51), 1980, pp. 62–3.

Guibert, Bernard, and Serge Latouche, eds, *Antiproductivisme, altermondialisme, décroissance*. Lyons: Parangon/Vs, 2006.

Gusdorf, Georges. *Les Sciences humaines et la conscience occidentale*, vol. 6: *L'Avènement des sciences humaines au Siècle des lumières*, Paris: Payot, 1973; vol. 8: *La Conscience révolutionnaire des idéologues*, Paris: Payot, 1978.

Hammond, Peter J. 'Charity: Altruism or Cooperative Egoism'. In Edmund S. Phelps, ed., *Altruism, Morality and Economic Theory*. New York: Russell Sage Foundation, 1975, pp. 115–31.

Heinsohn, Gunnar, and Otto Steiger. *Eigentumsökonomik*. Marburg: Metropolis Verlag, 2006.

Hénaff, Marcel. 'De la philosophie à l'anthropologie. Comment interpréter le don?'. *Esprit* 282, February 2002, pp. 135–58.

Insel, Ahmet. 'La part du don, esquisse d'évaluation'. In *Ce que donner veut dire. Don et intérêt*. Paris: La Découverte/MAUSS, 1993, pp. 221–35.

Iribarne, Philippe d'. 'Comment l'économie assure-t-elle sa clôture?'. *Revue du MAUSS* 15–16, 1992, pp. 58–78.

Jackson, Tim. *Prosperity without Growth? The Transition to a Sustainable Economy*. London: Sustainable Development Commission, 2009.

Jacob, Jean. *L'Anti-mondialisation. Aspects méconnus d'une nébuleuse*. Paris: Berg, 2006.

Jorion, Paul. 'Déterminants sociaux de la formation des prix du marché; l'exemple de la pêche artisanale'. *Revue du MAUSS* 9, 1990, pp. 71–105.

Keen, Steve. *Debunking Economics: The Naked Emperor of the Social Sciences*. London: Zed Books, 2007 (2004).

Kempf, Hervé. *Pour sauver la planète, sortez du capitalisme*. Paris: Seuil, 2009.

Keynes, John M. *The General Theory of Employment, Interest and Money*. London: Macmillan, 1961 (1936).

Kuhn, Thomas. *The Structure of Scientific Revolutions*. 2nd edn. Chicago: Chicago University Press, 1970.

Lane, Robert E. 'Le travail comme "désutilité" et l'argent comme mesure du bonheur?'. *Revue du MAUSS* 3, 1994, pp. 17–32.

Latouche, Serge. *Survivre au développement*. Paris: Mille et une nuits, 2004.

Latouche, Serge. *L'Invention de l'économie*. Paris: Albin Michel, 2005.

Latouche, Serge. *Le Pari de la décroissance*. Fayard: Paris, 2006.

Latouche, Serge. *Petit traité de la décroissance sereine*. Paris: Mille et une nuits, 2007.

Latouche, Serge. *Farewell to Growth*. Cambridge: Polity Press, 2009.

Latouche, Serge, ed. *L'Économie dévoilée. Du budget familial aux contraintes planétaires*. Paris: Autrement, 1995.

Latouche, Serge, and Didier Harpagès. *Le Temps de la décroisssance*. Paris: Thierry Manier, 2010.

Latour, Bruno. *We Have Never Been Modern*. Cambridge MA: Harvard University Press, 1993 (1991).

Lavignotte, Stéphane. *La décroissance est-elle souhaitable?*. Paris: Textuel, 2008.

Le Mercier de la Rivière, Pierre-François. *L'Ordre naturel et essentiel des sociétés politiques*. London: Jean Nourse, 1767.

Lebaron, Frédéric. *La Croyance économique. Les économistes entre science et politique*. Paris: Seuil, 2000.

Leenhardt, Maurice. *Do Kamo. La personne et le mythe dans le monde mélanésien*. Paris: Gallimard, 1985 [1947].

Lepage, Henri. *Demain le libéralisme*. Paris: Livre de poche, 1980.

Lepage, Henri. *Tomorrow, Capitalism: The Economics of Economic Freedom*. London: Open Court, 1982.

Lévi-Strauss, Claude. 'Productivité et condition humaine'. *Études rurales*, 159–160, July–December 2001, pp. 129–44.

Liaudet, Jean-Claude. *Le Complexe d'Ubu ou la névrose libérale*. Paris: Fayard, 2004.

Lizot, Jacques. 'Économie primitive et subsistance. Essais sur le travail et l'alimentation chez les Yanomami'. *Libre* 4, Paris: Petite Bibliothèque Payot, 1978, pp. 69–114.

Madelain, Camille. 'Pratiques de la décroissance'. *Notes et Travaux* 76, Geneva: Institut universitaire d'études du développement, 2005.

Malinowski, Branislaw. *Argonauts of the Western Pacific*. Long Grove IL: Waveland Press, 1984 (1922).

Malthus, Thomas R. *Definitions in Political Economy*. London: John Murray, 1827.

Malthus, Thomas R. *Principles of Political Economy Considered with a View to Their Practical Application*. 2nd edn. London: W. Pickering, 1836.

Malthus, Thomas R. *An Essay on the Principle of Population*. London: Penguin Books, 1979 (1798, 1830).

Marglin, Stephen A. *The Dismal Science: How Thinking Like an Economist Undermines Community*. Cambridge MA: Harvard University Press, 2008.

Maris, Bernard. *Lettre ouverte aux gourous de l'économie qui nous prennent pour des imbéciles*. Paris: Seuil, 2003 (1999).

Marx, Karl. *The Poverty of Philosophy*. London: Lawrence & Wishart, 1966.

Marx, Karl. *Capital*, Volume 1. Harmondsworth: Penguin/NLR, 1976.

Marx, Karl. *Capital*, Volume 3. London: Penguin/NLR, 1981.

Marx, Karl. *Grundrisse: Foundations of the Critique of Political Economy*. London: Penguin, 1993.

Mauss, Marcel. *The Gift: Forms and Functions of Exchange in Archaic Societies*. London: Cohen & West, 1966 (1923–4).

Meadows, Donella H., Dennis L. Meadows, Jørgen Rander and William W. Behrens III, eds. *The Limits to Growth*. New York: Universe Books, 1972.

Méda, Dominique. *Qu'est-ce que la richesse?* Paris: Aubier, 1999.

Meillassoux, Claude. *Terrains et Théories*. Paris: Anthropos, 1977.

Meo, Cyril di. *La Face cachée de la décroissance*. Paris: L'Harmattan, 2006.

Michéa, Jean-Claude. *Impasse Adam Smith. Brèves remarques sur l'impossibilité de dépasser le capitalime sur sa gauche*. Castelnau-le-Lez: Climats, 2002.

Michéa, Jean-Claude. *L'Empire du moindre mal. Essai sur la civilisation libérale*. Paris, Climats, 2007.

Michéa, Jean-Claude. *La Double Pensée. Retour sur la question libérale*. Paris: Flammarion, 2008.

Mill, John Stuart. *Principles of Political Economy*. London: Longmans, Green & Co., 1921 (1848).

Monsuttti, Alessandro. *War and Migration: Social Networks and Economic Strategies of the Hazaras of Afghanistan*. London: Routledge, 2005 (2004).

Mylondo, Baptiste, ed. *Pour une politique de la décroissance*. Villeurbanne: Golias, 2007.

Myrdal, Gunnar. *The Political Element in the Development of Economic Theory*. Edison NJ: Transaction, 1990 (1930).

Naredo, José Manuel. *La Economía en evolución. Historia y perspectivas de las categorías básicas del pensamiento económico*. Madrid: Siglo XXI de España, 2003.

Ndione, Emmanuel Seyni. *Dynamique urbaine d'une société en grappe: un cas Dakar*. Dakar: Enda, 1987.

Nodier, Luc Marie. 'Définition de l'utilitarisme'. *Revue du MAUSS* 6, 1995, pp. 15–30.

Partant, François. *Que la crise s'aggrave*. Paris: Solin, 1978.

Pasquinet, Jean-Luc. 'Développer l'esprit critique'. In Baptiste Mylondo, ed., *Pour une politique de la décroissance*. Villeurbanne: Golias, 2007, pp. 49–57.

Perrot, Marie-Dominique. 'Passager clandestin et indispensable du discours: le présupposé'. In Gilbert Rist and Fabrizio Sabelli, eds, *Il était une fois le développement....* Lausanne: Éditions d'En Bas, 1986, pp. 71–91.

Perrot, Marie-Dominique, and Gilbert Rist. 'Des Argonautes aux Internautes'. *Revue européenne des sciences sociales* 44 (134), 2006, pp. 203–14.

Perrot, Marie-Dominique, et al., eds. *Ordres et désordres de l'esprit gestionnaire*. Lausanne: Réalités sociales, 2006.

Perrot, Marie-Dominique, Fabrizio Sabelli and Gilbert Rist. *La Mythologie programmée. L'économie des croyances dans la société moderne*. Paris: PUF, 1992.

Place, Christophe. *Community Currency for Local Economy: A Grassroots Innovation for Prosperity through Democracy*. Paris: HEC, 2010.

Polanyi, Karl. *The Great Transformation*. Boston MA: Beacon Press, 1957 (1944).

Polanyi, Karl. *Primitive, Archaic, and Modern Economies: Essays of Karl Polanyi*. Ed. George Dalton. Boston MA: Beacon Press, 1968.

Polanyi, Karl. *The Livelihood of Man*. New York: Academic Press, 1977.

Rahnema, Majid. *Quand la misère chasse la pauvreté*. Paris/Arles: Fayard/Actes Sud, 2003.

Rahnema, Majid, and Jean Robert. *La Puissance des pauvres*. Arles: Actes Sud, 2008.

Raveaud, Gilles. 'Pluralism in Economic Teaching'. *Development Dialogue* 52, 2009, pp. 43–78.

Ricardo, David. *The Principles of Political Economy and Taxation*. London: Dent, 1973 (1817).

Ridoux, Nicolas. *La Décroissance pour tous*. Lyons: Parangon/Vs, 2006.

Riesel, René, and Jaime Semprun. *Catastrophisme, administration du désastre et soumission durable*. Paris: Encyclopédie des nuisances, 2008.

Rist, Gilbert. 'Le concept de "développement" est-il rationnel? Un concept occidental à l'épreuve de la démarche interculturelle'. In Fernand Ouellet, ed., *Pluralisme et École*. Québec: Institut québécois de recherche sur la culture, 1988, pp. 57–83.

Rist, Gilbert. 'Préalables à une théorie générale de l'échange'. *Nouveaux Cahiers de l'IUED* 7. Geneva: IUED/Paris: PUF, 1998, pp. 17–40.

Rist, Gilbert. *The History of Development: From Western Origins to Global Faith*. 3rd edn. London: Zed Books, 2008.

Rodinson, Maxime. *Islam and Capitalism*. New York: Pantheon Books, 1974 (1966).

Romaña, Alfredo L. de. 'Une alternative sociale en émergence: l'économie autonome'. *Interculture* 22 (3), 1989, cahier 104.

Rosset, Clément. *L'Anti-nature. Éléments pour une philosophie tragique*. Paris: PUF, 1973.

Rousseau, Jean-Jacques. 'Essay on the Origin of Languages'. In *On the Origin of Language*. New York: Ungar, 1966.

Rousseau, Jean-Jacques. *On the Social Contract*. New York: St Martin's Press, 1978 (1762).

Rousseau, Jean-Jacques. 'Preface to *Narcissus, or The Lover of Himself*'. In *The Collected Writings of Rousseau*, vol. 2. Hanover NH: University Press of New England, 1992 (1782).

Sahlins, Marshall. *Stone Age Economics*. Chicago: Aldine Atherton, 1972.

Sahlins, Marshall. *Culture and Practical Reason*. Chicago: University of Chicago Press, 1976.

Sapir, Jacques. *Les Trous noirs de la science économique. Essai sur l'impossibilité de penser le temps et l'argent*. Paris: Albin Michel, 2000.

Sapir, Jacques. 'Libre-échange, croissance et développement: quelques mythes de l'économie vulgaire'. *Revue du MAUSS* 30, 2007, pp. 151–72.

Saussure Thierry de. *L'Inconscient, nos croyances et la foi chrétienne. Études psychanalytiques et bibliques*. Paris: Le Cerf, 2009.

Say, Jean-Baptiste. *Catechism of Political Economy*. London: Sherwood, Neely and Jones, 1816 (1815).
Schroyer, Trent. *Beyond Western Economics*. London: Routledge, 2009.
Seers, Dudley. 'The Limitations of the Special Case'. *Bulletin of the Institute of Economics and Statistics* 25 (2), May 1963, pp. 77–97.
Smith, Adam. *The Wealth of Nations*, 2 vols. London: Methuen, 1961 (1776).
Smith, Adam. *The Theory of Moral Sentiments*. Oxford: Oxford University Press, 1979 (1759).
Steppacher, Rolf. 'La petite différence et ses grandes conséquences: possession et propriété'. *Nouveaux Cahiers de l'IUED* 14, Paris: PUF/Geneva: IUED, 2003, pp. 181–90.
Steppacher, Rolf. 'Property, Mineral Resources and "Sustainable Development"'. In Otto Steiger, ed., *Property Economics: Property Rights, Creditor's Money and the Foundations of the Economy*. Marburg: Metropolis Verlag, 2008, pp. 323–54.
Stiglitz, Joseph E. *Making Globalization Work*. London: Penguin, 2007.
Sugden, Robert. 'Reciprocity: The Supply of Public Goods through Voluntary Contributions'. *Economic Journal* 94, 1984, pp. 772–87.
Taguieff, Pierre-André. *L'Effacement de l'avenir*. Paris: Galilée, 2000.
Temple, Dominique, and Mireille Chabal. *La Réciprocité et la naissance des valeurs humaines*. Paris: L'Harmattan, 1995.
Terray, Emmanuel. *Marxism and Primitive Societies*. New York: Monthly Review Press, 1972 (1969).
Tertrais, Jean-Pierre. *Du développement à la décroissance. De la nécessité de sortir de l'impasse suicidaire du capitalisme*. Saint-Georges d'Oléron: Éditions libertaires, 2006.
Todorov, Tzvetan, Thierry Grillet and Yann Fauchois, eds, *Lumières! Un héritage pour demain*. Paris: Bibliothèque nationale de France, 2006.
UNDP. *Human Development Report 1991*. Oxford: Oxford University Press, 1991.
van Parijs, Philippe. 'Le modèle économique dans les sciences sociales: imposture ou nécessité?'. *Bulletin du MAUSS* 22, June 1987, pp. 67–86.
Veblen, Thorstein. 'Why Is Economics Not an Evolutionary Science?'. *Quarterly Journal of Economics* 12, 1898, pp. 373–97.
Ventelou, Bruno. *Au-delà de la rareté, La croissance économique comme construction sociale*. Paris: Albin Michel, 2001.
Vers une autre science économique (et donc un autre monde)?, Revue du MAUSS 30, 2007.
Viguier, Anne. 'Enfances de l'Individu, entre l'École, la Nature et la Police'. *Mots* 9, October 1984, pp. 33–55.
Walras, Léon. *Elements of Pure Economics*. London: George Allen & Unwin, 1954 (1874, 1900).
Walras, Léon. 'Economics and Mechanics' (1909). In Philip Mirowski and Pamela Cook, 'Walras' "Economics and Mechanics": Translation, Commentary,

Context'. In Warren J. Samuels, ed., *Economics as Discourse: An Analysis of the Language of Economists*. Dordrecht: Kluwer, 1990, pp. 189–213.

Watzlawick, Paul, John H. Weakland and Richard Fisch. *Change: Principles of Problem Formation and Problem Resolution*. New York: Norton, 1974.

WCED. *Our Common Future. Report of the World Commission on Environment and Development*. New York: University Press, 1987.

Weber, Max. *Economy and Society*, vol. 1. Berkeley: University of California Press, 1978.

Weiller, Jean, and Bruno Carrier. *L'Économie non conformiste en France au XXe siècle*. Paris: PUF, 1994.

INDEX

ABOUT ZED BOOKS

Zed Books is a critical and dynamic publisher, committed to increasing awareness of important international issues and to promoting diversity, alternative voices and progressive social change. We publish on politics, development, gender, the environment and economics for a global audience of students, academics, activist and general readers. Run as a co-operative, we aim to operate in an ethical and environmentally sustainable way.

Find out more at www.zedbooks.co.uk

For up-to-date news, articles, reviews and events information visit http://zed-books.blogspot.com

To subscribe to the monthly Zed Books e-newsletter,
send an email headed 'subscribe' to marketing@zedbooks.net

We can also be found on Facebook, ZNet, Twitter and
Library Thing.